BERMUDA

By Susan Irwin-Wiener

917.296

Irwin-Wiener

Bermuda

DATE DUE

IMPERIAL PUBLIC LIBRARY
P.O. BOX 307
IMPERIAL, TEXAS 79743

About the Author

Susan Irwin-Wiener is a New York public relations executive who has visited the island many times on business and pleasure trips.

Publisher: Frank A. Marshall
Senior Editor: E. R. Grusky
Cover Design & Illustration: Eric Walker
Map Design: Marit Jaeger-Kanney

All prices are based on those available at time of writing. It is inevitable that changes will have taken place by the time that this book is published. Please double check so as to be sure of latest figures. We will be delighted to hear from you, whether it be a recommendation or complaint at World of Travel Publishing, 106 South Front Street, Suite 2E, Philadelphia, PA 19106.

© 1989 by Fisher's World Inc.   ISBN 1-55707-040-7

All rights reserved. No part of this book may be reproduced or utilized in any form or by any means, electronic or mechanical, including photocopying, recording or by any information storage and retrieval system, without permission in writing from the publisher. All inquiries should be addressed to World of Travel, 106 S. Front Street, Suite 2E, Philadelphia, PA 19106. World of Travel is a division of Fisher's World Inc., Nutmeg Farm, Route 17, Laporte, PA 18626.

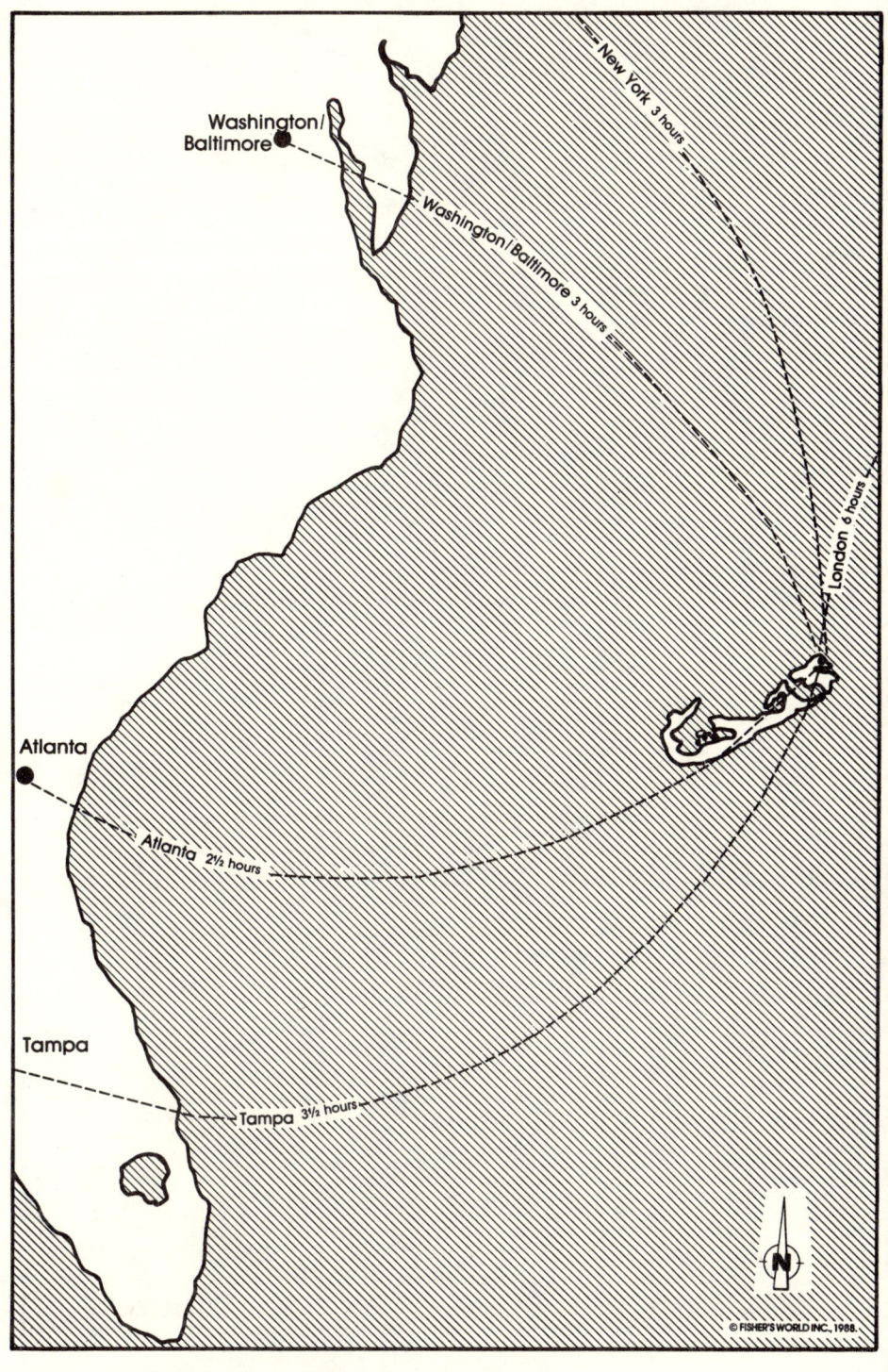

Table of Contents

Introduction 1

Bermuda's History and People 3

Food in Bermuda by *Mamie Crumbe* 11

Hamilton 15
   Along the Waterfront 17
   Moving Inland 17
   Outskirts of Hamilton 20
   The North Shore 21
   Nearby Hamilton 22

Shopper on the Go by *Janet Steinburg* 23

St. George's 27
   First Capital of Bermuda 27
   Walking Around St. George's 29
   Nearby St. George's 34

Bermuda is Another World by *Andrew Vladimir* 39

The Parishes - West to East 43
   Sandys 47
   Southhampton 51
   Warwick 52
   Paget 52
   Devonshire 54
   Smith's 54
   Hamilton 56

Some Rare Bermuda Pleasures 57
   by Elizabeth and Henry Urrows

Author's Choice
  Hotels 61
   Hamilton Parish 63
   Paget Parish 64
   Pembroke Parish 65
   St. George's Parish 66
   Sandys Parish 68
   Smith's Parish 69

Southampton Parish 70
Warick Parish 71
Private Clubs 72

Restaurants 73

Nightlife/Entertainment 85

Shopping 87

Sports 97

Sights Around the Island 111

What to Do When You Lose Your Wallet 115
  by Frances Sheridan Goulart

Index 118

Travel Planner

List of Maps

Beaches 100	Location Map iii
Bermuda, general map vii	Parishes of Bermuda 42
Bermuda Railway Trail -	Public Parks 108
Key to Railway Trail ..44-45	Restaurants 74-75
Bus System 84	Resorts & Hotels 62
Ferry Schedule 38	St. David's Island 35
Golf Course Locations ...105	St. George's 26
Golf Course I 110	St. George's Bike
Golf Course II 112	or Hike Tour 28
Golf Course III 117	St. George's Island 33
Hamilton 14	St. George's Shopping 92
Hamilton area 55	Somerset Island 46
Hamilton Bike & Hike	Tennis 103
Tour 28	Tucker's Town Area 37
Hamilton Shopping 88	Water Sports 96
Ireland Island 48	West End 50

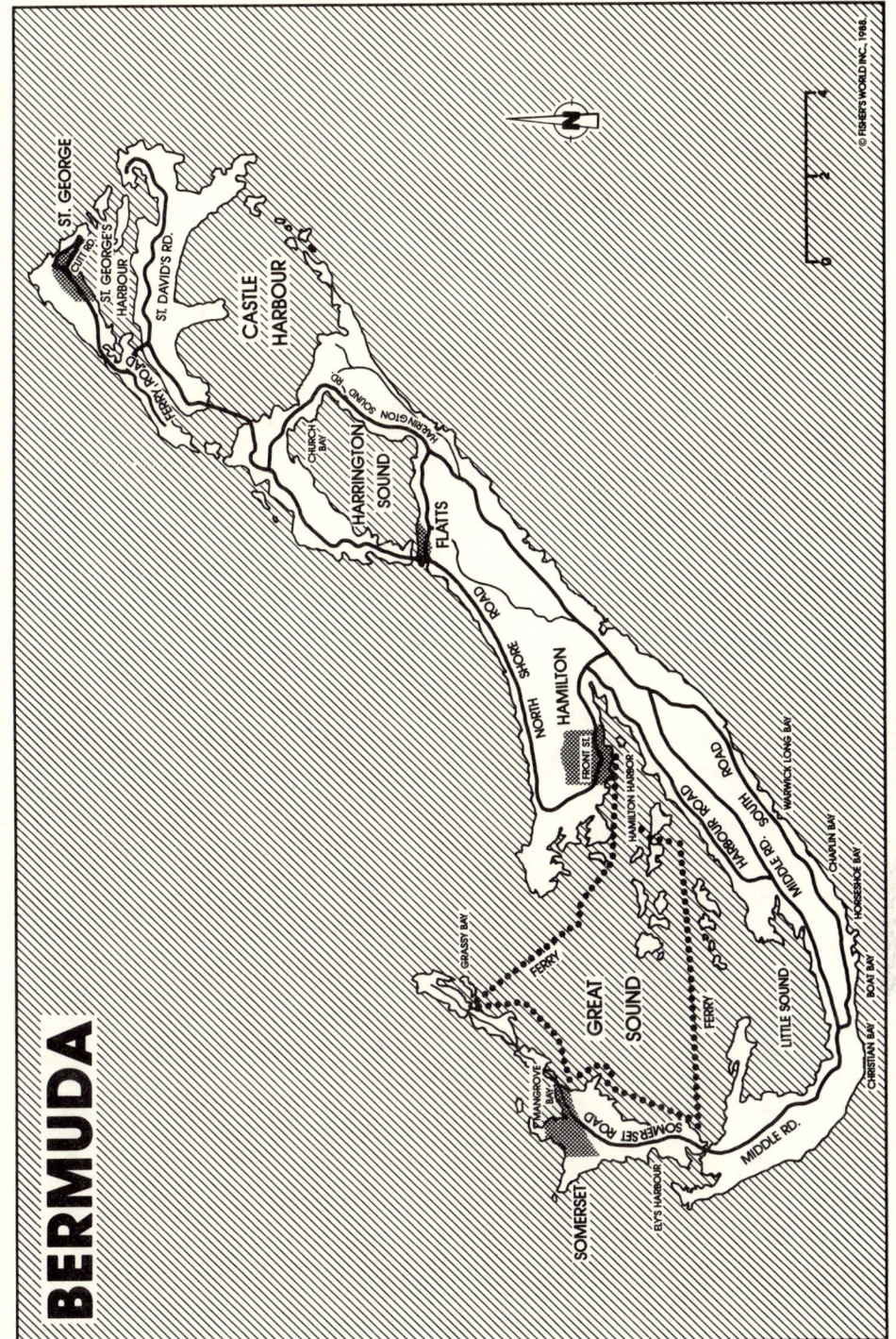

Introduction

There are few places in the world that live up to their travel poster representations. Bermuda is one of them—a truly pretty land of winding country roads, luxuriant flora, enthralling coastline vistas, and immaculate picturebook towns of pastel houses topped by sparkling white lime-washed roofs.

Bermuda's ties to the United States, Canada, and the United Kingdom are based on long association, friendship, and even kinship. Many leading Bermudians have been educated in the United States and have great sympathy for American cultural and economic prowess. The attachment to Britain, largely sentimental, is still strong, and there are few Bermudians who would radically change their present status as the oldest self-governing colony in the British Commonwealth.

In the past, fishing, whaling, farming, and even privateering helped support the economy. Today, in addition to its tourism mainstay, there is some light industry, including pharmaceutical manufacturing and liquor production. Thanks to favorable tax laws, some revenue comes from foreign companies that have established either real or "paper" headquarters here. There's no direct financial benefit to the government from having the U.S. Naval Air Station and Naval Annex here, since the land for both was a World War II rent-free, 99-year gift to the United States from Bermuda. Naval personnel do spend money on the island, but since their purchases tend to be similar to those of the average visitor, we circle back to the economic dominance of the tourism industry.

Bermuda's form of government is patterned after the English parliamentary system with a Cabinet, headed by a premier, a Senate, and a House of Assembly. The Senate, also known as the upper house, is composed of members normally appointed or reappointed every five years. The Assembly is made up of 40 elected representatives. Though general elections are scheduled at five-year intervals, the premier can call for a new election at any time (as in the English system). Titularly at the helm is a governor appointed by the queen, though power resides with the premier, presently the Honourable John W. D. Swan, Jr., leader of the United Bermuda party. The island's two opposition parties are the Progressive Labor party and the National Liberal party.

Bermuda is by inclination and design stoutly conservative. You won't find nude beaches here, or neon signs, or outdoor advertising. High-rise apartment buildings and hotels are prohibited. Cars are not allowed to proliferate and befoul the highways and the pristine air. Bermudians spurn proposals for casinos and superhighways. They proudly retain the vestiges of years past, as exemplified by colonial mansions with rambling gardens and by huge stretches of nature preserves.

One of the first visual distinctions to strike most visitors is the pervasive use of pink blush, sunk into the limestone walls of scores of Bermuda's houses and hotels. Why the predominance? I don't know, but like the music of Bach, with its endless variations of a compellingly simple theme, the island's pinks never strike a vulgar or discordant note. Rather, they provide the base of a melodic, restful harmony.

Much of the island's clientele tends to be what can loosely be categorized as the country club set and the honeymoon crowd. These visitors, when added to the 57,000 island residents, help perpetuate the island's basic character and texture.

Bermuda's History and People

Bermuda's discovery and certain facts about her colonization are shrouded in tantalizing mystery. Legend has it that an Irish monk named Saint Brennan may have sighted the island while crossing the Atlantic. Two Spanish historians credit Juan de Bermudez, a captain who commanded the *La Garza* (The Heron), with the discovery in 1503. Some believe that Columbus may have sailed past the islands after discovering San Salvador in 1492. That's a logical assumption since sailors on their way home from the Caribbean or South America relied on the westerly winds that accompanied the Gulf Stream to fill their sails and speed them back to Europe.

In 1511, an Italian atlas placed Bermuda very close to its actual location and gave it the name of La Bermuda. The first description of the islands, however, came from the pen of Spanish seaman-historian, Fernandez de Oviedo, who is supposed to have made a visit. In fact, he may have even released some pigs there to provide food for future conquistadores. Descendants of these pigs ran wild on the land for centuries, but there's little to suggest that the Spaniards ever returned. A group of Portuguese arrived around 1543, albeit involuntarily; they had been shipwrecked while en route home from Santo Domingo. Perhaps they were the ones who left behind some mysterious initials and a Maltese-style cross carved in a rock at Spittal Pond in Smith's Parish, a site now known as Spanish Rock. Some historians who've analyzed the Rock say that the cryptic initials mean *Rei Portugues* (King of Portugal), while the Maltese version of the cross was well known during the age of discovery as a Portuguese insignia. The Portuguese castaways probably reconstructed a vessel from Bermudian cedar and sailed back to Spanish Santo Domingo. Today, there is a bronze cast of the initials and cross at Spanish Rock and a plaster of paris reproduction in the Historical Society Museum in Hamilton. Another legend ascribes the markings to Spanish sea captain Teodoro Fernando Camelo, who may have reached Bermuda under royal grant and inscribed his initials there.

The French were shipwrecked on Bermuda's reef sometime in the 1560s, but they, like the Portuguese, built a ship and sailed away to French Canada. Again in 1593, a French ship called at Bermuda and ran against the Bermuda reef. One Englishman, Henry May, was among the survivors who came ashore on a raft. They stayed only long enough to build a new ship, then headed for Newfoundland.

Bermuda's reputation among Europe's maritime powers was that of an island inhabited by devils and enchanters. There is an account of a fleet of Spanish galleons under the command of Captain Diego Ramirez, en route to Spain from Mexico, Panama, or Colombia, which encountered a severe storm off Bermuda. The flagship struck a reef, and though not wrecked found itself forced into Great Sound, where the captain decided he would send a search party ashore to find fresh water. The screeching of birds sounded to Spanish ears like devils screaming, "Diselo, diselo!" (Tell it! Tell it!). When this frightened party sailed away, the captain took with him a map of Bermuda and left behind a cross and directions for finding drinking water, instructions that long afterward were mistaken as indication of a cache of buried treasure. Spanish Point at the western tip of Pembroke Parish and the entrance to Great Sound was the locale for this adventure.

It was not until 1609 that permanent European settlement began in Bermuda, and even then it was entirely by accident. It happened as the result of a gathering at Plymouth, England, of a royally chartered fleet carrying 500 would-be colonists to the new English settlement on the James River in Virginia. There were seven ships and two pinnaces, (smaller vessels). The flagship and largest vessel, carrying 150 hardy souls, was the 300-ton *Sea Venture*. The fleet was under the command of Admiral Sir George Somers. Sir Thomas Gates, deputy governor of the new Virginia colony, and Captain Christopher Newport, who had led the first colonial expedition to Jamestown, were also aboard. Another important passenger was John Rolfe, accompanied by his pregnant wife. They were the parents of the first child born in Bermuda, a girl named Bermudas who died soon after birth. Those familiar with the colonial history of Virginia will recall that when Rolfe became a widower, he married the Indian princess Pocahontas in that colony and took her to England, where she spent her remaining years.

Sailing from England, Admiral Somers's fleet was scattered by stormy weather as it approached Bermudian waters. One of the pinnaces turned back, but the rest of the fleet, except for *Sea Venture*, rode it out and made port in Virginia. The *Sea Venture* was shipwrecked on Bermuda's eastern-most reefs, but there was no loss of life. The survivors, salvaging all they could from the wreck, founded the first British colony, legitimized in 1612 by King James I.

Over the next nine months, despite clashes between Admiral Somers and Deputy Governor Designate Gates over command, the castaways made themselves two ships under the direction of ship's carpenter Frobisher. The vessels, *Patience* and *Deliverance*, were constructed of Bermudian cedar but the *Deliverance* had the advantage of structural materials salvaged from the *Sea Venture*. (Today, on the waterfront at St. George's, the visitor can see a replica of the *Deliverance*.) Meanwhile, Sir George Somers busied himself exploring and mapping the island of Bermuda. The little colony lived on wild pig, fish, and birds. Unfortunately, there was discontent and mutiny and even an execution under Gates's orders.

The two new ships sailed for Jamestown in May 1610; after ten days they reached that poor and bedraggled colony, which was then on the point of abandonment. In June 1610, Sir George Somers returned to Bermuda to seek supplies for his destitute colony at Jamestown. Unfortunately, Sir George died in Bermuda. His nephew, Matthew Somers, who succeeded him in command, decided to leave his uncle's heart in Bermuda where it is buried in Somers Gardens, St. George's, and take the body back to England aboard the *Patience*. Three men were left behind on the island, while those who returned related such favorable stories of the island that the Virginia Company decided to colonize it formally.

Official colonization dates from 1612 with the arrival of the *Plough* bearing 60 white settlers from England under the leadership of the first governor, Richard Moore. The *Edwin* arrived four years later from the West Indies and left behind an Indian and an African. Early settlers received a new Royal Charter in 1615 from the Bermuda Company (which obtained the rights of the Virginia Company) and found themselves governed by it for the next 69 years. The new charter granted Bermuda the right to create a General Assembly and to make laws that did not contradict laws made in England. A year later, Daniel Tucker became governor of the new colony.

Slavery was introduced around 1616; the masters wanted a plantation society similar to Virginia's. The slaves included Africans, American Indians, and later, Irish and Scottish opponents of Cromwell's rule in Britain. The slaves were used as handymen, shipbuilders, and servants rather than as field hands when the cultivation of tobacco and other products for export was found unprofitable. Meanwhile, the luxuriant forests of Bermudian cedar were decimated to build sailing ships, and a maritime tradition became fully established. In time of peace, the Bermuda-built ships roamed the Bahamas, Turk Islands, and the Caribbean, carrying produce from one English colony to the next. During wartime, they were supplied with letters of marque, empowering them to seize enemy ships without accusation of piracy. Nevertheless, there was considerable piracy in Bermudian waters, and ships under any flag, lured onto the perilous reefs, were plundered regardless of European alliance.

During the American Revolution, Bermuda's sympathies were divided between loyalty to the British Crown and ties to the colonies on the mainland, especially to Virginia. In 1775, Bermuda sent a delegation to Philadelphia's Continental Congress to ask for some desperately needed food. The response came from the commander-in-chief of the Continental armies himself, George Washington. Critically short of gunpowder for his troops, and aware of British supplies stored in Bermuda, Washington proposed a trade. In return for the much-needed food, Bermudians stole a hundred barrels of gunpowder and shipped it to the American rebels. After the war, since Britain could no longer maintain naval bases in what had become the United States, Bermuda became a focal point in the western Atlantic for the British navy as well as for commerce operating between British Canada, Newfoundland, and the Bahamas. The Napoleonic Wars, the War of 1812, the American Civil War, and both world wars focused British attention on the strategic position of Bermuda and led to considerable British military and naval investment in the island and its defenses. In fact, the 1814 attack on the United States that resulted in the burning of Washington, was launched from Bermuda's Royal Navy Dockyards.

There was a mild revival of agriculture in Bermuda during the 19th century, concentrating on onions, tomatoes, and potatoes, but despite the popularity of the large sweet Bermuda onion, the trend did not continue. Nor did another briefly profitable crop, the Easter lily, introduced from Japan in 1856. Nevertheless, a substantial number of Portuguese farmers and fishermen from the Azores were brought in. Today, their descendants contribute to the cosmopolitan makeup of the Bermudian people, which before was Anglo-Scottish-Irish and African.

As already noted, the institution of African slavery differed in Bermuda from that in other British colonies in the New World. Many slaves arrived in Bermuda from other colonies rather than directly from Africa. In 1602, the colony of Massachussetts, for instance, ruled that Indians captured in battle were to be sold or shipped off to the Bermudas. In 1670, the government made a first effort to stop further import of human cargo. Not all blacks in these early days were slaves; some arrived free while others earned their freedom, forming an element that caused the authorities to order all free blacks in Bermuda to be taken to Eleuthera in the Bahamas. This was only a stopgap measure, however, and there were numerous efforts by slaves in Bermuda as elsewhere to gain their freedom by force, especially during the latter half of the 18th century. There was a major uprising in 1761, which resulted in the execution of six blacks and the revival of harsh laws against all blacks, whether slave or free. Slaves were emancipated in Britain itself in 1772, and by 1807 the slave trade was abolished throughout the British Empire. In 1834, thanks to William Wilberforce and a determined abolitionist movement in Britain, slavery was abolished in the colonies. In Bermuda today, Cap Match, a two-day holiday at the beginning of August, commemorates the occasion. It is estimated that when emancipation came to Bermuda, it set free 4,000 black Bermudians, nearly half the population.

During the American Civil War, as during the American Revolution, Bermudian sympathies were divided between North and South. (A small element possibly contributing to the division may have been that in the mid 1800s, George Washington's first cousin, Marsden, was the publisher of Bermuda's *Royal Gazette*.) The Confederate government even established a mission in St. George's to advocate the Southern cause. As a vital military measure, designed to cripple the enemy and prevent shipments of cotton, tobacco, and other products to European markets, the North enforced a blockage of Southern ports. The blockade also prevented European shipments of war materiel, food, supplies, and manufactured goods to the Confederacy. Ingenious Bermudians developed blockade runners to avoid Northern warships. St. George's was the primary Bermudian port for this enterprise, which yielded enormous profits. The bubble burst in 1865 with the fall of Wilmington, North Carolina, to Northern troops. Dozens of Bermudian blockade runners were left with mountains of debt and unsalable merchandise.

One former South Carolinian, a slave named Joseph Haynes Rainey, whose freedom was purchased by his father, jumped ship and established himself as a barber in St. George's where his wife worked as a dressmaker. He was educated in Bermuda, but returned to South Carolina once the war had ended. During Reconstruction, he was elected to the House of Representatives from that state, the first black man to serve in the United States Congress.

With the advent of steamships in the mid-1800s, wooden sailboat building declined, and the colony had to turn to other means of support and prosperity. In 1852, a cornerstone was laid for the Hamilton Hotel, which was not completed until 1863. It flourished until it burned down in 1955. After a visit in 1883 by Princess Louise, daughter of Queen Victoria and wife of the governor-general of Canada, Bermuda built the first Princess Hotel which opened in 1885. During the last four decades of the 19th century, the development of steamship service to the mainland helped inspire a growth of tourism to Bermuda's relatively benevolent climate. In the early 1900s, the debate about whether to allow motorized vehicles on the island began to rage, and far from abating as other countries gradually lost their "get a horse!" attitude, the issue intensified through the years. In 1908, for instance, Woodrow Wilson, then staying on the island, was one of a long list of Americans who signed a letter warning of the dangers of motor vehicles in Bermuda. Samuel Clemens (Mark Twain) was another signer. The burning question of whether the island should continue to repel motorcars cropped up again in 1918 (leading to a secret session of the House of Assembly) and again in the 1940s. By 1943, doctors and then veterinarians and the governor were authorized private cars, but a poll conducted by the *Royal Gazette* revealed that its readers voted four to one against cars for general use and a full one quarter of those polled wanted to go all the way back to carless days.

Despite two world wars, the growth of tourism in this century has been phenomenal. The first Newport-Bermuda Ocean Yacht Race took place in 1906 with three vessels competing for the Sir Thomas Lipton Cup. In 1920, regular tourist service to Bermuda from the United States was inaugurated by the Furness-Withy Steamship Company.

Prohibition made Bermuda (like Canada, the Bahamas, and Cuba) a more popular travel destination for the thirsty, well-to-do American. Vessels sailing beyond the "three-mile limit" were free to uncork the world's best liquor, wines, and beers. There was also some rum-running to American shores by the various neighboring islands.

Bermuda, as a member of the British Commonwealth, was very much involved with both world wars, but perhaps more so with World War II. Hundreds of Bermuda's young men went off to fight, while many of those who stayed behind worked long hours at the dockyard preparing warships for battle. (In 1942 alone, some 142 ships were docked here.) Others took part, with British linguists, in a major intelligence operation involving the interception and decoding of secret messages passed between the Western Hemisphere and occupied Europe (with special emphasis given to correspondance heading for Portugal, where many of Germany's top spies were based). The operation was headquartered in the cellars of the Princess Hotel.

The island was also the site of a mini-drama involving the duke of Windsor. While in Portugal, he had been ceaselessly wooed by the German High Command, which had promised that if he helped negotiate a peace treaty with Britain they would, when they won the war, place him and his duchess on the throne of England. In order to remove the duke from temptation, the British government named him governor of the Bahamas and transferred him and his lady to the Caribbean for the duration of the war. The duke arrived on Bermuda August 8, 1940, reputedly torn between the assignment and the Nazi offer.

According to an account in the *Royal Gazette* written long after the war, the duke and duchess were kept busy during their week-long stopover in Bermuda with a continual round of social activities. Toward the end of the week, at a government house dinner, the duke emphatically stated that, "If I'd been King there'd be no war," an ill-considered remark that clearly enraged Bermuda's governor. Realizing that taking the Bahamian appointment would end any chance he had of returning to the throne, the duke sent off a telegram to Portugal, asking his Nazi contact if he should return to the continent. No answer was ever received. As William Shirer noted in *The Rise and Fall of the Third Reich*, "By the middle of August, Hitler had decided to conquer Great Britain by armed force. There was no need to find a new King of England; the island, like all the other conquered territory, would be ruled from Berlin. Or so he thought." A few days later the Windsors left Bermuda for the Bahamas.

Although the conflict interrupted the growth of Bermuda's tourist industry, it reemerged and grew in the 1950s, helped partly by two sets of special visitors who arrived amid great pomp and ceremony in 1953. The first was the newly-crowned Queen Elizabeth II, who toured the island with her husband, the duke of Edinburgh. Later that year, Bermuda hosted a Big Three summit meeting for Churchill, Eisenhower, and Laniel of France. The resulting worldwide publicity, plus the inauguration of regular airline service from both sides of the Atlantic, led to a veritable tidal wave of tourism.

Meanwhile, on the political scene, the Parliamentary Election Act, passed in 1963, helped kill some of the discriminatory practices that for centuries reserved special privileges for an elitist layer of society. (Only those who owned land valued in excess of L60 could vote and only those who owned over L250 worth of land could be elected to the Assembly, provisions originally designed to exclude emancipated slaves from government.) The act pushed the island into a more democratic phase by giving the vote to everyone over the age of 25, thus expanding the electorate from 5,500 to some 22,000 citizens, but it still allowed Bermuda's property owners an extra or "plus" vote. Three years later, by popular demand, the act was amended to enfranchise every Bermudian over the age of 21, and the plus vote was eliminated. The franchise now extends to those born in Bermuda, British subjects who are married to Bermudians, and to British citizens who have resided on the island for three years or more.

In 1968, a new Constitution slightly rearranged the institutions of government. Under the present system, the governor (officially known as His Excellency the Governor and Commander-in-Chief of the Bermuda or Somers Island) is appointed by the queen for a three- to five-year term. But unlike the queen, the governor's powers are more than honorary. He is charged with responsibility for police matters, internal security, national defense (though it is somewhat unlikely that Bermuda will be attacked), and external affairs. Following a general election, the governor must ask the leader of the winning party to serve as premier and to form a new government. The governor then formally appoints the cabinet members recommended by the premier. At least one must be a member of the Senate; the rest are chosen from the Assembly. The premier and Cabinet comprise the executive branch of government.

The two-house Parliament is composed of a Senate and Assembly. The Senate is made up of members appointed by the governor, four of whom are recommended by the premier, two by the opposition leader, and five picked by the governor. Its power is limited. It has no control over the national budget, for instance, and its veto of bills passed by the Assembly can be overturned. The 40-person House of Assembly is composed of elected representatives and it is here that most bills are introduced. As with the English system, the premier can ask the governor at any time to dissolve Parliament and call an election. Otherwise, elections are held every five years. Bermuda's Parliament, originally established in 1630, is the world's third oldest, after England and Iceland.

During the early part of the twentieth century, there was a considerable influx of black workers from the British West Indies, Leeward Islands, and the Bahamas. This new wave added to the strength of the black population enabling it to reach the three-fifths majority it counts today. According to the 1970 census, however, only 7 percent of Bermuda's blacks are not native born.

One of Bermuda's strong Afro traditions is that of the Gombey dancers, whose folkloric art is basically African and West Indian in origin and is closely related to similar art forms and celebrations in Jamaica and the Bahamas. The dancers, separated into groups for children and adults, don facial disguises and elaborate costumes frequently spangled with mirrors and perform to the accompaniment of drums, whistles, rattles, snares, and stomping feet. Several black clubs are active sponsors of Gombey groups, whose tradition began in the mid-18th century. Early Gombey dancers wore high headdresses suggesting buildings and even ships, while today for the most part the height desired for dramatic effect is obtained through the use of peacock feathers.

Like calypso from Trinidad and other islands in the southern Caribbean, and even Jamaica's reggae, Bermudian Gombey frequently has lyrics that comment sarcastically on local social problems and other injustices. Boxing Day, the day after Christmas, and New Year's Day, as well as Bermuda Day, May 23, are dates when Gombey dancers are certain to appear. An imitation of the exuberant Trinidad Carnival itself is also staged during the period of Cap Match in early August.

More Portuguese also arrived early in the present century. Like those who had come earlier, these immigrants were engaged largely in agricultural pursuits and today make up approximately one-fourth of the white population and one-tenth of the total.

Expatriates of all nationalities (English, American, Canadian, West Indian, and Portuguese) make up 29 percent of the Bermudian population and one-third of the labor force. Fifty-seven percent of all expatriates living in Bermuda are whites. In the hotel industry, there are some 5,000 employees, of whom 2,000 are expatriates of various races, including many British subjects who have become "floaters," working their way around the remaining scraps of the Empire. Recent estimates are that the tourist industry employs one-fourth of the labor force, building trades another quarter, business and commerce another quarter, so that three-quarters depend on an industry financed largely by foreigners.

But despite the presence of other nationalities, Bermuda is perhaps the most British of all colonies. Its government, its culture, and its society—still dominated by descendants of early settlers, sometimes unflatteringly referred to as the Forty Thieves—are firmly tied to the mother country, and monarchial symbols and allegiances are both an important part of its history and pervasive elements of everyday life.

Food in Bermuda

by
Mamie Crumbe

My father was lucky enough to have served in Bermuda during the last World War. I was in many ways a remarkably incurious child, for although I saw scattered snapshots of smiling young men in uniform, I studied them only as proof of my father's younger self. I remember only once, prodded by a classmate's boasts of his father's bloody exploits, questioning mine about his wartime service. I received the disappointingly inglorious answer, "Beautiful islands, beautiful people, and the best fish and chips I ever tasted!"

For years I accepted my mother's laughing dismissal of this culinary judgement as resulting solely from comparison with Uncle Sam's rations. With each successive trip to these isles, however, I become more convinced that anything eaten while watching a Bermudian sunset, even the franchised fried chicken now available, must be the "best ever-tasted."

This certainly isn't to say that I have never been subjected to an over-cooked and over-priced meal here, nor that the food keeps me coming back; however, the reputation Bermuda has in some circles for an undistinguished cuisine is undeserved. Since much of Bermuda's food stuffs have always had to be imported, in the days before rapid shipping and air transport, it's possible that Bermudian cooking warranted being called bland, particularly if this verdict were brought by one who disliked fish.

Bermuda always has relied on the bounty of its seas. Today, though the choices now range from New Zealand lamb to Midwestern beef, and from Maine lobster to European pheasant, I find fish the most reliable selection on most menus. This is true whether eating the Continental cuisine served at many of the hotels, the Chinese or Italian food available at some of the specialty restaurants that recently have sprung up, or even, when an extra bit of effort has been spent to find it, a native Bermudian meal.

Most restaurants serve their own version of the traditional rum-spiked fish and conch chowder, and the locally produced sherry peppers garnish many dishes, but only a smattering of other Bermudian dishes can be found on a typical hotel menu. Often the dessert list will make a gesture toward the local palate by including rum-glazed bananas, or the Bermudian version of syllabub (based on wine and cream, of course, but with the inspired addition of guava jelly).

Finding a more varied sampling of Bermudian cooking generally means leaving the hotel restaurants behind. Staying on the American plan is convenient, since all the time not spent on deciding where to eat, and then getting there, can be spent instead on enjoying all the activities which the resort and nature provide. Nevertheless, making time for meals on "the outside" can be a fun (and tasty) way of seeing another side of Bermuda.

From the first castaways, Bermudians have looked to the sea for their nourishment. That they have treated necessity with a creative flair was made clear to me the first time I timidly tasted shark hash and wanted to go back for more. Visitors excepted, almost everything that swims in the surrounding waters is considered fair catch for the cooking pot: Shark steaks; mussel pies and mussel fritters; curried conch, conch steaks, and conch fritters; as well as shrimp, rockfish, snapper, and other fish from local waters, served simply with rice, frittered, or simmered in savory chowders. One of the few limitations on what finds its way to the table is that "guinea chicks," the Bermuda spiny lobster, are in season only in the fall and winter months. That, however, is as good a reason as any to take advantage of the lower lodging rates generally in effect from mid-November to late February.

Many Bermudian dishes do not taste nearly as foreign as the concept of shark hash sounded to me. "Hoppin' John" undoubtably sounds peculiar, but its combination of rice and black-eyed peas will be familiar to many from the American South. This similarity is not really surprising, since the two areas were trading partners from earliest colonial times, and linked by common interests. There is even a Confederate Museum in St. George's.

Bermuda's history is reflected in many of its dishes. As one might expect, the Bermuda onion is widely used. Onion pie, onion soup with sherry peppers, cheese and onion sandwiches, and shrimp and onion salad are but a few of the guises in which this island native shows up on the menu. Though now grown in far greater numbers in Texas, the many imaginative recipes are a reminder that Bermuda gave this sweet onion to the world.

The penchant Bermudians have for tropical fruits, and bananas in particular, points to other historic trading partners, the islands of the Caribbean. Mangos, guavas, and avocados all find their way to the table with regularity, but it is the banana which has become an indispensable part of the local cuisine. From the traditional Sunday breakfast of salt cod and bananas, to every conceivable form of cooked bananas (frittered, fried, baked, or boiled), it is clear that Bermudians consider this fruit their own. Though the climate is not tropical, there are even a few banana groves to prove this claim.

By far the most important Caribbean import, however, is sugar cane. Without it, there would be no rum, and it is almost impossible to think of a meal here without thinking in some way of rum. From rum-laced chowders to rum glazed desserts, it is hard to forget that rum-running was once a major source of income here. Bacardi has an office in Bermuda, so rum is still important to the economy, as well as to the cuisine.

Perhaps the one meal which most clearly illustrates the wide range of influences on the island's cuisine is Christmas dinner. At Christmas, with poinsettias blooming outside, and decorated evergreens inside, it does not seem odd, but only happily Bermudian, to find two such seemingly incompatible dishes as the quintessentially English plum pudding and the tropically-derived cassava pie, side by side on the same table. The cassava, derived from the same root which gives us tapioca, is ground into a flour and used in baking the crust for savory meat fillings. Though cassava is now eaten only rarely in other seasons, the islanders enjoy maintaining this holiday tradition begun by their ancestors three hundred years ago, and almost every family has their own special recipe.

Despite the many good meals I've eaten here, it is not the food in particular that I remember. Breakfast after a lovely morning's ride on the beach, tea taken after a long afternoon of shopping, dinner on a terrace overlooking the harbor: The delightful surroundings are all more memorable than the meal. This is perhaps only fitting, for Bermuda's natural beauty is such that food does not seem as if it should be necessary, but only a delightful afterthought.

But, yes, the fish and chips, eaten after a day of swimming, with the shore still in sight, are the "best-ever!"

The author, Mamie Crumbe, raises peaches in Georgia when she isn't traveling around the world.

14 Bermuda

Hamilton

With a resident population of only 2,000 on a land area of just 180 acres, Hamilton, Bermuda, is one of the world's tiniest capitals. Nevertheless, with its attractive and busy waterfront, spectacular protected harbor (crisscrossed by ferries to other parts of the island), and docks where cruise ships may pull up right along Front Street (the city's main showcase), Hamilton is bustling, cosmopolitan, and attractive.

The town is situated on a narrow neck of land between Hamilton Harbour, an easterly extension of Great Sound, and the north coast of Bermuda fronting the ocean. Incorporated in 1790, around what was originally called Crow Lane Harbour, Hamilton became the capital of the colony in 1815 when British authorities felt more comfortable with a central, protected location on Great Sound than with the more remote northeastern capital of St. George's, where the British occupation of Bermuda started at the beginning of the 17th century. The new location was no doubt partly inspired by the uncertainties of British involvement in the long, drawn-out Napoleonic Wars and the War of 1812 between Britain and her former Thirteen Colonies.

The town is named for Henry Hamilton, one-time governor of Bermuda, who gave his permission to name the place for him in 1793. It is situated in Pembroke Parish, named for the third Earl of Pembroke, a major shareholder in the Bermuda Company, which in 1616 surveyed the land.

Most of present-day Hamilton has a fin de siecle Victorian colonial atmosphere. Many of its white terraced limestone roofs, atop pastel walls, are designed to catch rainwater stored in individual tanks below ground. The limestone roofs are whitewashed every two years and whitewash is often applied to bright red walls, thus creating an extremely popular Bermuda pink, which complements the green foliage and the pinkish sand of Bermuda's beaches.

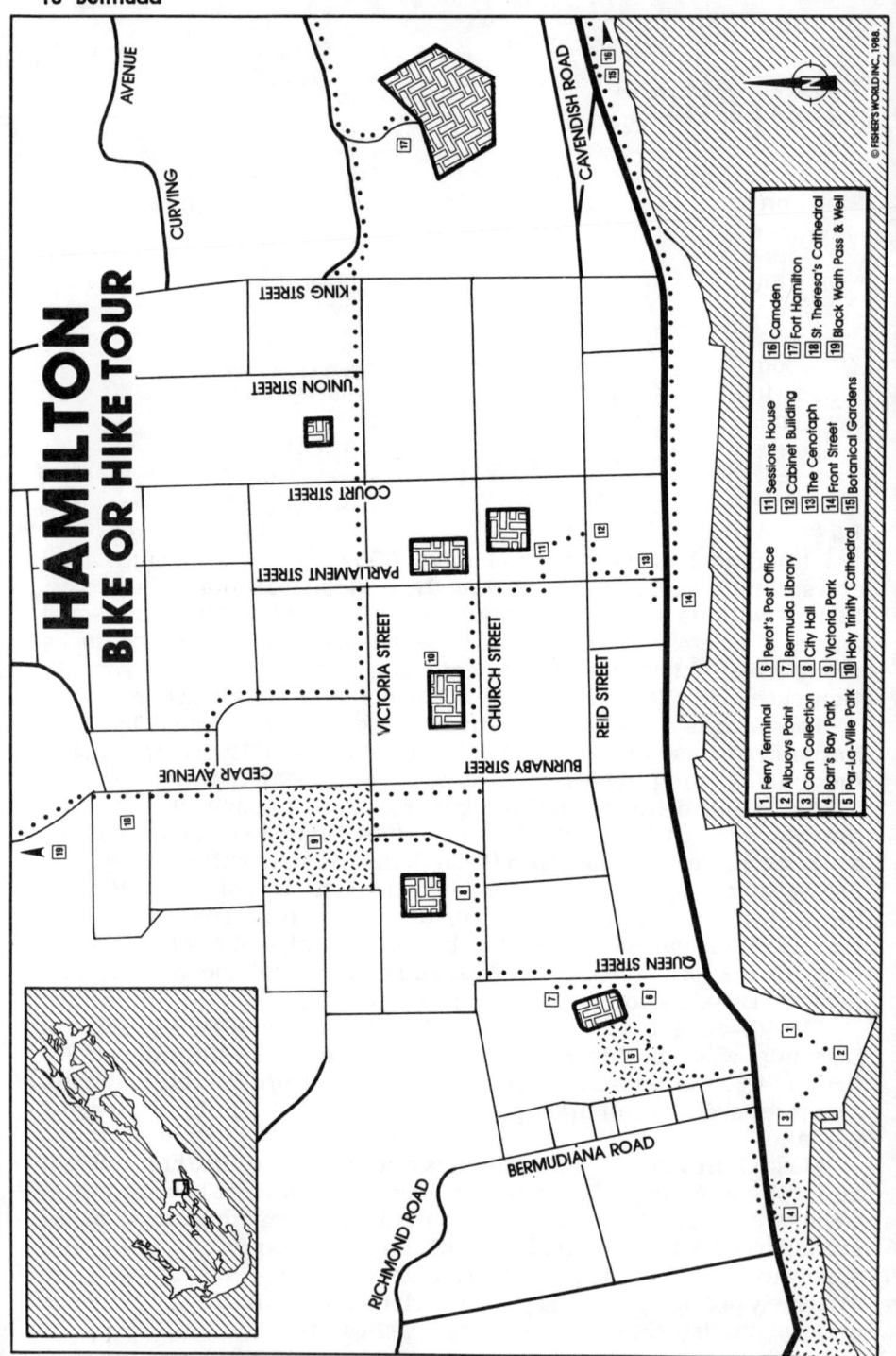

ALONG THE WATERFRONT

The capital's landmarks are numerous, and most are within easy walking distance of one another. Shaped like a horizontal grid along the harbor, the town is anchored by the elegant, elaborate Princess Hotel on the waterfront on the western end, and Fort Hamilton on the eastern end of town.

Horseshoe shaped, with its two wings facing the harbor, the Princess Hotel sits on its own little peninsula south of Pitts Bay Road. Around the corner from the Princess, in a graceful residential section, is a private house built in 1707 by the granddaughter of Richard Norwood, Bermuda's first surveyor. A polite sign at its gate still draws smiles from passersby: "Where tramps must not, Surely ladies and gentlemen will not trespass."

Eastward on the waterfront is the Royal Bermuda Yacht Club, founded in 1844. This is the club that sponsors the Newport to Bermuda race (even-numbered years) in which many of the the world's finest yachts compete. The finish line is at St. David's Head at the extreme eastern end of Bermuda.

Below the club is Albouy's Point, a small park jutting into the bay. Named in honor of a 17th-century professor of pharmacy who fought yellow fever in Bermuda, it provides a magnificent vantage point for viewing impressive Hamilton Harbour.

Behind the park, between Bermudiana Road and Par-la-Ville Road on Pitts Bay, rises the imposing United States Consulate. Beyond, on the harbor side is the Visitors' Service Bureau. Next door is a ferry station providing service to various points across the harbor and sound. At this point Pitts Bay becomes Front Street. Here, in downtown Hamilton, the Bermudian version of a "bobby" (British term for police officer) directs traffic from a "birdcage," one of the most photographed sights in town.

At this point Front Street begins unfolding its elegant shops along the street facing the passenger liner docks. This is prime shopping territory, and also the setting for a number of Hamilton's lively restaurants and night spots.

Continuing along Front Street past Walker Arcade, we arrive at Burnaby Street, another important commercial thoroughfare. The Front Street block between Burnaby and Parliament Street is lined with shops including airline offices.

On the wharf side of Front Street is Her Majesty's Customs, through which freight must pass before entering the country. Front Street continues along several less interesting blocks until it becomes Crow Lane, which leads to a southern road to suburban Page and east to Devonshire Parish.

MOVING INLAND

Turning away from the Front Street waterfront, we find several east-west parallel streets lined with important public buildings and commercial houses as well as residential property. Reid Street runs for four blocks between Queen Street and Par-la-Ville Park on the west side of town to King Street on the east. Three of Hamilton's most important structures may be found on the edge of Par-la-Ville Gardens, a public park between Par-la-Ville Road and Queen Street. They are the old Perot Post Office, facing Reid on Queen and, farther up, in the Gardens, the Bermuda Historic Society and the Public Library.

The Perot Post Office is named for Bermuda's first postmaster, who carried mail around in his top hat. Perot also created the first Bermuda stamp in 1848. As the story goes, it then cost a penny to send a letter to St. George's, but customers arriving after hours too often left insufficient payment. So Perot's friend Herl, who ran an adjoining apothecary, suggested the concept of creating a postage stamp. Perot made the stamps by hand and signed each one. Today, the post office still has a small-town feel. A well-used desk is usually occupied by someone dashing off a last minute postscript, and behind decorative grills is a friendly staff ready to assist both philatelists and those who just want to get off a postcard to home.

Bermuda Library

A century ago, the Bermuda Library was the home of Postmaster William Bennett Perot. Among the historic collections is one of all newspapers and magazines published in Bermuda beginning as early as 1787. The Historical Society Museum contains memorabilia from early colonial days such as portraits of Sir George Somers and his lady, and early maps of the colony, including a 17th-century map by Richard Norwood, who is credited not only with the first survey of Bermuda but its demarcation into tribes which later became parishes. Antique Bermudian cedar furniture, coins (including the "hog penny"), and old china are also displayed, as are models of the *Sea Venture* (the ship that first brought colonists to Bermuda, albeit by mistake), the *Deliverance*, and the *Patience*. There is also a copy of the famous letter written by General George Washington in 1775, asking Bermuda for gunpowder. Around the library are gardens planted by the first postmaster, including a soaring rubber tree that dates back to the mid-1800s.

City Hall

From Reid Street northward on Queen Street, the sightseer arrives at a slight turn to the left where Queen Street becomes Wesley Street. Across to the right facing Church Street, Hamilton's modern City Hall (built in 1960) sits in a little park of its own. The structure, topped by a weathervane shaped like the *Sea Venture*, houses a theater and an art gallery that exhibits Bermudian artists' work. During some of the most clement months, there are exhibits on the grounds. Exhibitors frequently offer works for sale through the Bermuda Society of Arts.

As for the theater in City Hall, it is probably the best in Bermuda, but is not entirely suitable acoustically for concerts. There is also a convention-concert hall at the Ruth Seaton James Auditorium, which has the unfortunate defect of allowing audiences to be conscious of rain on the roof at inopportune times.

Hamilton's Churches

The City Hall Park occupies the entire block between Church and Victoria streets and between Wesley and Burnaby streets. Across the latter, it faces another square block enclave occupied by the most imposing of Bermuda's churches, the Anglican Cathedral of the Most Holy Trinity, seat of the bishop of Bermuda. In religious, as in governmental matters, the colony is structured like a miniature Britain. Although freedom of religion is scrupulously respected, the Church of England stands high in nonsecular matters and its presiding bishop occupies a position of eminence and prestige. The present structure, dedicated in 1894, was built on the site of a previous cathedral destroyed by arson in 1884. It is built in Gothic style from Bermudian limestone, marble, and granite, with a commanding central tower that dominates the capital skyline. The interior has reredos sculpted by noted Bermudian artists in British oak and Bermudian cedar and a remarkable stained glass Window of Angels, which was the work of Bermudian artist Vivienne Gilmore Gardner. There is a flag-clustered Warrior Chapel, dedicated in 1977 to Bermuda's fallen soldiers, throne chairs for visiting royalty and ecclesiastical dignitaries, and priedieux and locally made prayer cushions, which are heavily hand-embroidered.

Across Parliament Street from the Anglican cathedral is Wesley Methodist Church, perhaps the leading church of its denomination on the island. One block east of Wesley, on Court between Church and Victoria streets, are two other churches of note: St. Andrew's Presbyterian and, above it, St. Paul's African Methodist Episcopal Church. The latter, historically one of the island's most prestigious black churches, is closely related to the same denomination founded in Philadelphia in 1793 and of which black American abolitionist Richard Allen was the first bishop.

Other important Hamilton churches are north of the Anglican cathedral complex. The Roman Catholic Cathedral of St. Theresa at the corner of Laffan Street and Cedar Avenue, a block above Victoria Park, is built in Spanish mission style and is noted for its exceptional carillon.

Sessions House

Due south of Wesley Methodist Church is the Victorian structure known as Sessions House, with its two Italianate towers of unequal height rising from either end. The taller clock tower was added to celebrate Queen Victoria's golden jubilee in 1887. The building itself has a parklike entrance facing the harbor and is the real seat of power of the Bermudian government. Upstairs, the Speaker of the House of Assembly presides in full wig and robe with mace before him under portraits of George III and his Queen Charlotte, while the Assembly itself, like the British House of Commons, sits on government benches and opposition benches accommodating a division of the house in approved British parliamentary style. Cabinet members are members of this House and must defend government policies on the floor. The premier sits in the place of honor on the government side while the opposition, led by a "shadow" premier sits opposite. As in Britain, the opposition chooses a "shadow" Cabinet, which may become the Cabinet if the opposition wins the next island-wide election. There is a visitors' gallery in both the Assembly and in the Supreme Court (the former City Hall) on Front Street, where the chief justice and barristers wear traditional English wigs and robes. The House meets on Fridays at a time that may be ascertained by telephone (292-7408). Visitors are welcome in both chambers but are requested to dress and behave decorously. For timing of court sessions, telephone 292-1350.

The Cabinet Building

Another imposing structure, the Cabinet Building, sits in a landscaped enclave bounded by Front, Parliament, Court, and Reid streets. In this building the Senate, the "upper house" of the Bermudian parliament, meets and the governor has his office here. The Senate, roughly equivalent to Britain's House of Lords, is composed of senators who are appointed for terms rather than for life and who have an advisory role much less powerful than that of the Assembly in Bermudian affairs. It convenes on Wednesdays at 10:00 A.M. For information, phone 292-7408.

At the opening of Parliament in October each year, the governor assembles Parliament in joint session in the Senate chamber where he reads the equivalent of Queen Elizabeth's "Speech from the Throne," an outline of government policy prepared for him by the premier and his advisers. On this occasion, he stands before a carved Bermudian cedar "throne" dating from 1642 and the term of Governor Josiah Forster.

Standing in front of the Cabinet Building on Front Street is an imposing monument or, to use the British term, cenotaph, to Bermuda's dead of World War I. The cornerstone was laid by the late duke of Windsor while he was prince of Wales.

THE OUTSKIRTS OF HAMILTON

Fort Hamilton

Hamilton's immediate surroundings offer other sightseeing objectives, not the least of which is Fort Hamilton on the east side near Cavendish Road and Crow Lane on the road to Paget Parish. It is a relic of the post-Napoleonic era during which the Duke of Wellington, along with other British statesmen, thought it would be wise to convert Bermuda into the "Gibralter of the West." Fort Hamilton, like many others of its kind in Bermuda and elsewhere, was later assumed to be useless because it never fought an engagement with an enemy, but who is to say how many attacks its presence forestalled?

Once allowed to fall into ruin, Fort Hamilton has now been imaginatively restored. It is a pleasant spot from which to contemplate the beauty of Hamilton and its spectacular harbor. The grounds have been beautifully landscaped with oleander, ponciana, poinsettia, coleus, and other plants that thrive in Bermuda. There is no admission charge and children especially seem to enjoy the excursion.

NORTH SHORE

Government House

On the northern edge of downtown Hamilton, just past St. Theresa's Roman Catholic Cathedral, one comes upon the Tennis Stadium where important tournaments are held. There are all-weather courts at most of the resort hotels and tennis professionals in residence at the more affluent ones. (Tradition says that a Bermudian lady, Mary Outerbridge, brought the game to the United States in 1874 and that it was first played in the States at the Staten Island Cricket Club in New York.) Nearby are Victoria Park, created to commemorate the queen's golden jubilee in 1887, and historic St. John's Anglican Church, which dates from 1625. Originally known as Spanish Point Church, its graves bear the names of many of those who nutured Bermuda through its infancy and passage to modern times. Up the hill of Mt. Langton, one arrives at Black Watch Well, dug by members of that famous Scottish regiment at the request of the governor during the severe dry spell of 1849.

On the north shore itself, beyond the Tennis Stadium, are the impressive grounds of Government House atop Mount Langton, where the governor of Bermuda resides during his term of office.

As the queen's representative in Bermuda, the governor is the ceremonial head of state taking precedence over all other officials and serving as a living link to the Crown itself. The head of government, of course, is the premier, who is responsible for the day-to-day conduct of the affairs of state. The gardens and residence of Government House are closed to visitors except on special occasions when invitations are issued. The distinguished guests at Government House have included Queen Elizabeth II and Prince Philip, Charles, Prince of Wales, Sir Winston Churchill, President John F. Kennedy, and others.

In 1973, Governor Sir Richard Sharples and his aide-de-camp, Captain Hugh Sayers, were assassinated in the gardens of Government House and Bermuda was plunged into an unaccustomed crisis. The assassins, who were tried and executed in 1977, were obviously unhinged, but the event exacerbated relations between the privileged and underprivileged in Bermuda and led to rioting and bitter feeling, which have since abated.

NEARBY HAMILTON

Spanish Point.

At the top of the Pembroke Parish is Spanish Point, where Captain Diego Ramirez may have camped when he stopped to draw a rather detailed map of the island in 1603. At the end of the point is Cobbler's Island.

Admiralty House

Built in the early 1800s when the Royal Navy reigned here, Admiralty House has been empty since British forces withdrew from the island in the 1950s. Though it's not open to visitors, it's worth mentioning in passing that beneath the house is a series of caves specially built for an admiral with a passion for spelunking.

Depending on your interests, I suggest you combine Hamilton sightseeing, perhaps including an hour of observing the legislature at work, with shopping on Front Street (see Shopping in Author's Choice). There are a host of eating options, from pubs to fine restaurants to tea break spots (see Restaurants in Author's Choice).

Special events in Hamilton range from turnouts by Gombey dancers in the streets on Boxing Day (the day after Christmas) to sunset hour Beating the Retreat on Front Street by the volunteer corps of the Bermuda Regiment (400 men) and a cadet pipe band. This follows the medieval British tradition of summoning people within the fortified walls of castle towns for safety at night.

During Rendezvous Time, the winter season from December to March, there are military, sports, choral, and other special events.

Shopper On The Go

by

Janet Steinberg

Ho hum . . . another perfect day in paradise. Send the beachers to their pink spun-sugar beaches. Let the golfers challenge water holes such as the Atlantic, and tennis buffs test approximately 100 courts..

But shoppers, you come along with me. Crisscrossing the striking unspoiled island known as Bermuda, I'll show you shopping you didn't know existed. Like the rest of the jocks that sport in Bermuda, you will also work up a sweat shopping the island from A to Z.

Archie Brown & Son has been bringing fine British knitwear and woolens to Bermuda for over 50 years. "The Pringle Shop," as it is dubbed on its distinguished pink and green shopping bag, is the exclusive dealer of these fine Scottish cashmeres that cost approximately 40 percent less than the U.S. price. Check out the hidden corners on the second floor. They often reveal clearance racks jammed with bargains in cashmere and Harris tweed.

Bermuda bottle bargain . . . Liquor is a good buy with considerable savings over U.S. and Canadian prices. You can take home ready mixed bottles of Bermuda's exotic Rum Swizzle or that other island refresher Dark 'n' Stormy. Locally made liqueurs such as Bermuda Gold, Bermuda Banana, and Bermuda Creme are also a taste treat. Check U.S. Customs and state liquor laws for importation quotas.

Coins provide a field day for numismatists in Bermuda. These duty-free purchases are a favorite of collectors, investors, and souvenir hunters. You'll find everything from ancient "pieces of eight" to royal wedding commemoratives. Before you buy, you might want to view the Bermuda coin collection at the Bank of Bermuda in Hamilton.

Davison's cable-knit, 100-percent cotton, V-necked sweater was priced from $70 to $90 in New York (depending on the neighborhood). The identical sweater was $39.95 at Davison's in Bermuda. But, get this—Bermuda's English Wool Shop undersells even Davison's. The sweater was only $35.95 there.

Early Riser, the historic pilot gig (oared sailing boat) that was lost in 1876, is one of Bermuda's Wrecks, a commemorative issue of stamps on sale at the Bermuda Philatelic Bureau. Located in the general post office in Hamilton, the bureau services visiting philatelists and maintains a mailing list so you can continue your purchases once you go home.

Friendship goblets, turned from a single piece of Bermudian cedar, are as aromatic as they are beautiful. The single ring around the stem denotes friendship. The double ring is usually given as a wedding gift. Goblets from this precious wood remain prized possessions for a lifetime.

Genuine Bermudian-made products are identified by a round emblem with the words Bermuda Product encircling it. This distinctive sticker guarantees that you are purchasing an item made in Bermuda. The staggering selection of Bermuda products is growing in both quantity and quality.

Highland flinging is never out of fashion on this tartan filled island where there's a huge choice of kilts, including one called "Bermuda Blue."

Whether or not you have some Scottish blood in you, you'll want to take home a plaid kilt. Those at Archie Brown & Son are not the heaviest on the island, but they are the cheapest.

Iceland's oldest and largest knitwear manufacturer, Alafoss, (est. 1869) is represented at the five Chameleon Sweater Shops located around the island. Alafoss is no ordinary wool. The unique conditions found on the volcanic island of Iceland have produced sheep whose wool is longer, silkier, and more water repellent than that of any other breed. Alafoss designers lead the way in contemporary Icelandic woolen fashions.

Jay Fox, one of Bermuda's popular singing troubadours has two delightful records, *Signature* and *Reflections,* which are wonderful ways to preserve memories of Bermuda. They're available at gift and record shops throughout Bermuda and, of course, from Jay himself.

Knick Knack is a reasonably-priced, multi-level department store with entrances on Washington and Reid streets in Hamilton. The store features good quality clothing, footwear, beachwear, and a nice selection of Bermuda T-shirts. On Fridays and Saturdays only, you can pick up extra savings in the bargain basement.

Let them eat cake. The recipe for an old traditional Bermuda cake has been revived and is now being packaged for visitors to take home. The recipe for this intoxicatingly different confection is a closely guarded secret. However, it has been revealed that one ingredient is a generous splash of black rum.

Moongates, the graceful arches scattered around the island, have been executed in porcelain by Lladro of Spain. Moongates, brought to Bermuda by a 19th-century sea captain who had seen them in China, symbolize unity, peace, and happiness. The porcelain version, complete with a pair of lovers, is approximately $90 for the 10-inch size.

Natural Nailfiles, available in drug and gift shops, are actually the scales of very large Amazon River fish called Pirarucu. There are three different surfaces on the nailfiles: a waxen texture on the inside of the curve, a hornlike colored surface on one-third of the outer curve, and a fine abrasive surface on the remaining two-thirds of the outer curve. This is the nailfile surface that is used as you would use an emery board.

Outerbridge's Sherry Pepper Sauce has been an island tradition for years. Made originally by families for their own use, this spicy condiment became so popular that two men began producing it. They called their product Outerbridge's Original Sherry Peppers and used a secret family recipe that requires steeping selected bud peppers and more than a dozen different spices in casks of sherry for months. The resulting liquid proved to be a favorite seasoning.

Pottery, handcrafted at Bermuda Pottery in Blue Hole Hill. The glazes are made of a secret formula and have been designed to reflect the spectacular Bermudian colors of the green sea, blue sky, leafy greens, and sunny yellows. The Longtail, the dramatic seabird that is the harbinger of Bermuda's summer, is a favorite subject of the potter. So too, is the hibiscus which flowers throughout the year on the island.

Questions about any item you're looking to buy and can't find will be answered at the Visitors' Service Bureau at the Ferry Terminal on Front Street in Hamilton (9 A.M. to 5 P.M., Monday-Friday). Other bureaus are located at King's Square, St. George's, and Somerset.

Rock watches . . . time in stone. Tissot, the fine Swiss watchmaker, has created a watch that is like a granite sculpture. Inspired by the endless variations of color, grain, and structure of the stone, artists create timepieces that are as individual as a fingerprint . . . as personal as a signature. Available at Astwood Dickinson in Hamilton and Southampton.

Scents make sense if you confine your purchase of local fragrances to those of the Royall Family. Royall Lyme, the world famous line of island fragrances is justly famed for their cool understated scents. Royall Lyme and Royall Spyce, with a base of native limes and allspice leaves respectively, come in soaps and toilet lotions. So too, does Royall Bay Rhum, a very masculine fragrance and Royall Muske, the elegant sophisticated addition to the line.

Trimingham's is Bermuda. This Front Street landmark (with branches throughout the island) has been family owned and run since 1842. A tradition of providing quality in British and European merchandise has earned Trimingham's its well- deserved reputation for excellence. British cashmeres and woolens, Scotch tartans, French perfumes, and Irish crystal are offered here.

Upstairs Golf and Tennis shop caters to the needs of the golf and tennis enthusiasts. Located on Church Street, at the traffic light opposite City Hall, this specialty store offers well known brands of clothing and accessories that will enhance your favorite sport.

Videos now let you take a little bit of Bermuda home with you. Six videos (VHS or Beta) keep Bermuda as close as your video recorder. *Bermuda Bound, Paradise Found, Bermuda Highlights,* and *Flower Paradise Bermuda* are three of the videos that capture the beauty and sensations of the island.

Windjammer Gallery is housed in a charming yellow cottage on the corner of Reid and King streets in Hamilton. Exhibited here are outstanding collections of work by local and international artists, including signed silk screen prints by Graeme Outerbridge.

Xpressions is a fashionable boutique located at 29 York Street in the quaint town of St. George's. Featured are collections of ladies' wear and accessories by Canadian designers. There is also an interesting selection of designer jewelry.

Yankee Store, on Reid Street in Hamilton, features lovely Bermudian cedar items that are made in Bermuda. One of the island's most beautiful natural resources is lovingly carved, molded, and polished into a lasting memento. You can choose from a selection of clocks, boats, candleholders, bookends, salad servers, and plaques.

Zee whiz! What can you buy with a Z? Zillions of enticing items are bursting the seams of Bermuda's boutiques, department stores, art galleries, coin, and jewelry shops. Let the golfers swing their clubs. Let the tennis jocks hit their racquets. But those of you who are now in the know can just stamp your credit cards. You'll score high in Bermuda.

Janet Steinberg is a contributing editor to Travel Agent magazine and a regular travel columnist for several magazines.

26 Bermuda

ST. GEORGE'S

St. George's

FIRST CAPITAL OF BERMUDA

Imagine, if you will, being one of 150 would-be English colonists aboard the *Sea Venture*, bound for Jamestown in 1609. An angry storm has scattered six sister ships, provisions are running low, and frightened fellow passengers rue their decision to leave the comparative safety of England. Through the sheets of rain and ocean spray, land appears and hope glimmers. But with a sudden shudder, the ship careens from soaring surf onto solid reef and there hangs precariously.

Such was the introduction of Admiral Sir George Somers and his charges to the shores of Bermuda. The wreck of the *Sea Venture* occurred on the rocks below the site of Fort St. Catherine, near the serene town of St. George's.

The ship's company were able to transfer themselves and the bulk of their possessions to land. They also managed to salvage much of the timber from the *Sea Venture*, and with the single-mindedness characteristic of so many early pioneers, set about building new ships to transport them to their original goal, Jamestown.

In the spring of 1610, the company set sail for Virginia aboard new transportation, the *Deliverance* and the *Patience*. Later that same year their courageous leader, Admiral Somers, died. In 1612, 50 adventurous American colonists sailed back to Bermuda aboard the *Plough*. On arrival, they officially founded the town of St. George's, named in honor of St. George, patron of England, and probably Sir George Somers as well. Sir George's heart was interred in Bermuda and his body returned to England for burial. In tribute to him, companions named Bermuda in his honor and Somers Isle is still an alternate designation for the island cluster originally named for Juan de Bermudez.

28 Bermuda

ST. GEORGE'S BIKE OR HIKE TOUR

Legend:
1. Visitors Information Centre
2. Deliverance Ship
3. Town Hall
4. Bridge House
5. State House
6. Somers Garden
7. Unfinished Church
8. St. George's Historical Society Museum
9. Featherbed Alley Printery
10. The Old Rectory
11. St. Peter's Church
12. Tucker House
13. Carriage Museum
14. Confederate Museum

© FISHER'S WORLD INC. 1988.

Although St. George's was christened in 1612, it was inhabited for almost two years by only three men, left behind when the *Plough* continued on to England. When the first full-fledged colonists arrived, they were jubilantly greeted by these three "kings" of Bermuda, who were by now bedraggled, sun baked, and prone to fighting among themselves. That they had successfully held the island for England had more to do with a lack of invaders than their military prowess.

The colonists found dense woods of dark cedars and palmettos, which they used for housing. A profusion of wild pigs, fish, sea turtles, berries, and birds were used for food. (Legend has it that many of the landbirds were so tame that they obligingly landed on settlers' shoulders and were promptly gobbled up.) The only eerie sights on the island were the gloomy groves of mangroves, their roots sunk deep into shadowy inlets.

Before long, it was apparent that cedar housing was not hurricane resistant. After some experimentation, the settlers hit upon limestone as the ideal building material, both for houses and for the forts they erected to stave off the conquerors who never came. These early citizens of St. George's turned to the task of tobacco growing in an effort to nourish the economy. Bermuda, however, was ill suited for this enterprise, so gradually ship building became the colony's special focus.

Today St. George's still retains much of the feel of those early times. And unlike its slightly older sister Jamestown, now merely a reconstruction of its former self, St. George's is still actively inhabited by some 1,600 residents. The town is situated in the Parish of St. George's, composed of two islands linked to Hamilton Parish by a causeway. The southern island, shaped like a boomerang, is almost entirely occupied by Bermuda's international airport, equipped to accommodate the largest airliners, with terminal facilities to match. The northern island across St. George's Harbour is St. George's Island proper.

The town was the capital of Bermuda until 1815 when the colonial government moved to Hamilton, which offered a central location and greater security. St. George's is the second most important destination for visitors, and some cruise vessels elect to anchor off its shores and use tenders to bring passengers ashore. Public service buses make the trip out from Hamilton in about an hour and at certain times of the year it seems that all Bermuda gathers here for special events, such as the April Peppercorn Ceremony, in which the governor traditionally receives a peppercorn as payment for a year's rent from the Masons for the use of the historic State House, which dates from 1620.

WALKING AROUND ST. GEORGE'S

It is customary, and sensible, to begin a walking tour of St. George's at King's Square. There's plenty of bike parking here, as well as a Visitors Information Centre and, in a special theatre atop St George's

Town Hall, continuous showings of *The Bermuda Journey*, a 25-minute presentation that imaginatively captures 375 years of Bermudian history. After the show, look for a small bridge near the White Horse Tavern, which anchors one corner of King's Square. Across the bridge is tiny Ordnance Island.

Sitting high and dry on Ordnance Island is a full-sized replica of the *Deliverance*, one of two vessels built by Sir George Somers and his shipwrecked crew. The original *Deliverance* was actually built on the adjacent mainland while her sister ship, the smaller *Patience*, was constructed on Ordnance Island. In 1610 both ships set sail for Jamestown, Virginia, temporarily abandoning the then inhospitable shores of Bermuda. This duplicate, dating from 1970, is open to visitors.

Nearby is a model of a colonial dunking stool, a cantilevered contrivance resembling a seesaw with a seat at the far end. In early times, gossips, scandalmongers, and obstreperous wives were tied into the seat and doused in the cold sea water. In the mid-1600s, when witchcraft hysteria surfaced in Bermuda, dunkings also were administered to determine the guilt or innocence of women accused of being in league with the devil. Drowning proved one's innocence. Those who survived the experience were taken to the gallows to be hanged as witches.

Back on King's Square, known in the past as King's Parade and Market Square, are replicas of colonial stocks and pillories that held heads, hands, and feet by means of sliding wooden panels. These were used for the humiliation of those found guilty of petty crimes and misdemeanors.

Take a moment from this vantage point to look again at the handsome Town Hall, a near duplicate of the original building constructed in 1782. It contains offices of the mayor and the town corporation, consisting of three aldermen and five counselors. The facade of the building is emblazoned with St. George's coat of arms, and there are two flanking stairways that lead to the second story. Inside, furniture made of Bermudian cedar and portraits of mayors are displayed.

King Street enters the square at its northeast corner. Here, in a little triangular garden is a bust of the Irish poet Tom Moore. A few steps farther, on the left, is Bridge House, built around 1700. During the American Revolution it was home to the infamous "Honorable" Goodrich, a Virginia privateer who preyed on both American ships and Bermudian vessels trading with the Americans. Although the British honored his exploits by erecting a memorial in St. Peter's in his name, the tribute to the "Honorable" was instantly defaced, presumably by one or more Bermudians not keen about his choice of targets. Today, Bridge House is an art gallery devoted to the works of Bermudian artists.

At the end of King Street is the State House, the oldest building in Bermuda, dating from 1620, built in what Governor Nathaniel Butler thought of as Italian style with a flat roof, inviting leaks. When St. George's was the capital of the colony, the House of Assembly met in this building, which also provided the setting for receptions and other festivities under governmental auspices. Now it is rented to the Masons who ceremoniously pay one peppercorn annually. From Duke of York Street, behind the State House, One Gun Rum Alley leads down to the waterfront.

A little farther north on Princess we come to Duke of York Street, which forms the southern boundary of the irregular quadrangle of Somers Gardens. Dedicated by the then Prince of Wales in 1920, the gardens are the burial place for Sir George Somers's heart.

Through the park and up a hill (crossing the point where Governor's Alley meets Slippery Hill) is the Unfinished Chapel, a Gothic stone structure ambitiously begun in 1874 when St. George's was still the capital and intended to replace St. Peter's. Quarrels within the church a few years later led to the abandonment of work and Bermuda's only cathedral was subsequently built in Hamilton.

Back down Duke of Kent Street is the Historical Society in a house dating from 1725 that contains a collection of antiques illustrating life in 18th- century Bermuda. It was in front of this building, in 1801, that a Methodist missionary named John Stephenson broke the law by preaching to blacks. He was both fined and imprisoned but continued undeterred to preach from the barred windows of his basement cell (now the home of the post office on the corner of Water and Queen streets).

If you turn right here, you'll be on Featherbed Alley, home of the noteworthy Featherbed Alley Print Shop, housing a working model of a 17th-century press with movable type, a copy of the original invented by Gutenberg in Germany during the mid-15th century. The street name supposedly derives from featherbeds that once lined the street as a convenience for drunks to sleep off their intoxication!

Going westward, one comes to Church Street and the imposing edifice of St. Peter's Church and Rectory. The latter is said to have been built in the early 18th century by a reformed pirate, and only served briefly as the rectory. The building is owned by the Bermuda National Trust and is occupied by a private tenant but is open to visitors on Wednesdays and Saturdays (except holidays). St. Peter's churchyard contains many graves of slaves, dating back to the 17th century, but among the more modern ones are those of assassinated Governor Sir Richard Sharples and his aide Captain Hugh Sayers. Some Americans, including Richard S. Dale, a seaman during the War of 1812, and a U.S. Consul, John W. Howden, who died of yellow fever in 1852, are also buried here.

St. Peter's Church lays claim to being the oldest Anglican church in the hemisphere still used for worship. The present building dates from 1713; its clock tower was added in 1814. The original wooden church was built in 1612 and replaced seven years later by a stone edifice that lasted nearly a century. It was here that the first meeting of the Bermuda Parliament was held in 1620, and until the State House was constructed legislative sessions also convened here. The Bermudian cedar altar dates from the 1620s and is enhanced by a triple-tiered pulpit and cedar roof beams. The baptismal font of ironstone is believed to be of 15th-century origin, and there is a silver communion service, which was the gift of William III, co-monarch with his wife, Mary II, for whom the College of William and Mary in Williamsburg, Virginia, was named. The knife marks on the silver paten are attributed to the irreligious Governor Samuel Day, who allegedly used it as a dinner service! The interior walls of the church are lined with memorials to distinguished St. Georgians, including Joseph Stockdale, the island's first printer.

Returning to Church Street and heading left, you'll run into Printer's Alley, named for Stockdale who arrived in Bermuda in 1783 with his own printing press. For 20 years he published the *Bermuda Gazette*. Not far away is Hillcrest, a guest house with a traditional Bermudian moon gate. At the beginning of the 19th century, this establishment was host to Tom Moore, the well-known Irish poet, who was apparently smitten with his neighbor's wife, "Nea" Tucker, to whom he wrote passionate verses. It's no wonder that the the westward extension of Printer's Alley has been named Nea's Alley.

South of Nea's Alley, on Aunt Peggy's Lane, is St. George's Library, located in Stuart Hall. A circulation library set in an old private home, it boasts cedar-beamed rooms and Bermuda-made furniture in a cozy atmosphere.

Two lanes take one back down to Duke of York Street. One is Old Maid's Lane because, yes, a century ago there were some unattached older women living here. The other is Silk Alley, sometimes called Petticoat Lane, where two freed women are reputed to have cavorted in silk petticoats after the abolition of slavery in 1834.

If you follow Silk Alley, you'll bump into Barber's Alley, named in honor of Joseph Rainey (1832-1887). Rainey, a free black man from South Carolina, escaped to Bermuda with his wife aboard a blockade runner during the American Civil War and set himself up as a barber in St. George's. He returned to the States after the war to become the first black congressman.

Farther down, on Water Street, one comes upon Tucker House, where the fugitive American rented the kitchen from the owner during his Bermuda exile. Tucker House, is now a museum owned by the National Trust. It was built in 1752 and housed several generations of the distinguished Tucker family, one of the most famous in Bermuda. The house was named in honor of President Henry Tucker, whose title came from his presidency of the town council. President Tucker was the son of Colonel Henry Tucker, the son-in-law of Bermuda's governor and related to the Tuckers of Williamsburg, Virginia, some of whom sided with the Americans during the Revolutionary War. The house contains family portraits and a generous legacy of furniture presented by a centenarian cousin from Baltimore, Robert Tucker. Among distin-

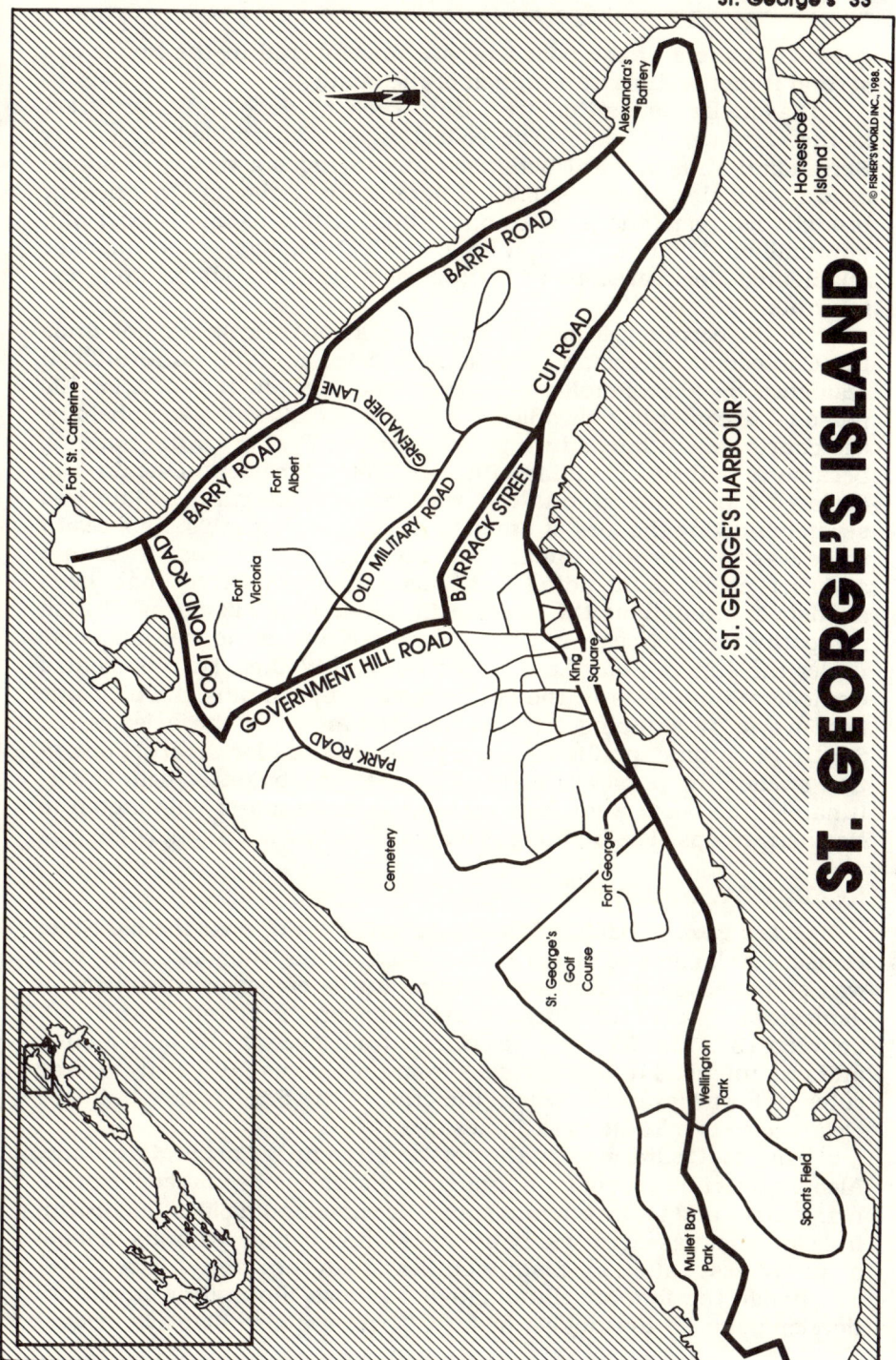

guished Tuckers of the past who are remembered in the house are several from the American branch of the family.

Diagonally across the street from Tucker House on Water Street is the Carriage Museum. The collection was assembled largely by Bermudian Mrs. Bernard Wilkinson and includes a variety of horse-drawn vehicles from small children's run-abouts to elegant broughams, phaetons, and an opera bus. The museum is part of a multimillion dollar restoration project, which has converted the once dilapidated dock area to an attractive setting for shops and restaurants.

On the corner of King's Square at Duke of York Street, one finds the Confederate Museum, a building erected in 1700 as an official residence by a Bermudian governor, who sued to retain it for his personal use after leaving office. He died before his suit was upheld by the courts. Much later, during the American Civil War, the building became a hotbed of military intrigue. After President Lincoln had declared a blockade around the rebellious Confederacy, Britain was severely hurt by the loss of American cotton for her mills. As a result there was widespread sympathy for the Confederate cause in Britain and her colonies including Bermuda, although slavery had been abolished throughout the Empire in 1834. Capitalizing on British sympathy for their cause, Confederate authorities opened an office under the supervision of one Major Norman Walker. He represented Confederate interests in the British colony by running the blockade both ways: by shipping arms in and cotton out of the beleaguered South. For a time, profits from the blockade and black market operation swelled the purses of many of St. George's businessmen. Unfortunately, the boom went bust in 1865 with the fall of Wilmington to Northern troops. The building is maintained by the National Trust.

NEARBY ST. GEORGE'S

Gates Fort. Taking Water Street out of town, past the old State House, you'll come to Gates Fort, named for Sir Thomas Gates, who was shipwrecked on the *Sea Venture* and later became governor of Jamestown. One of the oldest fortifications on the island, it was built between 1612 and 1615 by the colony's first governor, Richard Moore, and was intended to repel attacks from the Spanish. Close by are the ruins of Fort Alexandra, where the crew of the *Sea Venture* built the *Deliverance* to take them to Jamestown.

Fort St. Catherine. On the northeastern tip is Fort St. Catherine. Also a project of the colony's first governor, it has been reconstructed many times and today is a museum. The commanding location, frowning cannons, passageways, battlements, and parade grounds make it a special destination for history buffs and adventurous children.

Inside the fort are illuminated dioramas illustrating important developments in Bermuda's history. There are also displays of flags

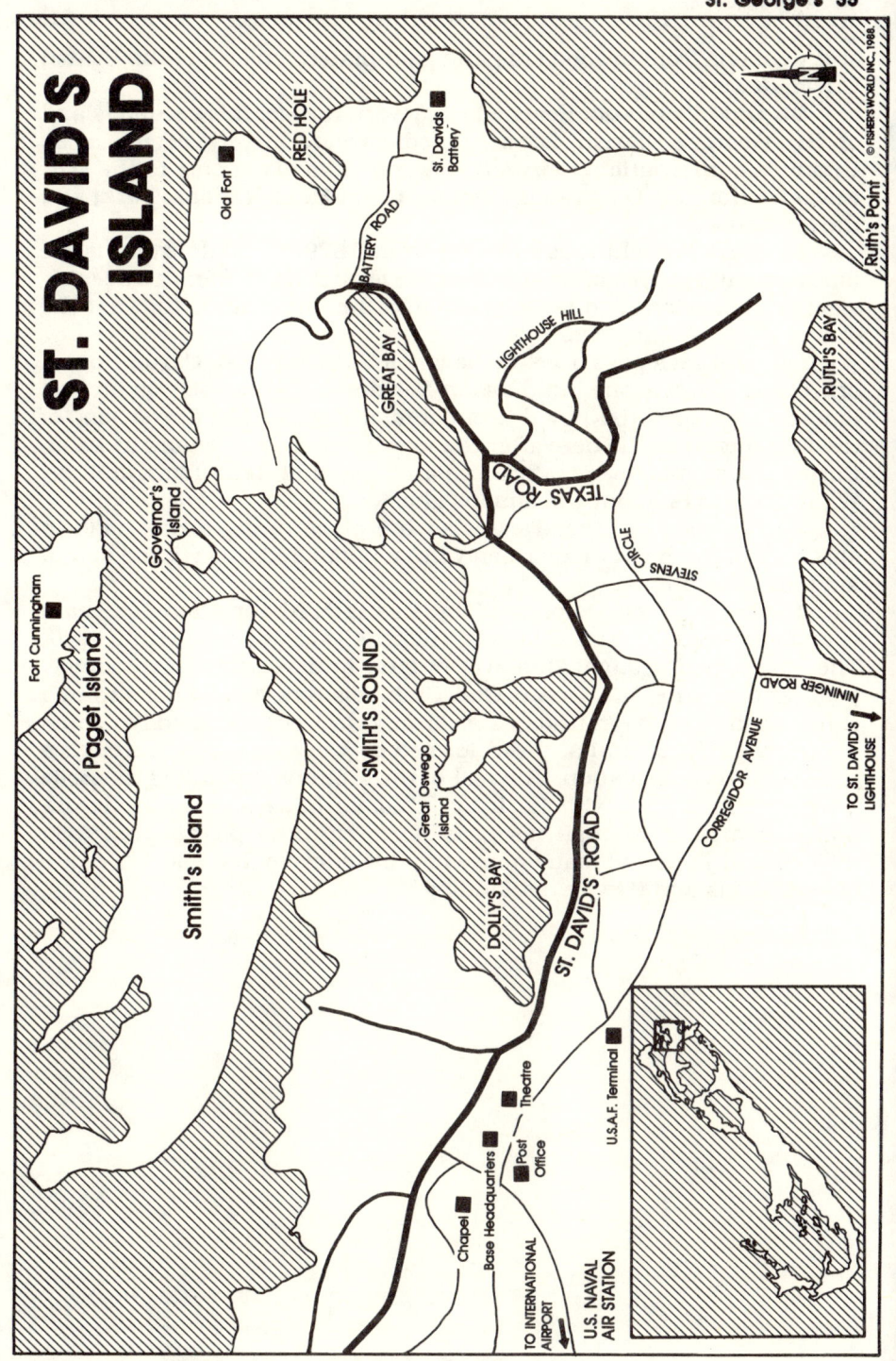

and weapons from bygone eras and gold-plated replicas of the British Crown Jewels.

St. David's Island. Reached via Severn Bridge, this second island of St. George's Parish is, as noted earlier, largely occupied by Bermuda's international airport. However, it is also home to the U.S. Naval Station, St. David's Lighthouse, Great Head National Park, and Carter House.

St. David's Lighthouse, dating from 1879, is made from native limestone and rises a modest 55 feet. Nevertheless, it offers a sweeping view of the eastern end of Bermuda and the tiny islands that dot the Castle Harbour entrance.

One can get a pass from the Naval Air Station to visit Carter House, one of the oldest stone buildings in Bermuda. The house was built of limestone around 1640 by descendants of Christopher Carter, one of the first men to settle here after the wreck of the *Sea Venture* in 1609. Carter House has been restored as a museum of Bermudian culture. While there, ask about the famous ghost.

By the way, St. David's is also the place to get shark hash, a specialty of the hearty fishermen who've populated this rugged spit of land for generations.

Tucker's Town. Separated by Castle Harbour from the main islands that comprise St. George's, Tucker's Town is a world unto itself. The government bought this arm of land to develop the exceedingly posh and private Mid Ocean Golf Club. Visitors can swing through some of the club grounds, specifically to visit Bermuda's much photographed "natural arches," formed by waves crashing through a once solid rock formation. The rest of the grounds, including the Belle Cove neighborhood, with its truly fabulous houses, are strictly off-limits. (Warning: Though it's possible to zip onto private roads via motorbikes, there are many houses in this enclave that sport "Beware of Dog" signs and they're not kidding.)

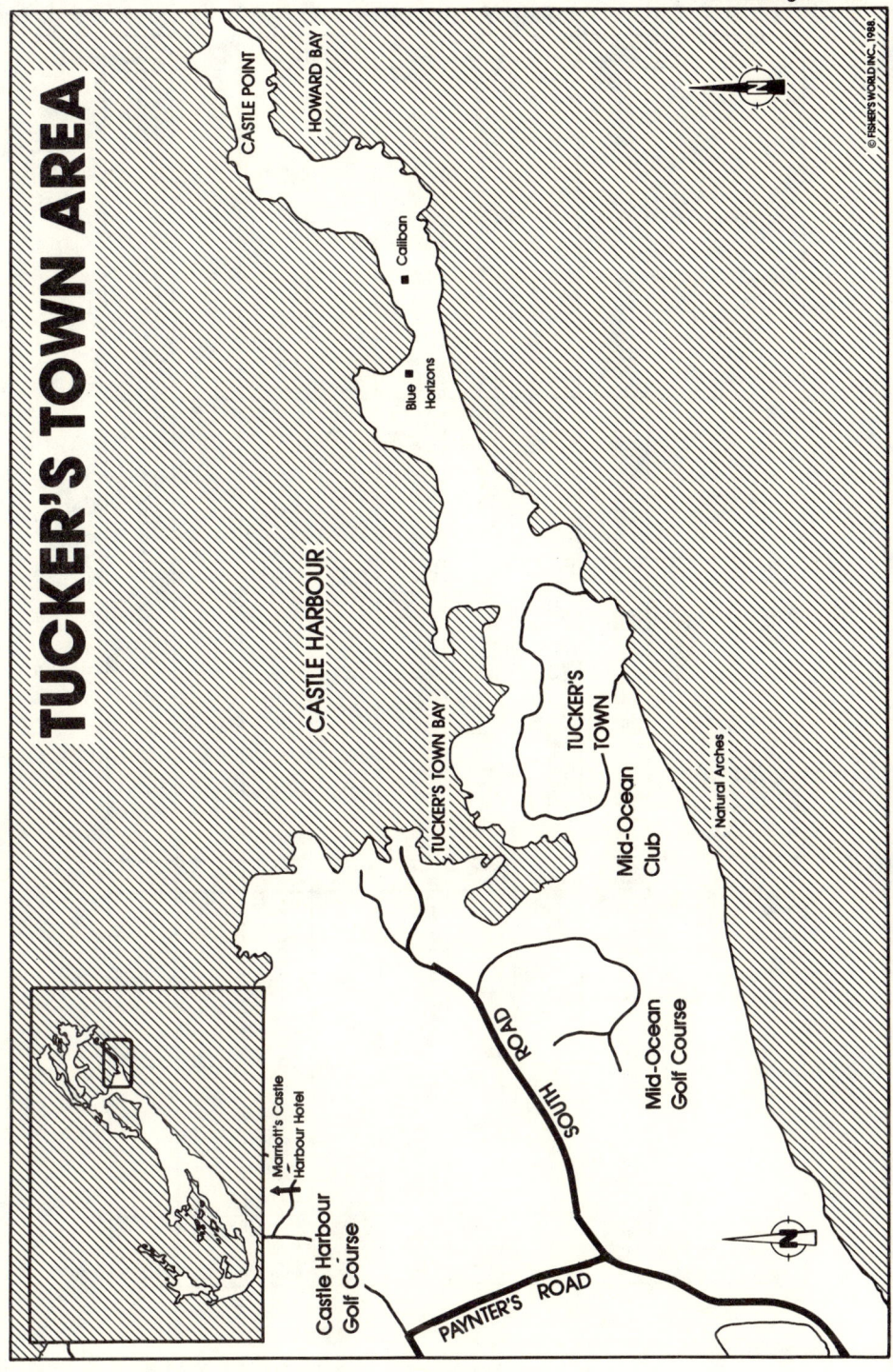

FERRY SCHEDULE

	Leave Hamilton	Hinson's	Belmont	Darrell's Wharf	Salt Kettle	Hodson's	Lower Ferry	Arrive Hamilton
Hamilton ▶ Paget Warwick	7:15am	7:25am	—	7:30am	—	—	—	7:40am
	7:45	—	7:55	8:00	8:05	—	—	8:10
	8:15	—	8:25	8:30	—	—	—	8:40
	8:45	—	8:55	9:00	—	—	—	9:10
Monday through Friday	9:20	—	9:30	9:40	—	—	—	9:50
	10:00	—	10:20	10:10	—	—	—	10:30
	10:40	—	10:50	11:00	—	—	—	11:10
	11:20	—	11:40	11:30	—	—	—	11:50
(Saturday's	12 Noon	—	12:10pm	12:20pm	—	—	—	12:30pm
first ferry	12:40pm	—	1:00	12:50	—	—	—	1:10
leaves Hamilton	1:20	—	1:30	1:40	—	—	—	1:50
at 8:45 am)	2:00	—	2:20	2:10	—	—	—	2:30
	2:40	—	3:00	2:50	—	—	—	3:10
	3:20	—	3:30	3:35	—	—	—	3:45
	4:10	—	4:30	4:20	—	—	—	4:40
Hinson's Island	5:10	—	5:20	5:25	—	—	—	5:35
Stops only	5:40	—	6:00	5:50	5:45	—	—	6:10
on request	6:15	—	6:25	6:35	6:45	—	—	6:50
	7:00	—	7:10	7:15	7:20	7:25	7:30	7:35
	7:50	—	8:10	8:00	7:55	—	—	8:20
	8:36	—	8:45	8:55	9:00	—	—	9:05
	9:20	—	9:40	9:30	9:25	—	—	9:50
	10:05	—	10:15	10:20	10:25	10:30	10:35	10:40
	10:45	—	11:05	10:55	10:50	—	—	11:15
	11:20	—	11:30	11:35	11:40	—	—	11:45
Sundays and Public Holidays	10:10am	—	10:20am	10:25am	10:30am	10:35am	10:40am	10:45am
	11:00	—	11:20	11:10	11:05	—	—	11:30
	11:45	—	11:55	12:05pm	12:10pm	—	—	12:15pm
	12:30pm	—	12:50pm	12:40	12:35	—	—	1:00
	1:15	—	1:25	1:35	1:40	1:45	1:50	1:55
	2:30	—	2:50	2:40	2:35	—	—	3:00
	3:15	—	3:25	3:35	3:40	—	—	3:45
	4:00	—	4:20	4:10	4:05	—	—	4:30
	4:45	—	4:55	5:00	5:05	5:10	5:20	5:25
	5:40	—	6:00	5:50	5:45	—	—	6:10
	6:25	—	6:35	6:45	6:50	—	—	6:55
	7:10	—	7:35	7:30	7:25	7:20	7:15	7:45

	Leave Hamilton	Lower Ferry	Hodson's	Salt Kettle	Arrive Hamilton
Hamilton Paget ▶	7:45am	—	—	8:05am	8:10am
	8:15	8:20	8:25	8:30	8:35
Monday through Friday	8:45	8:50	8:55	9:00	9:05
	9:15	9:20	9:25	9:30	9:35
	9:45	9:50	9:55	10:00	10:05
(Saturday's	10:15	10:20	10:25	10:30	10:35
first ferry leaves	10:45	10:50	10:55	11:00	11:05
Hamilton at 8:45 am)	11:15	11:20	11:25	11:30	11:35
	11:45	11:50	11:55	12:00pm	12:05pm
*Does not return to Hamilton Terminal	12:15pm	12:20pm	12:25pm	12:30pm	12:35
NOTE: See Hamilton	12:45	12:50	12:55	1:00	1:05
- Paget - Warwick	1:15	1:20	1:25	1:30	1:35
Ferry Schedule	1:45	1:50	1:55	2:00	2:05
for ferry schedule to	2:45	2:50	2:55	3:00	3:05
Paget stops after	3:15	3:20	3:25	3:30	3:35
5:45 pm Monday	3:45	3:50	3:55	4:00	4:05
through Friday,	4:15	4:20	4:25	4:30	4:35
Saturdays, and Sundays	4:45	4:50	4:55	5:00	5:05
	5:15	5:20	5:25	5:30	5:35
	5:45*	5:50	—	—	—

	Leave Hamilton	Dockyard	Watford Bridge	Cavello Bay	Somerset Bridge	Arrive Hamilton
Hamilton Somerset	6:15am	—	7:00am	—	6:45am	7:30am
	6:25	6:55	7:15	7:25	7:40	8:10
Dockyard ▶	7:35	8:05	8:15	8:25	—	8.50
	9:00	9:30	9:50	10:00	10:15	10:45
Monday	10:00	11:15	10:55	10:45	10:30	11:45
through	11:00	11:30	11:50	12:00pm	12:15pm	12:45pm
Friday	12Noon	1:15pm	12:55pm	12:45pm	12:30pm	1:45pm
	1:00	1:30	1:50	2:00	2:15	2:45
	2:00	3:15	2:55	2:45	2:30	3:45
	3:00	3:30	3:50	4:00	4:15	4:45
	4:00	5:15	4:55	4:45	4:30	5:45
	5:20	6:35	6:15	6:05	5:50	7:05
	6:00	7:05	6:55	6:45	6:30	7:35
Saturday ▶	7:00am	7:30am	7:50am	8:00am	8:15am	8:45am
	9:00	9:30	9:50	10:00	10:15	10:45
	10:00	11:15	10:55	10:45	10:30	11:45
	11:00	11:30	11:50	12:00pm	12:15pm	12:45pm
	12Noon	1:15pm	12:55pm	12:45pm	12:30pm	1:45pm
	1:00	1:30	1:50	2:00	2:15	2:45
	2:00	3:15	2:55	2:45	2:30	3:45
	3:00	3:30	3:50	4:00	4:15	4:45
	4:00	5:15	4:55	4:45	4:30	5:45
	5:20	6:35	6:15	6:05	5:50	7:05
	6:00	7:05	6:55	6:45	6:30	7:35
Sunday and Public Holidays ▶	9:00am	9:30am	9:50am	10:00am	10:15am	10:45am
	11:00am	12:15pm	11:55	11:45am	11:30am	12:45pm
	1:00pm	1:30pm	1:50pm	2:00pm	2:15pm	2:45pm
	3:00	4:15	3:55	3:45	3:30	4:45
	5:00	5:30	5:50	6:00	6:15	6:45

Bermuda is Another World
by
Andrew Vladimir

It was a sunny day in March 1984 when I first walked down Front Street as Bermuda's new director of tourism. I was the first American, indeed, the first non Bermudian, to hold this post. As I left my hotel room and walked past elegant shops like Trimingham's and Smith's, I faced the fact that I had been handed more responsibility than I had ever had in my entire career. Sixty thousand people who received seventy-five percent of their gross national product from tourism were depending on me to create better jobs and more opportunities for them.

I did not know very much about Bermuda when I accepted the job. I had spent my honeymoon there 20 years before but had not been back since. I did know that Bermuda's Department of Tourism had been ranked as one of the most successful and best managed in the world.

It was an honor to have been chosen. The department had a substantial staff of dedicated and experienced people to help me do my job. I had met Premier John Swan, and my impression was that he wanted very much to have me succeed and had gone out on a limb to bring me to Bermuda.

A key part of understanding Bermuda is to appreciate its size and character. Here you have a group of islands consisting of scarcely more than 20 square miles on which close to 60,000 people live. That works out to 3,000 people per square mile, making it one of the most densely populated places in the world. The average household income is $34,000, so Bermudians are also some of the most affluent people in the world. Considering that the island has no marketable natural resources—not even a natural supply of fresh water, it is a miracle that Bermudians have been able to attract more than half a million visitors annually to what is essentially a crowded coral reef 600 miles out in the Atlantic.

You can't live on an island the size of Bermuda and not be a sociable person. The extraordinary friendliness every visitor has noted for a hundred years is real, and has nothing to do with a desire for tourist dollars. Most Bermudians have to like one another, and if they don't, they have learned how to coexist peacefully.

My wife and I were fortunate in being able to live in one of Bermuda's most beautiful and historic homes—Blackburn Place on Harbour Road right across from Darrell's Wharf ferry stop. The house is furnished with antiques dating back to the 18th century and overlooks Hamilton Harbour. Our neighbors and landlords Gordon and Shirley Asbury couldn't have been more gracious. They invited us to use their swimming pool and share their vegetable garden. Connie Englehardt, who owns the Inverurie Hotel across the street, offered the use of his tennis courts. We discovered the nearby Friendly Supermarket, where it is still the custom to charge your groceries and pay monthly. Every morning when I rode to work on the ferry, everyone said good morning, and it was considered good form to inquire about work and family.

In 1975, Bermudians realized that the way to expand their economy was not by building more hotels but rather by improving the quality of the ones they already had as well as the entire experience of visiting Bermuda. So a moratorium on building was declared and no new rooms have been added. There were, however, several proposals on my desk to improve existing properties. Loew's wanted to sell its hotel in St. George's to Club Med. Marriott wanted to buy the Castle Harbour Hotel and rebuild it. Both proposals required the approval of the Department of Tourism. Home Lines Cruises also wanted to build a new ship, the *Homeric*, to serve Bermuda.

The problems involved in all these cases reflected the concern Bermudians have for maintaining the delicate balance between the interests of tourism and the interests of society. There was a real concern that Club Med might attract a new kind of visitor to Bermuda, Europeans, for instance, who would want to go swimming topless as they did on the French Riviera. Jobs were at stake at both hotels. If Castle Harbor closed while Marriott rebuilt it, how many people would be out of work and for how long? Would the Club Med continue to employ Bermudians or want to bring in a large international staff?

The concerns about the Home Lines proposal were of a different nature. Unlike many other tourist destinations the shops and the restaurants the Bermudians patronize are the same ones that the visitors use. For all practical purposes there are no "tourist traps" in Bermuda because they would also have to trap Bermudians to survive. The total number of visitors on the island has always been controlled. Since cruise ships bring in 1,000 or more visitors at a time, too many can easily crowd the shops and eating establishments to a point where service is noticeably affected. While visitors might be willing to accept this, Bermudians are not—their island is their home, and who wants a home so full of guests that no one gets taken care of?

These questions were all aired publicly in local parish and church meetings and in the pages of the *Royal Gazette*. Irving Pearman, the minister of tourism, whom I admired greatly, would have to defend my actions in Parliament as well, and I did not want to do anything that might embarrass either him or the government. At first, I found this disconcerting as a professional manager—it was not a process I could control or manage. But I recognized that I was not a Bermudian and my children and grandchildren would not have to live with the consequences of my decisions. There is a Tourism Board in Bermuda appointed by the premier and they too gave me a good deal of guidance as to what areas were likely to cause the most problems. In the long run, the extended public debates proved helpful because the director of tourism, like elected officials, is a public servant, and when I was able to appreciate what Bermuda wanted and needed, I had a clearer direction and mandate to work with.

Besides the internal problems of managing and controlling growth, the Tourism Department is also in charge of various attractions and activities. I discovered Fort St. Catherine was run by our department and a new curator needed to be appointed. Then there were activities like the Newport to Bermuda race to which we contributed funds and staff, and College Weeks, when 2,000 students invaded our shores and needed to be cared for.

Finally, my job involved promoting Bermuda all over the world. We had a multimillion dollar advertising and public realtions budget and we utilized newspapers, magazines, television, and direct mail extensively. We had our own staff of photographers and writers and routinely hosted programs like "Lifestyles of the Rich and Famous" which came to Bermuda to do broadcasts. We also had sales and information offices in New York, Boston, Atlanta, Chicago, Toronto, and London. These offices mainly worked with travel agents, groups, and meeting planners who were interested in Bermuda.

Every year the department hosted more than a thousand agents whom it invited to visit Bermuda, as well as hundreds of members of the press and other media representatives. In cooperation with the Hotel Association the department organized training and informational seminars and receptions that were presented in major cities all over the United States and Canada. My role was to tell audiences how much we had to offer and how proud and honored I was to represent Bermuda. On these trips, my colleagues and I wore powder blue Bermuda shorts (even in a snowstorm in Boston), a blue blazer with the crest of Bermuda embroidered on it, and a special Bermuda tie. Often we would take entertainers like the famous Talbot Brothers with us or the Bermuda Regiment Band. St. George's famous town crier Bob Burns, who has been called the loudest man in the world, was also an employee of our department. He was in demand whenever we could spare him from his regular duties of making the rounds and assuring the populace that all was well!

Another aspect of my job that was new was the routine formal appearances and functions that are an important part of Bermudian life stemming mainly from her British heritage. For example, there was the Queen's Birthday Party and the annual Peppercorn Ceremony at St. George's. There were formal calls to Government House to meet with the governor and his aides. Although I worked for the civil service, I had been formally appointed by Lord Dunroissil under the authority granted him by the queen. Bermuda's 375th Anniversary was in 1984 and Princess Margaret arrived to open our Parliament. I was excited to learn that I ranked 23rd on the government protocol list. That was high enough so that I would be presented to Her Royal Highness. All of us so honored received two pages of instructions on how to act in her presence. I was told that while I was expected to answer her questions, it was not proper for me to address any of my own, nor should I engage in any conversation unless first invited by the princess to do so. In fact, Her Highness was truly interested in the outlook for Bermuda's tourism industry and I enjoyed telling her about it!

I am often asked, as an American who was fortunate enough to be part of the inner workings of the government, what I really think of Bermudians. It is not an easy question to answer. The most important thing to any Bermudian is the future of their island—where it is going and how it will get there. The net effect to a visitor is that the troubles and concerns of the outside world seem to receive little attention on the island. But this is a superficial impression. Bermudians are literate and well traveled. They are concerned about world affairs and are interested in participating. Bermuda is not simply "another world", as the song you are bound to hear during your visit there goes. It is a world where you will always be welcome if you take time to understand and appreciate it.

After many years of running various advertising agencies (his own included), Andrew Vladimir is currently a visiting assistant professor at F.I.U. in the School of Hospitality Management.

PARISHES OF BERMUDA

The Parishes—
West to East

The division of Bermuda began around 1618 when 400 strips were traced across the island from shore to shore. Every other strip was designated a "tribe road"; land falling within the strips was sold both to the 600 pioneers then in residence on the island and to London-based backers of the colony. Thus began the establishment of a first coterie of landed gentry whose descendants form much of Bermuda's present aristocracy. (Modern maps still refer to tribe roads, but individual land holdings today tend to be modest.)

As most visitors know, Bermuda is not chock-a-block with must-see monuments and museums. Still, the island offers much that is pleasantly diverting, and there are a few attractions well worth a special trip. Of course, renting your own car for sightseeing is out of the question, but Bermuda's bus system is efficient and taxi drivers may well be the best in the world in terms of helpfulness and knowledge of their country's sights and history. And do-it-yourself motorbike touring is a Bermuda tradition. When biking, just remember to stay on the left—and when approaching an intersection or traffic circle, look to the right. Bemudians do drive cautiously; nevertheless, each year there are many bike accidents involving wrong-way visitors.

One way to avoid traffic contact is to take advantage of the Bermuda Railway Trail. The trail was turned over to bikers and walkers in 1984 as part of the island's 375th anniversary. It follows a stunningly picturesque route along the coast, through quiet forest glades, from St. George's to Somerset (excluding three miles around the city of Hamilton). Here and there are benches and picnic tables. Graceful white longtails glide overhead; cedars, fiddlewoods, and hibiscus line some stretches.

KEY TO BERMUDA RAILWAY TRAIL

1. Somerset Bus Terminal
   The original railway building
2. Springfield & Gilbert Nature Reserve
3. Harman's Bay
   Rich Woodland of Fiddlewood
4. Heydon Trust Estate
5. The Bermuda Cedar
   View over the Great Sound
6. Fort Scaur
7. Somerset Bridge
   Smallest drawbridge in the world
8. Evans Pond
   Stands of native flora
9. Old Bermuda houses
10. Franks Bay
11. Relaxing view of Little Sound
12. Geological history
13. Dunes
    One of the largest
14. Black Bay
15. Gibbs Hill Lighthouse
16. Jews Bay
17. Princess Park
18. South Shore Beach Parklands
19. Tall Allspice Woodland
20. Khyber Pass, huge quarry
21. Warwick Pond, a bird sanctuary
22. Belmont Golf Course
23. Old Bermuda houses
24. Elbow Beach
25. Surinam Cherry
26. Superb view of the City of Hamilton
27. Paget Marsh Nature Reserve
28. Old Railway Tunnel, 450 feet long
29. Palmetto Park
30. Palmetto Hotel, 18th Century
31. Panoramic Views
    of the North Channel
32. Penhurst Park
33. Gibbet Island,
    where witches were burned
34. Lovely Flatts Inlet
35. Coney Island Park, Cricket Pitch
36. Bailey's Bay
37. Shelly Bay Park and Nature Reserve
38. Flatts Inlet, Harrington Sound
39. Aquarium
40. Tiger Bay Gardens
41. Mullet Bay Park
42. Rock Hill Park
43. Sugarloaf Hill
44. Lover's Lake Nature Reserve
45. At Ferry Point Park

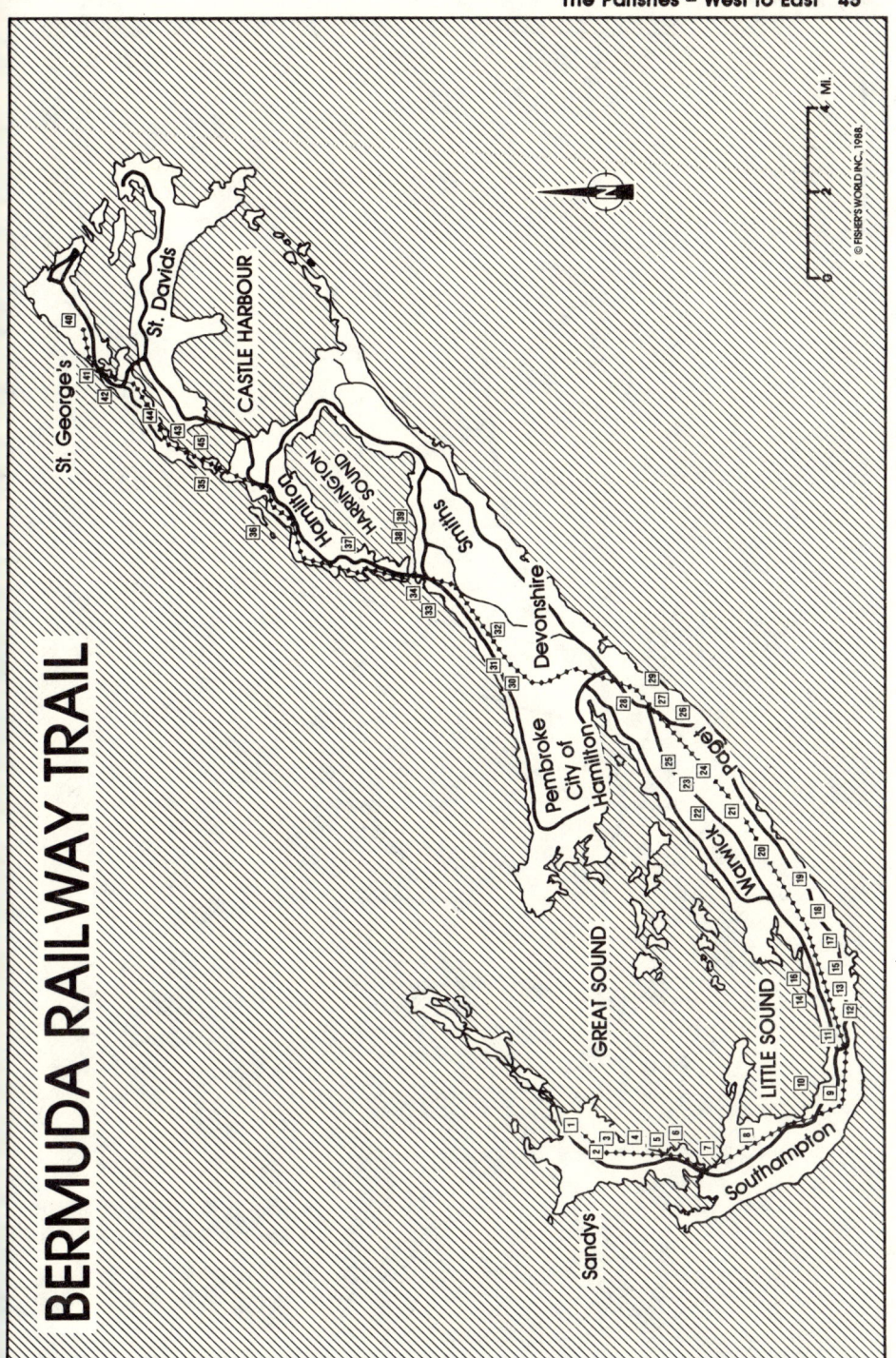

46 Bermuda

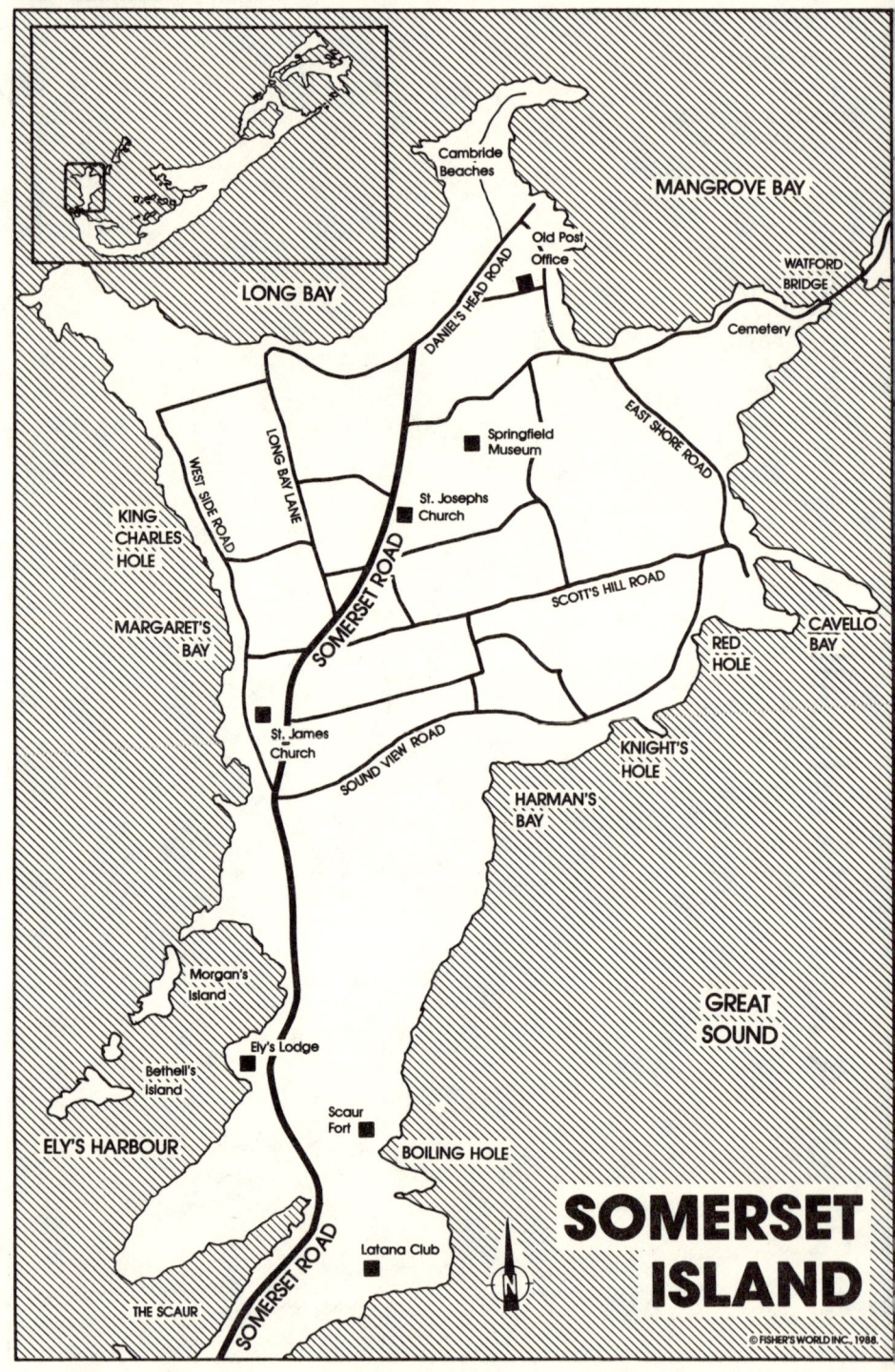

Bermudian homes exhibit several interesting architectural details. One of the most famous is the "welcoming arms" staircase, a design in which stairs leading up to a house taper gradually as they approach porch level. This creates a feeling of being graciously drawn into the heat of the home. You'll also notice that while all island houses sport bright whitewashed roofs, there are two roof styles. Newer houses have stepped roofs; older models have less practical flat roofs. All have a cistern system that allows Bermuda's precious rainfall to be caught by rooftop pipes, channeled down through the walls and deposited in a basement tank. (The pipe opening can be closed in the event of a hurricane.) Harder to spot is the difference between old and new building materials. Houses dating back to the 1700s were usually constructed of limestone, which though sturdy, has a tendency to hold dampness. Contemporary homes are built of cement blocks with holes that allow the structure to "breathe."

The following describes much of what there is to see in each of the parishes - with the exception of St. George's and Pembroke/the City of Hamilton, which are covered in separate sections.

Sandys

Sandys (pronounced "sands") Parish, named for Sir Edwin Sandys, a large shareholder in the original Bermuda Company, covers Ireland Island North, Ireland Island South, Somerset Island, and several islets off the coasts of the Atlantic and Great Sound. It also includes the northernmost tip of the Bermudian "mainland" just below Ely's Harbour.

Bermuda's premier attraction, one I highly recommend, is the indoor-outdoor Maritime Museum, located on the windswept tip of North Ireland Island. Part of the fun of visiting the museum is getting there from Somerset Village, via a series of little bridges along a narrow spit of land. On a balmy summer day, the biking is easy. In winter months when the wind gusts mightily, the ride can be rigorous.

On the ocean side are strips of beach, some with picnic tables and stretches of rock formations, buffeted by waves and spray. The inland side is mostly tangled greenery, but do look for a small old cemetery. It's worth a stop because the quirky gravestones not only record centuries-old names and dates, but also the manner of death: by drowning, cannon ball, hanging, etc.

You'll know you're nearing the museum when you pass a series of standard issue military barracks. The museum property is solidly dominated by a massive fortress, with ancient stone walls that rise toward the sky in fierce resolve to repel marauders. At its feet is the working dockyard complex, which until 1950 served as one of the British Navy's bastions of power. That the fortress and dockyard were not allowed to crumble is to the credit of the West End Development Corporation, which began restoration work in 1974 and projects completion by 1992, in time for the 500th anniversary of Columbus's discovery of the New World.

48 Bermuda

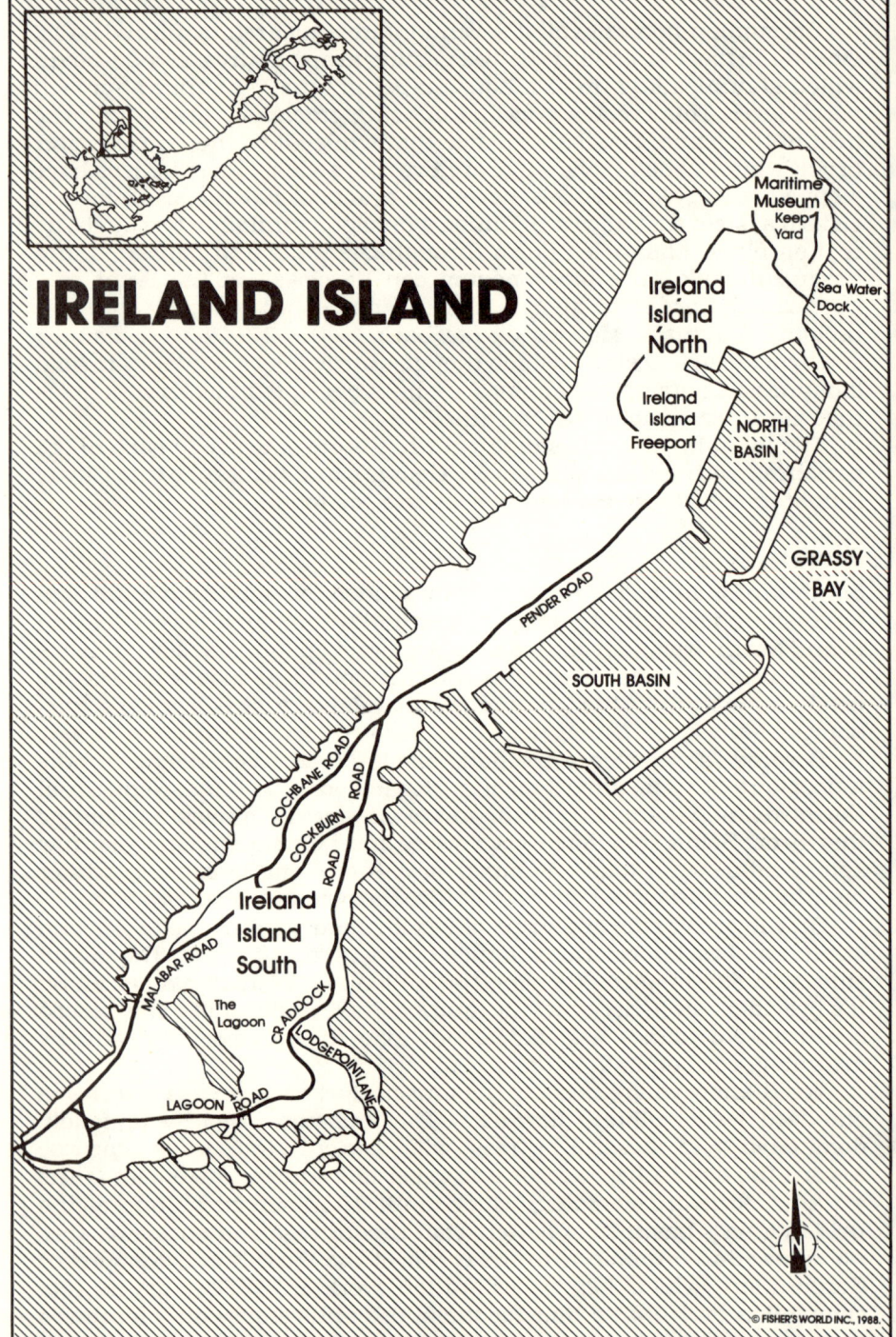

There's plenty to see right now, however. Entering via the fortress keep, once used to store gunpowder, the visitor is free to meander through exhibits of Bermuda's 300-year seafaring history. There are exhibitions of boats and boatbuilding, of pearl and treasure diving, the whaling industry, and collections of treasure wrested from the sea. On the parade grounds is a giant figurehead of King Neptune, taken from the wooden battleship HMS *Irresistible;* the Forster Cooper building offers a history of the dockyard, and up on the ramparts one can relive the heady experience of being one of Bermuda's early defenders.

Across from the museum entrance is the Old Cooperage where an excellent hour-long multimedia show, *The Attack on Washington,* tells the story of Bermuda's history and the island's role in the War of 1812.

In the Arts Centre at the dockyard is a craft market where local artists display a variety of goods: hand-made quilts, delicate, whimsical cards and signs for the younger set, botanical prints (some from Carole Holding, whose work I particularly admire), stained glass boxes and ornaments, hand-dipped candles, pottery, and, of course, T-shirts. The setting is informal, leading to pleasant interchanges between artists and visitors.

As part of the ongoing restoration, the dockyard's marina has been given a new lease on life. Visiting yachts now tie up at its once cobwebbed piers; there's a marina clubhouse and informal restaurant; and cruise ships (but by law, only one at a time) will make Dockyard stops. In addition, the Terrace Pavilion offers regularly scheduled concerts during summer months.

I suspect that you'll want to linger beneath the fortress walls, and perhaps grab a fish sandwich and a beer, and sea-gaze and take snapshots. Unless you hit the museum grounds on a particularly crowded day, there's a bit of magic in the air. But do save some time for the nearby snug and sleepy little village of Somerset, home to three ferry terminals and fishing boats, which unload their catch on the Mangrove Bay docks. On East Shore Road, near Cavello Bay, is the Gladys Morell Nature Reserve, a Bermuda National Trust property acquired in 1973 from the Sandys Chapter, Imperial Order, Daughters of the Empire, to which the late Mrs. Morell left the acreage as a nature preserve. A short walk away, on Somerset Road, is The Springfield Museum and Gilbert Nature Preserve. The mansion was owned by the Gilbert family from 1700 to 1973 and is now one of the Bermuda National Trust Houses. The most handsome of the mansion's rooms are used as the Somerset Library (open Mondays, Wednesdays, and Saturdays). Outbuildings house the original kitchen, slave quarters, and buttery (a high-ceilinged cooling shed built over a stream). The surrounding five-acre reserve of rambling woodland is open to visitors every day, year round.

On the Atlantic side of Somerset, near Church Bay, is beautiful old St. James Parish Church (Anglican). The present building, dating from the 18th century, replaced the original, which was probably destroyed by a storm. About 1836, additional aisles were added on both sides of

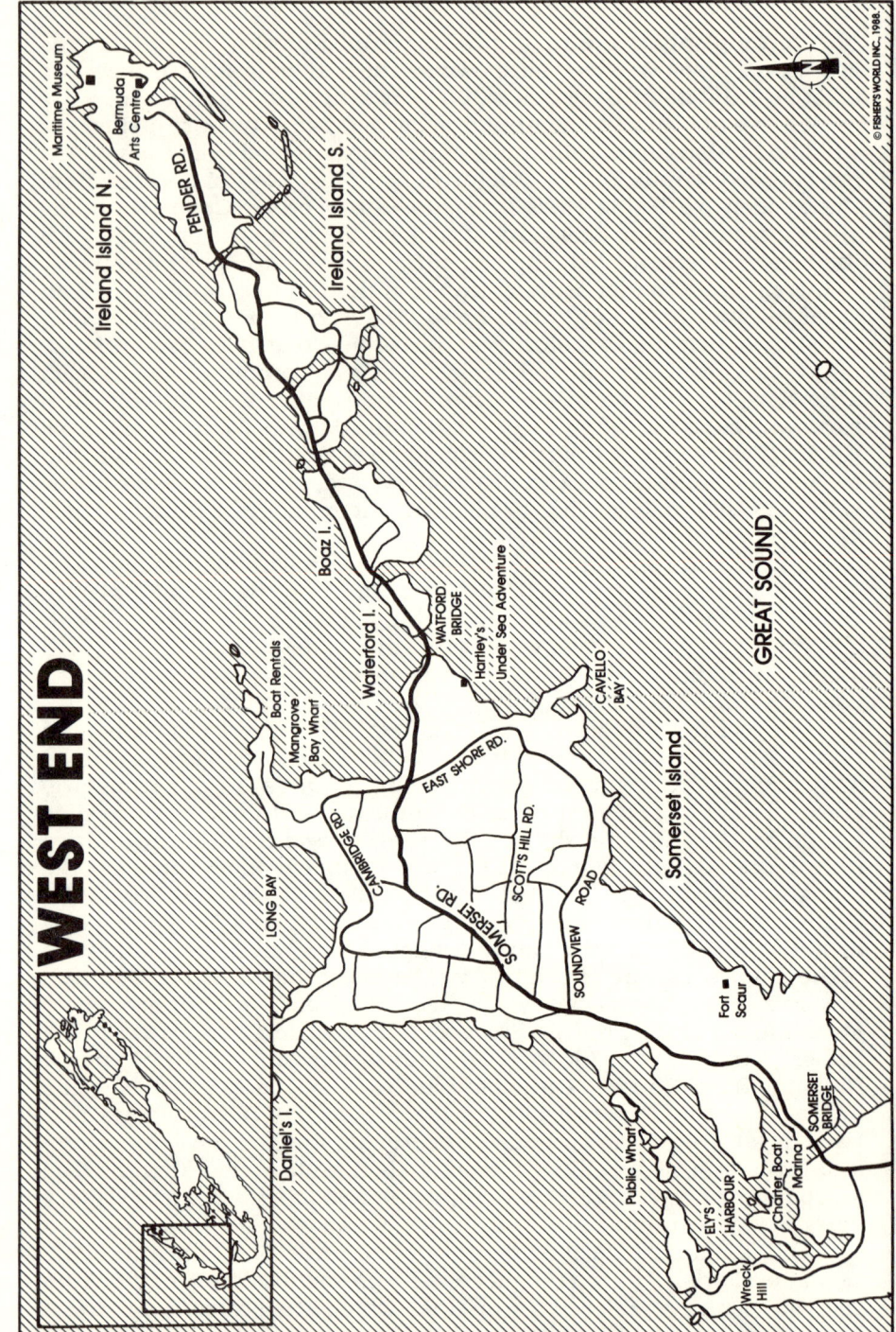

the main aisle, and much later a spire was built to replace one that was struck by lightning.

Due south is Scaur Lodge, overlooking Cathedral Rocks and Ely's Harbour, a protected haven for yachts and other pleasure craft on the Atlantic side. Fort Scaur, near the Scaur Lodge property, was built by the Iron Duke, Arthur Wellesley, Duke of Wellington, victor at Waterloo and later prime minister of Great Britain. The site, a historical landmark, has picnic accommodations.

Also of interest is Somerset Bridge, built in the 17th century to connect Somerset Island to the rest of Bermuda. The world's smallest and narrowest drawbridge, it opens a mere 18 inches, just enough to allow topsail masts at high tide to pass between Ely's Harbour and Great Sound. From this point the main road, now called Middle Road, progresses southward with a spur along Ely's Harbour to swank Wreck Hill, where in centuries past privateers and pirates looted wrecks lured onto the rocks offshore.

Southampton

Southampton Parish is a great favorite with visitors to Bermuda. The little bays on its northern shores offer fine views of the harbor and its tableau of ships: the little local fishing boats heading off for secret spots known only to their captains, ferries plying their routes, and pleasure craft skimming the waves, bound for snorkeling sites or just exuberant races with the wind. The south shore boasts a series of resorts—the Pompano Beach Club, the Reefs, the Sonesta, and the Southampton Princess—and truly excellent beaches. Most famed—and photographed—is the stretch along Horseshoe Bay where a six-mile line of offshore reefs called The Boilers creates ceaselessly breaking surf and a boiling foam.

Here and there, you'll see small, mostly hand-tended patches of farmland where onions and potatoes are grown. Only some 500 acres of island land are devoted to agriculture, thus the need to import most produce from the United States and the Caribbean. Look too for examples of Bermuda blinds, slatted shutters that sensibly open vertically instead of horizontally, allowing light and air in but keeping sudden showers and direct sunlight away from drapes and furniture.

Near the Sonesta, up Lighthouse Road, is the Gibbs Hill Lighthouse. Built over a century ago, it is nearly 120 feet tall on a hill nearly 250 feet high. Its beam may be seen forty miles away by ships and 120 miles away by planes. Electricity supplemented other power in the 1950s, and today there is a huge 1,500 watt electric bulb located in the center of a giant lens, which takes less than a minute to make its complete circuit. Until 1964, the mechanisms were wound by hand every 30 minutes. Today, all is automated. Visitors may climb to the top (slightly less than 200 steps) to admire the celebrated view this aerie provides.

At the northern end of Lighthouse Road are the grounds of the Riddell's Bay Golf Course. The high hedges on both sides of the road and the stretches of green, interspersed with small, well-tended gardens, give an English countryside feel, though admittedly planted with more exotic flora than is found in the Cotswolds. Nearby is St. Anthony's, with its Spanish-influenced architecture.

Warwick

Warwick Parish is named after the second Earl of Warwick (yet another major stockholder in the Bermuda Company of 1610). Harbour Road, one of the island's most important thoroughfares, hugs the parish's northern shoreline, passing the Belmont Golf Course and assorted smaller hotels and guest cottages. Farther on is Darrell's Wharf, where the Hamilton ferry pulls in, and off to the west is Darrell's Island, site of the island's first airport. Too small, you say? Well actually, it was originally the home of a squadron of New York-to-Bermuda Pan Am seaplanes that once provided the only air passenger service to Bermuda.

The clipper service was begun in 1937 and continued through World War II. During the war, these flying boats would set down in Bermudian water and unload mail, which was then screened by the British government's Imperial Censorship staff to uncover U.S.-based spies. The planes would then continue on to Portugal and circle back with more mail. (Bermuda's espionage operation was one of many mounted by William Stephenson, the real-life British agent played by David Niven in the film, *A Man Called Intrepid*.) More recently, Darrell's Island served as the movie location for *Mandrake the Magician*, and today it is a government-owned camping site.

The stone walls you'll pass in this area, separating pavement from water, proved necessary but not infallible during Hurricane Emily. In a few places, the force of the wind hurled boats through the wall, and one 45-foot yacht was picked up and deposited atop a section of the wall.

While traversing Warwick via the South Shore Road, one finds Warwick Camp, with its blue and red barracks, which once headquartered British troops; today it's the base for the volunteer Bermuda Regiment. You may hear shooting off in the distance as you pass. Not to worry—there's an artillery range on the property. Down the road are Jobson's Cove and Warwick Long Bay, popular picnicking spots, with cliffs, boulders, and sand that glistens brightly in the sun.

Paget

Where South Road joins Middle Road is Paget Marsh, a 26-acre preserve owned jointly by the National Trust and the Audubon Society. This is the only area on the island untouched since colonial times. The marsh holds some of the island's best examples of palmetto and cedar trees as well as a mangrove swamp. Because of the delicately balanced environment, those who wish to visit must first gain permission from the Trust Office. To the south is the placid Grape Bay, as well as Hungry Bay where, true to its name, the sea roars in with ravenous force.

On the northern shore, near the Warwick-Paget border, is the Salt Kettle Bay neighborhood. There are no historical landmarks here, but the road twists and hairpins to reveal a wealth of stately homes as well as inviting guest houses and the popular Glencoe Hotel. You'll notice that the homes all have names, ranging from the practical to the fanciful; you may note too that especially along the water's edge there are a few recurring themes with a penchant for the obvious ("Waterview," etc.). Farther along Harbour Road, look for Clermont, a magnificent example of pure Bermudian architecture. Built in 1801, it is large, symmetrical, and sits splendidly alone on a large lot overlooking the water. In fact, all through Paget, named for the fourth Lord Paget, are superb examples of fine homes, a number built in the 1600s. A few, such as Inwood in the Rural Hill neighborhood, boast multiple powder rooms which accommodated ladies and gentlemen who needed, literally, to powder their wigs before dinner.

Yet another home of note, just west of the Foot-of-the-Lane roundabout, is Waterville House, headquarters of the Bermuda National Trust. While the 18th-century house isn't open to visitors, you can take a stroll on the lawn, populated by a noisy group of friendly ducks. Nearby is the Royal Hamilton Amateur Dinghy Club, host of an alternate-year yacht race from Marion to Bermuda. The big white house across the harbor was once an unsightly mishmash of apartments; now it's the handsomely restored headquarters of the Fidelity Life Insurance Co.

At the top of Paget Parish is Bermuda's Botanical Gardens, operated since 1898 by the Department of Agriculture. Spread over some 36 acres, it once displayed every plant grown in Bermuda as well as a large selection of imported blooms. The variety is still impressive. Unfortunately, the gardens were hit hard by Hurricane Emily. One heartbroken Bermudian commented that in the aftermath of Emily all was chaos, particularly the once magnificent formal rose gardens, which "looked like the victim of a rocket attack." Nevertheless, the garden's flowering shrubs, hedges, flower beds, and trees are slowly coming back to life. Admission is free, and there are guided tours of the grounds and greenhouses.

One may still see surviving cedars, giant banyan trees, many varieties of cacti and some 75 varieties of hibiscus, including a red-flowered hybrid called Scotsman's Purse. Match Me If You Can, also called the Beefsteak Bush or Copper Plant, is sometimes used as a poultice for home remedies and its luxurious scarlet-yellow-green-russet leaves are a visual delight. Poinsettia, pink oleander, and the famous Bermuda Easter lilies are special seasonal treats at the gardens, as well as along highways and byways throughout the island.

There are special exhibitions and shows throughout the year, including periodic dog, horse, and bird shows; among the permanent attractions is a garden for the blind. In the center of the gardens is Camden House, the official residence of Bermuda's premier. It is open to the public on Tuesdays and Wednesdays. The wide lawn in front of

Camden House is a popular venue for children's parties. Parents often hire a clown to entertain and feed the celebrants, balloons bob in profusion, and laughter mixes merrily with beauty.

Devonshire

There's not a lot to see in Devonshire. It's a green, hilly expanse, home to very few hotels, no restaurants, and only one night spot, the pink Clay House Inn—one of the only places on the island that boasts native entertainment. Once, the Old Devonshire Church was worth visiting, but unfortunately an explosion on Easter Sunday, 1970, tore apart the original structure and destroyed its organ, font, and many of its trappings. Some of its silver, dating from 1590, did survive, as did a lovely cross, a candelabrum, and an old cedar armchair. On a hot day, this is a cool, serene stop.

Nearby is Devonshire Marsh, which today, thanks to a large distillation plant, supplies much of the island's fresh water; and the Arboretum, which is a quiet, leafy place ideal for wandering. Along the South Shore Road are the Edmund Gibbons Nature Reserve and the Palm Grove Gardens. The former is a marshland (closed to the public) which provides sanctuary for rare Bermudian flora. The latter, set on the grounds of an old estate, offers lush greenery and a collection of tropical birds. It is open daily, except Sunday.

On Devonshire's Atlantic shore is Palmetto Park, yet another bucolic haven, and Palmetto House, an early 18th-century manor home built in the shape of a cross. Called a "Cruciform" house, three of its rooms are open for viewing on Thursdays only.

Incidentally, Devonshire was originally called Cavendish Tribe, in honor of the principal shareholder William, Lord Cavendish, governor of the Somers Island Company. When Lord Cavendish became the Earl of Devonshire, the name of the parish was changed.

Smith's

To the south, on Collector's Hill, off South Shore Road, is one of Bermuda's most historic old colonial houses, Verdmont, also a property of the Bermuda National Trust. The ground floor of this 1700s mansion features a fireplace in every room, and near the parlor chimney sits a powder closet. You'll see fire screens, used to separate the ladies from the blazing logs—and to protect their wax-based makeup from melting! Of particular interest to connoisseurs is the classic cedar staircase that leads upstairs to an Oriental room and two bedrooms, one dominated by a handsome four-poster mahogany sleight bed. The house was probably built by Captain William Sayle, three-time governor of Bermuda. The last person to live here was a somewhat eccentric spinster who spurned all notions of installing electricity or plumbing.

Also along South Shore Road is the Spittal Pond Nature Reserve, a 60-acre wildlife sanctuary run by both the National Trust and the Bermuda Audubon Society. In the winter months (between November

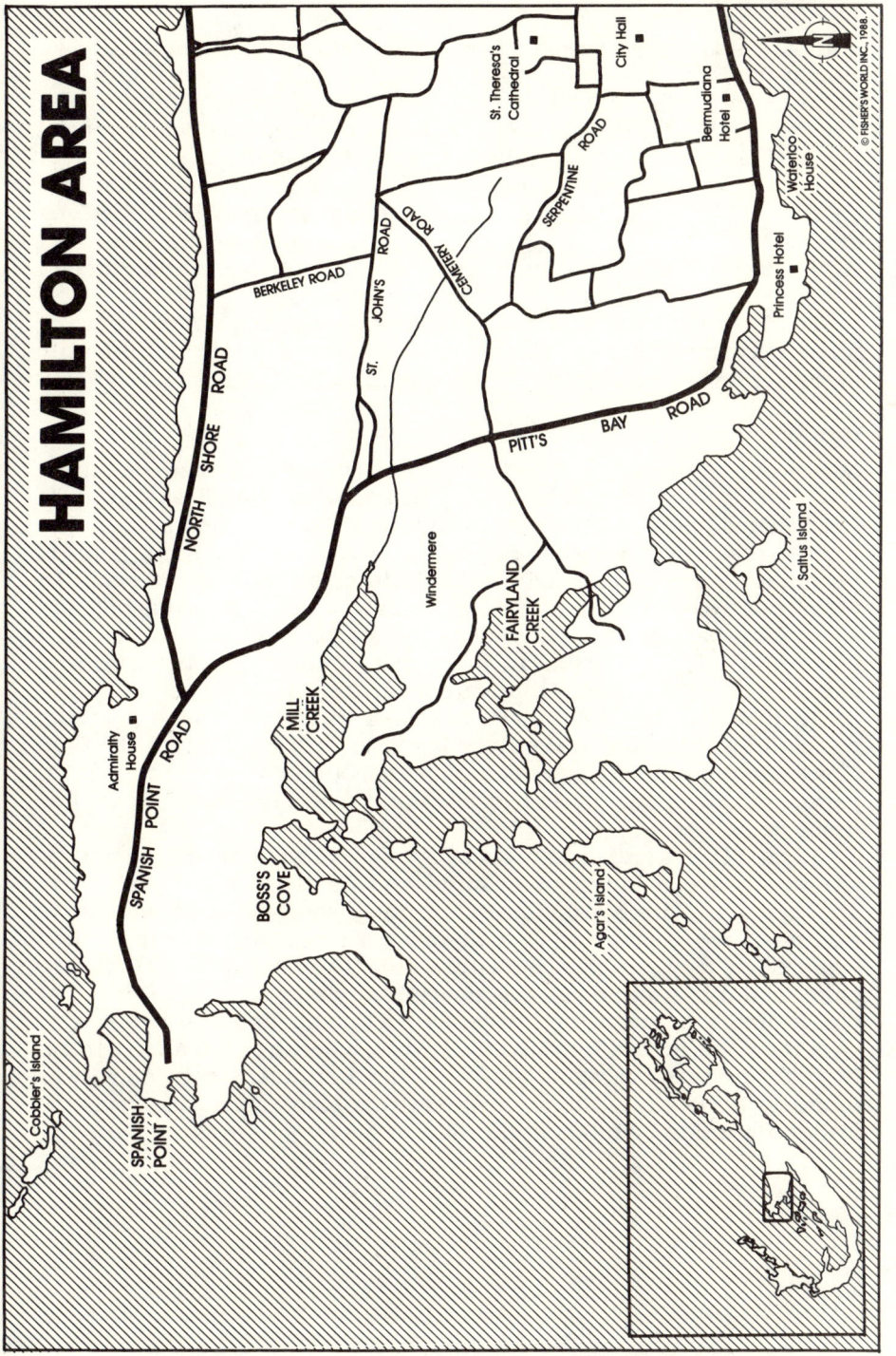

and May) it is visited by some two dozen species of migrant waterfowl. One of the Reserve's triumphs is saving Bermuda's national bird, the Kahow, once almost extinct, now flourishing happily. Within the reserve is a bronze replica of Spanish Rock, which has held a special mystery for centuries. The Reserve is open daily. No admission charge.

East of Spittal Pond is Devil's Hole, a commercial concession that dates to 1843, where sharks, eel, barracuda, etc. may be "fished" by customers, but when caught are safely returned to the pool; and Winterhaven Farm Cottage, displaying antique farm and kitchen equipment. Open Monday and Thursday afternoons.

The North Nature Reserve at Mangrove Lake, a forest of living mangroves growing in brackish water, is an area of interest primarily to nature lovers who appreciate marsh flora and fauna.

Hamilton

Somewhat confusing to first-time visitors is the fact that the city of Hamilton is located in Pembroke Parish, while Hamilton Parish is sandwiched between the parishes of Smith's and St. George's. In this parish, just beyond Flatt's Bridge, once a haven for smugglers, is Bermuda's Aquarium Museum and Children's Zoo, home to some 75 varieties of marine life native to Bermudian waters. Also living here are some giant tortoises from Ecuador's Galapagos Islands, a collection of parrots and flashy Caribbean flamingos, Archie, a harbor seal who splashes happily in his own private pool, and lots of monkeys.

Farther on, past the Bailey's Bay area, is a cluster of sightseeing possibilities including the Perfume Factory, Bermuda Pottery, the Blue Grotto Dolphin Show, where dolphins, responding to voice commands, perform in their own natural deep water pool. Performances are five times daily.

Crystal Caves and Leamington Caves are to be found on the narrow isthmus between Harrington Sound and Castle Harbour just above Tucker's Town. Both are impressive, but if you opt for only one cave excursion, we recommend Crystal Caves. You'll enter via a ramp, then explore (on pontoon bridges, with a guide) the subterranean Cahow Lake. A flip of a switch brings special fairyland lighting effects that dazzle almost as much as the stalactites and stalagmites themselves.

Also in this area is Tom Moore's Tavern, where a calabash tree trunk is enshrined as the spot on which the Bermuda Yacht Club was founded in 1844 and the place where Tom Moore, the Irish poet who visited Bermuda in 1804, wrote some of his famous verses.

Some Rare Bermuda Pleasures

by
Elizabeth and Henry Urrows

Tucked away from the gleaming hotels, the scenic golf courses, and the flowering hedges lies a magical Bermuda only the luckiest tourists ever see.

For a few hours, abandon the pink beaches and enticing shops. Explore the island that Bermudians know and love.

In ancient St. George's, crowning a long flight of steps, St. Peter's church displays touching reminders of island tragedies. All around the walls tablets memorialize Bermudians lost at sea, and those who died of yellow fever. Near the choir door the parents of Philadelphian Richard Dale placed a tribute to the people of St. George's, who tenderly nursed and reverently buried the 20-year old American midshipman injured in a sea battle between a U.S. frigate and a squadron of British ships in 1815.

The haunting incense of cedar permeates the church, from the huge beams and the altar table that dates back to 1624.

The Bermuda cedars that carpeted the island are now largely gone,—ravaged by a scale infestation in the 1940s. Fragrant and indestructible cedar wood supplied material for the framing and furniture of early cottages and mansions. Above all, it formed the small vessels that once dashed as far as Sandy Hook, off New York Harbor, to pilot steamships back to St. George's.

Replacing the cedars is an astonishing profusion of plant life. Protected from killing frosts by the Gulf Stream and from blistering tropical sun by its position off North Carolina, trees, shrubs, and vines from around the world flourish on these bountiful islands. At the end of a short walk from Hamilton Harbour, the Bermuda Botanical Gardens display the exotic and the beautiful. Giant banyans, with their scores of aerial roots, shelter hybrid hibiscus with their rainbow of shades and forms. The Royal Poinciana vies with the Sword Tree, the Golden Wattle, the Cabbage Tree, and the Orchid Tree in spectacular bloom.

In the northeast corner of the Gardens is Camden Museum. Among the memorabilia of the island's history, one can read the exultant reactions of such famous visitors from the past as Mark Twain, Woodrow Wilson, Eugene O'Neill, and Noel Coward. They returned, time and again, to enjoy the mild winters. And much else that unfolds to the observant.

Another outdoor treat is Spittal Pond bird sanctuary, where stately herons play host to flocks of migrating birds—fallinules, ibis, warblers, waterthrush, and more than 25 species of waterfowl. The sanctuary is a seasonal stopover on the Atlantic flyway from eastern Canada to Central and South America.

Rock formations in giant checkerboard pattern lie just inshore from strange circular potholes scoured out by the swirling waves. This quiet retreat delights photographers.

Visitors with eyes for architectural detail find treasures at every turn of the road. Bermuda roofs are unique: built up of thin coral slates, they channel rain into holding tanks that provide the main source of water. Roofs are kept gleaming white by regular painting that assures both clean water and visual beauty.

Old cottages still sport the peak-roofed butteries needed in the days before mechanical refrigeration. Massive chimneys and push-out hurricane blinds, hinged at their top edges, can still be seen. Welcoming Arms doubled stairways enrich older homes. Quarry gardens nestle in pits left where limestone was sawn out, mined to build the house nearby.

More than most popular resorts, Bermuda lovingly preserves many pockets of historic and natural interest for residents and visitors alike. A force for such cherishing preservation, founded by the same late Dr. Henry Wilkinson who organized both the Health Department and King Edward VII Memorial Hospital, is the Bermuda National Trust. At least two of its several properties are well worth careful, unhurried inspection.

In Smith's Parish on a green hill overlooking the South shore stands Verdmont, a small manor house. It is as gracious, and as inviting, today as when it was new more than three centuries ago.

The National Trust acquired Verdmont in 1951. There's no cold museum-like formality here. No velvet ropes separate friendly visitors from close and wondering scrutiny of the numerous treasures. This is a home, as warm and welcoming as the dwelling of a fortunate friend.

Architecturally, Verdmont has fine proportions. The well balanced 12-over-12 windows still hold many of the original panes. Look closely at the center of the sash rails. Holes show where a metal pin is inserted, to fasten upper and lower sashes together. The pins are simpler, and more effective, than many of our contemporary windows catches. The paneling and interior shutters reveal the depth of the exterior walls.

The heavy cedar doors bear marvelous brass fixtures. So do many of the highboys and tables. Balls atop andirons are kept gleaming.

The 17th and 18th century cedar pieces, wrought by local craftsmen, are as handsomely proportioned and meticulously detailed as their mahogany English counterparts.

Among the objects memorable, odd, or diverting that repay close examination are the fireplaces with their graceful cedar moldings; a secretary fashioned from a massive pillared doorway; the ship's desk resting on an upstairs table, with a section that can be taken out to use when seated in an easy chair; a toy collection in the nursery.

The attic is worth close attention. Its neat cedar staircase leads to the naked inside of the roof. There you can see the traditional lapped slate construction.

Verdmont is one of Bermuda's oldest homes. Captain William Sayle, its first owner, was colonial governor of Bermuda. He commanded the expedition which settled South Carolina. A later owner was Admiralty Court Judge the Honorable John Green, an ardent Loyalist who left the American colonies before the Revolution. When privateers brought captured American ships into Bermuda, Green dealt ruthlessly with their cargos.

Green had begun as a portrait painter. Several of his studies of Bermudians embellish the rooms at Verdmont. His painting of a young boy with his dog recalls the works of his more renowned contemporary Benjamin West.

Allow time to wander in the grounds. The north entrance is an informal garden with old-fashioned Bermuda roses, in the English style. Tall hedges conceal the ancient outdoor kitchen and slave quarters, with its immense chimney. The south front has a small formal terrace above the sloping lawns. Except for the other building visible down below on the South Shore road, Verdmont survives virtually as it was in the 1650s.

Another elegant National Trust showplace is Tucker House, hidden away on the narrow Water Street in St. George's, Bermuda's first capital. This structure stands guardian to a period that was stately, and more gracious than today's rushed bustle. The house once dominated an imposing vista that ran from Duke of York Street to the vessel-crowded harbor. Now shorn of lawns, gardens, and view, only its interior rewards the visitor. But the reward endures in memory. Five superbly proportioned rooms contain the Tucker family furnishings. Henry Tucker was eminent in Bermudian civic and social life. Married to a colonial governor's daughter, and father of a talented and large family, he was a shipping merchant who prospered: colonial treasurer, colonial secretary and, finally, president of the council. Host to most of the visiting dignitaries of his era, a descendant and namesake was head of the Bank of Bermuda and prime minister when the island because a self-governing Crown Colony.

The Tucker dining room table, crafted of polished birdseye mahogany, can comfortably seat 24 guests. Above it a Waterford glass chandelier hangs from a carved, painted cedar rosette. Matched carving crowns the doorway. At the west wall handblown glass doors of one of three Chippendale breakfronts permit us to see some of the family's china. Chippendale had brass hardware for these cabinets made in China; through their gold-washed finish, delicate chasing still shows.

The master bedroom has a Bermuda-made cedar tallboy. Its brass fittings are exuberant. On the bed is a "three-dimensional" quilt made of tiny silk patches.

By far and away the most original piece of furniture in Tucker House is in its nursery:- a Bermuda cedar cot—a compromise between a crib and youth bed. Rails on three sides of this cot are sturdy. When you put the open side up against the wall, there's protection for an infant. When that open side is next to the mother's bed, she has easy access to the child at night. As the baby becomes a tot, the open side lets him climb in and out without help.

Three other pieces of furniture deserve mention, and are worth study. A cedar blanket chest on legs has intricate dovetailing that is the "signature" of the anonymous, forgotten craftsman. A child's table of birdseye cedar shines with an especially lovely grain. Perhaps the most remarked-upon piece dominates the parlor: a tilt-top table made from one 43-inch wide mahogany crotch. The raised rim is part of this same single plank. Curators from other museums drool at the triumphant simplicity of the French craftsmen who were responsible for this work of art.

Note the one-hand Cromwellian clock in the entrance hall. See Queen Victoria's citation to St. George Tucker, Henry's son, for his distinguished service in India and her accompanying autographed portrait. Examine the bust of Dr. Samuel Johnson, carved of Bermuda cedar. Marvel at the miniature perfume bottle carved from a moonstone, amid the family jewelry in one resplendent exhibit case. So profuse are the Tucker House masterpieces that you will undoubtedly select several for the imaginative gallery of wonders in your own mind's eye.

In the compass of 21-1/2 square miles, including the array of more than 300 surrounding islands, the Bermudian archipelago is an inexhaustible store of finely-grained pleasures.

Elizabeth and Henry Urrows are free-lance writers based in Ridgefield, Connecticut.

Author's Choice

HOTELS

While it's difficult to make a wrong hotel choice, for maximum enjoyment I suggest you take into consideration how you intend to spend your time in Bermuda. For those who wish an activity-filled stay, there are "one-stop" properties that offer morning through midnight action. Those who would like to spend time in the handsome old city of Hamilton would do well to select a hotel either in town or on the south shore of Hamilton Harbour, linked to Hamilton by ferry service. You'd like a taste of proper Bermudian style? Many of the smaller hotels oblige nicely. A fishing holiday or a launch-point for sailing forays? There are a number of options. A secluded hideaway? Yes, they're available, too. Whatever you choose, you're in good hands. Bermudians are professional, sophisticated hosts who take guest comfort seriously.

Costs: My cost breakdowns are based on the median cost of a double room, BP (Bermuda Plan: full breakfast only) in season. (In season is generally considered May through November, though each hotel has its own seasonal definition, so do inquire.) Most hotels offer a choice of BP or MAP (Modified American Plan: breakfast and dinner). Those hotels that offer rooms only on MAP, which usually adds around $40-$80 per night to the cost, are noted. When looking at prices, do keep in mind that dining out in Bermuda's better restaurants is expensive. Many of the cottage colony resorts that offer only MAP (and in general, very good fare) may actually end up being less expensive than some of the large resort hotels offering BP. All room rates are subject to a 6 percent Bermuda government tax, payable at check-out time. Almost all hotels add a service charge of between 3.75 percent and a hefty 10 percent. Some of the smaller hotels have an energy surcharge—inquire before making reservations.

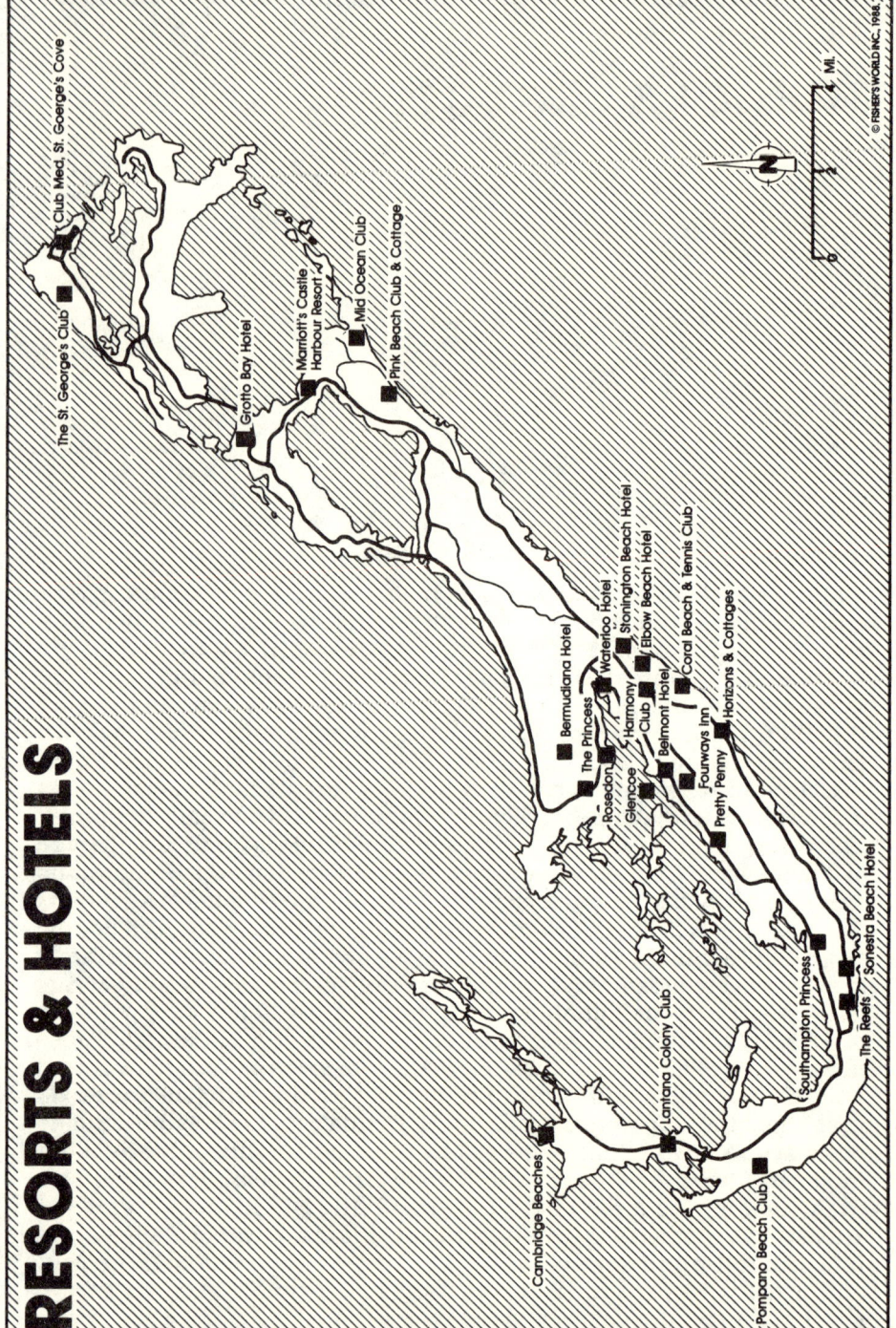

Very Expensive	over $200 per night, BP
Expensive	$150-200
Moderate	$100-150
Inexpensive	under $100

Most hotels offer money-saving "Honeymoon Specials" for stays of 3 to 6 nights and off-season rates dip by about 30 percent.

Of special interest, seven of the top cottage-style colonies have joined together to create The Bermuda Collection, to give guests exchange dining privileges. The seven are: Lantana Colony Club, Cambridge Beaches, The Reefs, Stonington Beach Hotel, Glencoe, Newstead, and Pompano Beach Club.

Many of Bermuda's guest houses are both inexpensive and fun. A number have their own strip of beach or a pool; all are shiny clean and well maintained. You're on your own for sports activities, meals, and entertainment, but Bermuda has plenty to offer in all three categories. Since there are some 70 official housekeeping cottages/apartments and guest houses, we haven't attempted to describe them. Your best bet is to get recommendations from your travel agent or friends. Or write to the Bermuda Department of Tourism for a list of what's available.

HAMILTON PARISH

Marriott's Castle Harbour Resort

Hamilton Parish. Phone toll free (800)223-5388. Set on a hilltop in Tucker's Town and surrounded by 250 well-groomed acres, this newly refurbished and enlarged hotel (purchased and polished to its former 1930s splendor, then reopened by Marriott in 1986), boasts harbor and ocean views every bit as spectacular as its brochures proclaim them to be. And for sports enthusiasts, there are a host of options, including golf on the resort's own 18-hole course (complete with pro shop and a pro staff); six tennis courts (two night-lit); swimming (at a choice of three pools or two beaches); snorkeling, boating and all manner of other water sports organized and launched from the hotel's own dock. New eight-story pyramid-style buildings, complete with generously-sized private patios augment the original seven-story hotel complex and two-story wing. In total, 1,000 guests can be accommodated. Naturally, there are restaurants (one Japanese—the only one on the island) and entertainment nightly. For those who like all the choices only a big resort can offer, this is a good bet. *Very expensive.*

Grotto Bay Beach Hotel and Tennis Club

Hamilton Parish. Phone (809)293-8333. Bring your kids and your tennis racquet. There's a resident tennis pro here to sharpen your game, four courts (two night-lit) on which to practice new moves, and a full range of supervised children's activities to keep the youngsters happily occupied. Some 171 rooms, distributed among nine three-story balconied lodges on 21 acres, all face a private beach, protected coves, and Grotto Bay. The emphasis here is on water sports including waterskiing, sailing, snorkeling, and scuba diving all of which cast off from the hotel's deepwater dock (where some half dozen different boats from Boston whalers to yaks, rock gently until called into service). Swimming is in the Bay or a pool, dining is poolside or in the mainhouse restaurant, and there's entertainment nightly in season, as well as dancing in the Cheek to Cheek Cave Disco. *Expensive.*

PAGET PARISH

Horizons And Cottages

Paget Parish. Phone toll free (800)468-0022. An island standard, and the only member of the prestigeous Relias & Chateaux in Bermuda. The Horizon's 50 rooms, suites, and 10 cottages are scattered along 25 acres on Bermuda's south shore, overlooking (but not in quick walking distance to) Coral Beach. The attractions here include very personalized attention (e.g., each cottage has a cook assigned to prepare and serve breakfast); immaculately kept grounds offering a pitch-and-putt nine-hole course, a putting green, tennis courts, and a pool; and a European flavor of elegant informality, all orchestrated by German-born manager, William Sack. Golf (full course) is available nearby, as are all water sports, and there are exchange dining privileges with two other small hotels, Waterloo House and Newstead. Hamilton is only a ten-minute ride away. No credit cards. MAP only. *Expensive to Very expensive.*

Elbow Beach Hotel

Paget Beach. Phone toll free (800)223-7434. Overlooking its own south shore beach dotted with blue and white umbrellas, the Elbow Beach offers 300 well designed rooms (some in real need of refurbishing), most in the main hotel set on the crest of a hill. Other guests are housed in posh lanais and suites sprinkled amid bougainvillea-filled gardens on the 34-acre grounds. There are five first-rate tennis courts (two lit for night play), pool and beach clubs, a health club for adults and a playground for children, a shopping enclave, restaurants, and entertainment most nights either at the Surf Club and Beach Terrace, or in the Peacock Room, which features local shows. For groups and individuals favoring a host of activity options, this hotel fills the bill. Perhaps service isn't always all it should be, but most guests seem contented. *Very expensive.*

Glencoe

Paget Parish. Phone toll free(800)468-1500. It's no accident that the sailing crowd has adopted Glencoe. Hugging a protected curve of Salt Kettle Bay, this is the perfect place from which to cast anchor for forays into the Atlantic, and between excursions an excellent spot from which to watch the multicolored sails glide by. Owned and managed by Reggie Cooper for some 30 years, this 40-room property centers around an 18th century manor house surrounded by a collection of cottages decorated in wicker with tropical accents. Other sailing pursuits include free Sunfish use, and windsurfing available from the Glencoe-based Wind Surfing School. There are two pools on the grounds, one with a whirlpool. Other sports can be arranged as can transportation via road or ferry to near-by Hamilton. *Expensive.*

Stonington Beach Hotel

Paget Parish. Phone (809)236-5416. Set on a sweep of beach on Bermuda's South Shore, this is both a luxury hotel and a working classroom, operated by Bermuda College, for hoteliers and chefs-in-training. The young, anxious-to-please staff is supervised by professional managers to ensure continuity of service. But for most guests, lapses in service (and there are a few) are offset by the enthusiasm and genuine caring of the students, many of whom will finish their training in top U.S. and European hotel and restaurant schools. The hotel has 64 balconied rooms and suites, all with water views and framed prints of work done by Alfred Birdsey, one of Bermuda's favorite artists; a library; a restaurant; a pool, ocean sunning and swimming, some water sport facilities; and tennis courts. Golf and Hamilton shopping are minutes away. *Expensive.*

Fourways Inn

Paget Parish. Phone toll free (800)223-5581. Opened in 1988 and adjoining the excellent Fourways restaurant, this small complex of five, two-story villas, each with two suites of rooms, manages to be both cozy and elegant. The former quality comes via the surrounding landscaping that embraces and shields the villas from the outside world and such welcome room extras as fluffy curl-up-in terry robes and slippers. The rooms themselves are simple, verging on stark, but each furnishing was selected with an eye for quality. Each unit also has a kitchenette, although a Continental breakfast is served with flourish in the room. On the grounds are a pool and small gym with Nautilus equipment. While the villa patios supply a water view, beaches are a motorbike ride away, as are other sports options, all of which (golf, tennis, water sports) are arranged by the staff. *Expensive.*

Harmony Club

Paget Parish. Phone toll free (800)223-5672. To compensate for the lack of an ocean view, the gardens here have been pruned and prodded into splendid masses of color sculpted around a putting green, two tennis courts, a shuffleboard area, saltwater pool and sun terrace. The 72 large, marble-bathed cottage and cabana rooms are as neatly furnished as the gardens, and most face banks of flowers. In late 1987, the

Harmony Club transformed itself into a couples-only, all-inclusive resort, which means that the room tariff covers all food, drinks, wine, motorbike rental, taxes, and gratuities. As part of its metamorphosis, its public rooms were handsomely redone, with antiques, chintz, marble, and soaring greenery. *Expensive.*

Pretty Penny

Paget Parish. Although many of Bermuda's guest houses offer special, personalized touches, this one is in a class of its own. Its name may or may not reflect the "pretty penny" that obviously went into its furnishings, but it was money well spent. Owner Stephen Martin's impeccable taste and eye for detail have made this a property that brings delight. Each of the nine one-of-a-kind studios, all with kitchenettes (and all with money names: Six Pence, Shilling, Farthing, etc.), has pastel walls, setting off tiled floors, luxurious bedspreads, simple paintings, wicker accents, plants, and furniture you wouldn't mind having in your own home. One of the studios, the one that opens onto the redwood deck pool area, has a fireplace for brisk Bermuda evenings. Surrounding the house are gardens and trees, which lend privacy. Once a week the owner (since 1984) holds a cocktail party for guests in his own home. For those who can live without an on-site restaurant and sports facilities, this is a find. *Moderate.*

PEMBROKE PARISH

The Princess

Hamilton. Phone toll free (800)223-1818. Named for Princess Louise (a daughter of Queen Victoria), who visited Bermuda in 1883. The Princess has been a favorite of visitors since it opened its doors in 1885. Part of the allure is its Hamilton Harbor-side location, allowing easy access to both shopping and sailing. Another bonus is its style. While there are now 452 rooms (many recently decorated, most with balconies), the hotel has maintained a sense of graciousness without lapsing into stodginess. It offers not only top-notch accommodation, but also one of the liveliest nightclubs on the island, with shows imported from Broadway and dancers who strut their stuff with pizzazz. For other diversions, there are exchange privileges with a sister property, the Southampton Princess (a more convention-driven resort), including use of the beach club, 18-hole golf course, and array of restaurants. The Princess has her own restaurants as well as a pool, watersports, and mini shopping arcade. *Expensive.*

The Bermudiana Hotel

Pembroke Parish. Phone toll free (800)223-5672. Like its near-neighbor, the Hamilton Princess, the Bermudiana's site in the heart of the capital makes it geographically desirable to many visitors. But unlike the Princess, location is this hotel's prime asset. The original and highly regarded Bermudiana burned in 1958 in one of the island's most spectacular blazes. Two years later, the new Bermudiana rose from the ashes. Unfortunately, new didn't equal improved, and today's clientele tends to come in group form and often skews toward the young and rambunctious. Still, the 233 balconied rooms are fine, if not wonderful, the waterfront rooms and public areas are newly redone, and the facilities are good, including: two pools, one indoors, the other outdoor and saltwater; a beach club offering free snorkeling equipment; an alleyway of shops; two tennis courts; two restaurants as well as dining exchange privileges with the Belmont Hotel. Entertainment by local talent is featured twice weekly. *Expensive.*

Waterloo House

Pembroke Parish. Phone toll free (800)468-4100. A 34-room beige and white compound with a small pool and trim courtyard gardens. There is a sense of seclusion here even though bustling Hamilton is but a stroll away. On chilly nights, guests gather around the hearth of a cheerful fireplace or adjourn for bridge in the library. Daytime sporting diversions are easily arranged. Depending on one's inclination, dinner is served either in the hotel's small restaurant or delivered to one's room. This is a genuinely friendly place where staff members go out of their way to please. *Moderate.*

Rosedon

Pembroke Parish. Phone (908)295-1640. A handful of Rosedon's 43 rooms are on the second floor of the big square villa that dominates the estate grounds; most are in new wings spread out in nearby gardens. Breakfast is served either on the villa's wide breezy veranda or poolside. Once a week, a local entertainer comes to perform, but for other diversions, lunch and dinner guests stroll or scooter into nearby Hamilton—or head to the Princess, some one hundred yards away. Sports, too, are close at hand (and free) thanks to an arrangement with Elbow Beach, which makes available to Rosedon its excellent beach and tennis facilities. *Moderate.*

ST. GEORGE'S PARISH

The St. George's Club

St. George's Parish. Phone toll free (800)268-1332. Built on the ashes of the old St. George Hotel, The St. George's Club officially opened in 1983. It now operates as a buy into time-sharing resort and as a cottage colony . . . handling both with distinction. Each of the 61 botanically-named cottage suites, all with terraces or decks, overlooks the complex's three pools (one heated) and the town of St. George's. And since many units are second homes to their owners, they've extras not found in many Bermuda hotel rooms: color televisions with cable hookup, radios, books and games, and fully equipped kitchenettes, which will be provisioned for you on request. The color scheme skews to soft beiges and blues, with sailing prints on the walls, Wedgewood accessories and wicker touches. One-bedroom options, while very pleasant, are on the small side; the two bedroom duplexes ($450, in season, EP) are far grander. In addition to the spiffy accommodations, a major draw for many guests is the 18-hole St. George's Club golf course designed by Robert Trent Jones. Also on the property are a warm-up putting green and tennis courts; a fine restaurant, the Margaret Rose; and a small, well-stocked grocery store where cottage supplies can be purchased. *Very expensive.*

Club Med, St. George's Cove Village

St. George's Parish. Phone toll free (800)528-3100. Those used to the somewhat rustic sprawl of most Club Meds are in for a surprise. This one has thick plush carpeting, balconied rooms decorated with taste and style, and the feel of a luxury hotel. Part of the explanation is that it used to be a Loews hotel (and before that, a Holiday Inn), but Club Med completely refurbished the property and in the process added flair and fun. The unique French concept that has made Club Med so successful has not been abandoned here. There are non-stop activities, including a full range of water sports launched from the Club's own long stretch of beach. The room charge covers meals (at a choice of five restaurants) and most sports (except golf and deep-sea fishing), and there is ample opportunity to mingle with and meet a good selection of the 688 guests who can be accommodated here. A noteworthy extra: The town of St. George's, with restaurants, boutiques, bars, museums, and nightlife is a mere ten minute walk away. *Moderate.*

SANDYS PARISH

Lantana Colony Club

Sandys Parish. Phone toll free (800)468-3733. A scattering of permanent guests (actually life-sized statues) sprawl under shade trees or gaze endlessly at Lantana's justly acclaimed botanical gardens, created and ceaselessly tended by their owner, John Young. Complementing the alfresco collection of statues (including a few by Desmond Fountain, one of Bermuda's premier artists) is an outdoor display of paintings gathered from Bermuda, Italy, Spain, and California. The personal touch continues in the 65 suites (bedrooms and sitting rooms) and dotting of cottages, each of which sports an eclectic mix of pieces built of Bermudian cedar and furnishings shipped back from jaunts around the world. Managers Paul and Penne Leseu not only pay careful attention to all the niceties that make this a comfortable, caring retreat, but are entertaining hosts who with some prompting will unfurl the history of Bermuda with mesmerizing eloquence. Activities include swimming, snorkeling, windsurfing, sailing, etc. from Lantana's own stretch of beach; tennis, shuffleboard, croquet on a meticulously clipped lawn court, rum punches by the bayside pool, and golf at a nearby course. A longish walk away is a government ferry, which heads to and from Hamilton nine times a day for sightseeing/shopping expeditions. No credit cards. MAP only. *Very expensive.*

Cambridge Beaches

Sandys Parish. Phone toll free (800)468-7300. Set on a 25-acre peninsula jutting out into the Atlantic, this is Bermuda's original cottage colony and still one of its best. All of the 78 cottages (13 with fireplaces) are furnished with quiet good taste and scrupulous attention to detail (with such extras as hairdryers, umbrellas, and a folding bridge table tucked into roomy closets. The most spectacular is Pegem, a 200-year-old high beamed cottage (with three fireplaces), originally built by a pirate and now open to a maximum of four guests ($800 MAP). Handsome antiques and examples of Bermudian artwork are liberally distributed throughout guest rooms and in public areas; gardens flourish everywhere on the grounds. There are three tennis courts, a pool, a putting green, and five private beaches, one offering an array of water sports launched from the hotel's own marina. This is a place to which people return; over half of its bookings are by repeat guests. To ward off dining ennui, menus are remarkably varied and inventive, and nightly entertainment only slightly less so. Golf is only ten minutes away, and the hotel's launch makes twice-weekly excursions to Hamilton. No credit cards. MAP only. *Very expensive.*

SMITH'S PARISH

Pink Beach Club

Smith's Parish. Phone toll free (800)293-1666. Many guests (particularly Europeans and celebrities in hiding) have been coming here for years, drawn by the resort's exquisite setting and distinctly British tone. Twenty-five cottages containing a total of 88 rooms are scattered throughout beautifully landscaped gardens surrounding a private beach along the south shore. The roomy old main house containing a restaurant, upstairs changing rooms, bar, and library sits on a hill overlooking the ocean. Nearby are two tennis courts, a pool, and patio. Golf, at either the Mid Ocean or Castle Harbour courses, is five minutes away. While the often rough Atlantic is only steps away and good for swimming and snorkeling, close-by reefs make other water sports risky (arrangements can be made to sample such sports elsewhere on the island). Each of the cottages has a shared kitchen where maids prepare the daily breakfast and serve it on guests' private patios. Other times of day, the help-yourselves kitchens are open to guests. Nights bring quiet local entertainment. No credit cards, or checks unless you've a letter from your bank. MAP only. *Very expensive.*

SOUTHAMPTON PARISH

Sonesta Beach Hotel

Southampton Parish. Phone toll free (800)343-7170. Care for croquet? There's a croquet field here, as well as miniature golf. But that's only the beginning. Also offered are scuba, helmet diving, and windsurfing via the resident South Side Scuba Ltd. schools; six tennis courts (all night-lit) and an accompanying tennis pro; fishing, boating (including a glass bottom boat for touring), and swimming in either indoor or outdoor pools or from the beaches of three private coves. Nights are similarly well equipped. There's dining in six restaurants including the Greenhouse with its wraparound terrace, as well as a special spa menu and entertainment seven nights a week. Set atop a rocky sweep of shore, the hotel offers 403 recently redecorated balconied rooms. There are lots of nice touches here—in decor and service—and proper emphasis on giving guests their money's worth. But best of all, there's the Sonesta Spa. I've sampled lots of famous spas, so we can tell you with conviction that this one is world class . . . offering very professional, very personal fitness programs, top-flight equipment and massages that are positively addictive. (Spa programs are open to unregistered guests.) MAP only. *Very expensive.*

Southampton Princess

Southampton Parish. Phone toll free (800)223-1818. This is perhaps Bermuda's glitziest hotel and by far its largest. There are 600 rooms and suites, most facing the ocean, accommodating up to 1,500 guests. Convention planners love it. With the possible exception of its sister property, the more regal Hamilton Princess, it has the island's most glittering nightclub shows, complete with leggy showgirls and Broadway musical transplants. The hotel property, on its own spit of land, contains so many activities that there is no need to explore elsewhere (though we urge you to do so). A partial list of the sports offerings includes: golf (3-par, 18 holes), eleven tennis courts (seven night-lit), a health club, all water sports, numerous swimming options (including ocean forays from a private beach), volleyball, and a children's playground. One of the island's best restaurants, the Newport Room, is here along with five other dining spots ranging from casual to elegant, including Windows On The Sound, with dinner, dancing, and exchange dining privileges with the Hamilton Princess. There are seven bars and a gallery of shops. But lest we leave you with the impression that all is semiperfection, we must point out that occasionally, a puzzling—and inexcusable—spree of sloppiness, in service and maintenance, rears its head. MAP only. *Very expensive.*

Pompano Beach Club

Southampton Parish. Phone (809)234-0222. A family-owned and operated hotel for over 30 years, it was originally opened as a fishing club. Its small private beach still lures its share of fishermen and fish (yes, including pompano). The 56 rooms, 22 of which are suites, are distributed in a scattering of pink low-slung buildings with pink and green furnishings, steps away from the ocean (a few steps at high tide, but a fun walk at low tide when the water recedes some 250 pink sand yards). Dining is in the Cedar Room, drinks are on the pool terrace or in the Fo'c'sle Lounge, and there's entertainment nightly in season. In addition to fishing, snorkeling and tennis are offered and other sports can be arranged. On the Surfside Deck is a hot tub, perfect for tired post-sports muscles. *Expensive.*

The Reefs

Southampton Parish. Phone toll free (800)223-1363. The Reef's lanai cottages, nestled along a terraced cliff, all have breath-catching water vistas, and each of the 65 rooms has been newly refurbished. On the upper level is an ocean-view pool and terrace, and a clubhouse with a library, dining room and a particularly comfortable bar area that encourages guest meeting and mingling. Down on the shore, where snorkeling among the nearby reefs is a favorite activity, is the casual Coconuts restaurant offering sustenance between dips. There are tennis courts on the grounds (and right next door at the Sonesta), and shuffleboard in the garden. A very good staff—a few with over three decades of experience— have a no-request-too-silly to be ignored attitude. Open since 1947, the Reefs has one of the highest percentages of repeat business on the island, which is the best recommendation any hotel can offer. But owner David Dodwell takes nothing for granted. All guests receive newsletters between visits, and returnees are presented with a box of Godiva chocolates and a personal note of thanks. *Expensive.*

WARWICK PARISH

The Belmont Hotel, Golf and Country Club

Warwick Parish. Phone toll free (800)223-5672. The name of this 154-room hotel helps tell its story; it offers first-rate facilities for the golfers who congregate here, and a clublike sense of bonhomie. Many of its 110 acres, on the shores of the Great Sound, are devoted to an 18-hole golf course. It also boasts a pool with underwater viewing windows, a private dock, three tennis courts, an array of water sports (via special arrangements), entertainment nightly, dining in a choice of two restaurants (neither exactly casual or inspired) and a selection of shops. Its style is somewhat well worn, with an amiable, if sometimes absentminded management. Those not fascinated by chit chat about double bogeys or the woes of water hazards may not appreciate the Belmont's special charm. But those who live the links are apt to feel cosily at home here. *Very expensive.*

PRIVATE CLUBS

There are two private clubs in Bermuda, both posh, both requiring an introduction from a member before reservations can be contemplated. One, located in Paget Parish, is the 65-room Coral Beach & Tennis Club, with eight tennis and two squash courts, lawn bowling, a 9-hole golf course, a swimming pool, private beach, and club house with bars and a restaurant.

The other is the famous and ultraprivate 14-suite Mid Ocean Club, where the arrival of such members as Ross Perot can up the already super security to "invasion" status. Located in Tucker's Town overlooking Castle Harbour, it offers three secluded beaches, a superb 18-hole golf course, two tennis courts, water sports, clubhouse dining and occasional dinner dances. Over the years, the club has hosted its share of world leaders, often for highest level meetings. In 1953, for instance, it was the venue for a Big Three conference between Winston Churchill, Dwight D. Eisenhower, and French Premier Joseph Laniel. Yes, President Eisenhower—and many of the dignitaries since drawn to the club—did manage to fit in rounds of golf between rounds of diplomatic deliberations. (In fact, off the fifth hole fairway is Eisenhower Path, built to accommodate the president's golf cart.)

RESTAURANTS

Most of Bermuda's restaurants offer a selection of fresh local fish with a special oceanic flavor that the chef quietly abets with a simple butter sauce. But since most chefs find simple fare not adequately challenging, there's also a good deal of razzle-dazzle on island menus, much of it poured into intricate sauces that don't always succeed. In fact, too few restaurants strive for a disciplined and harmonious menu, with spices and sauces that enhance, not smother. Nevertheless, there is much to admire on many menus including some Bermudian dishes that we urge you to try at least once. Most have been well loved for centuries, which alone constitutes a recommendation, though you may not add all to your list of most favorite fare.

The decor of the restaurants tends to be simple. While many of the restaurants request jacket and tie or what they persistently refer to as "smart casual" during dinner hours, "drop-dead chic" is an alien form of dress, which may well make the wearer feel more uncomfortably conspicuous than cosmopolitan.

Prices: Based on the cost of an average dinner per person, with a drink before dinner and dessert, but without a bottle of wine or tip, I've divided the restaurants thusly: Very expensive, $50 and up; Expensive, $30-$45; Moderate, $18-$25; Inexpensive, under $18. Lunch menus, of course, are less expensive in all categories. Most places automatically add a 15 percent gratuity to the bill.

Newport Room
Southampton Princess. Phone 238-8167. Before being seated, take a moment to admire the room's glowing, no surface left un-teaked, yacht salon elegance. This is a truly handsome setting and the menu aptly reflects the opulence. A traditional opener is beluga caviar; another option might be the Bisque d'homard, a creamy Bermuda lobster soup

KEY TO RESTAURANTS

SANDYS PARISH
- 2   Lantana Colony Club
- 22   The Somerset Country Squire

SOUTHAMPTON PARISH
- 9   The Waterlot Inn

WARWICK PARISH
- 1   Newport Room
- 10   The Greenhouse
- 16   Glencoe
- 18   Henry VIII Pub and Restaurant
- 21   The Gold Hind

PAGET PARISH
- 3   Horizons
- 5   Fourways Inn
- 14   The Norwood Room

PEMBROKE PARISH
- 4   Penthouse
- 7   Once Upon A Table
- 8   Romanoff
- 11   The New Harbour Front
- 12   Fisherman's Reef
- 17   The Tiara Room
- 19   Bombay Bicycle Club
- 20   Chopsticks
- 23   Loquats
- 24   M.R. Onions
- 25   Rolan Hood Pub
- 27   Conch Shell
- 28   The Red Carpet

HAMILTON PARISH
- 6   Tom Moore's Tavern
- 13   Plantation Club

ST. GEORGE'S PARISH
- 15   The Margaret Rose
- 26   White Horse Tavern

RESTAURANTS

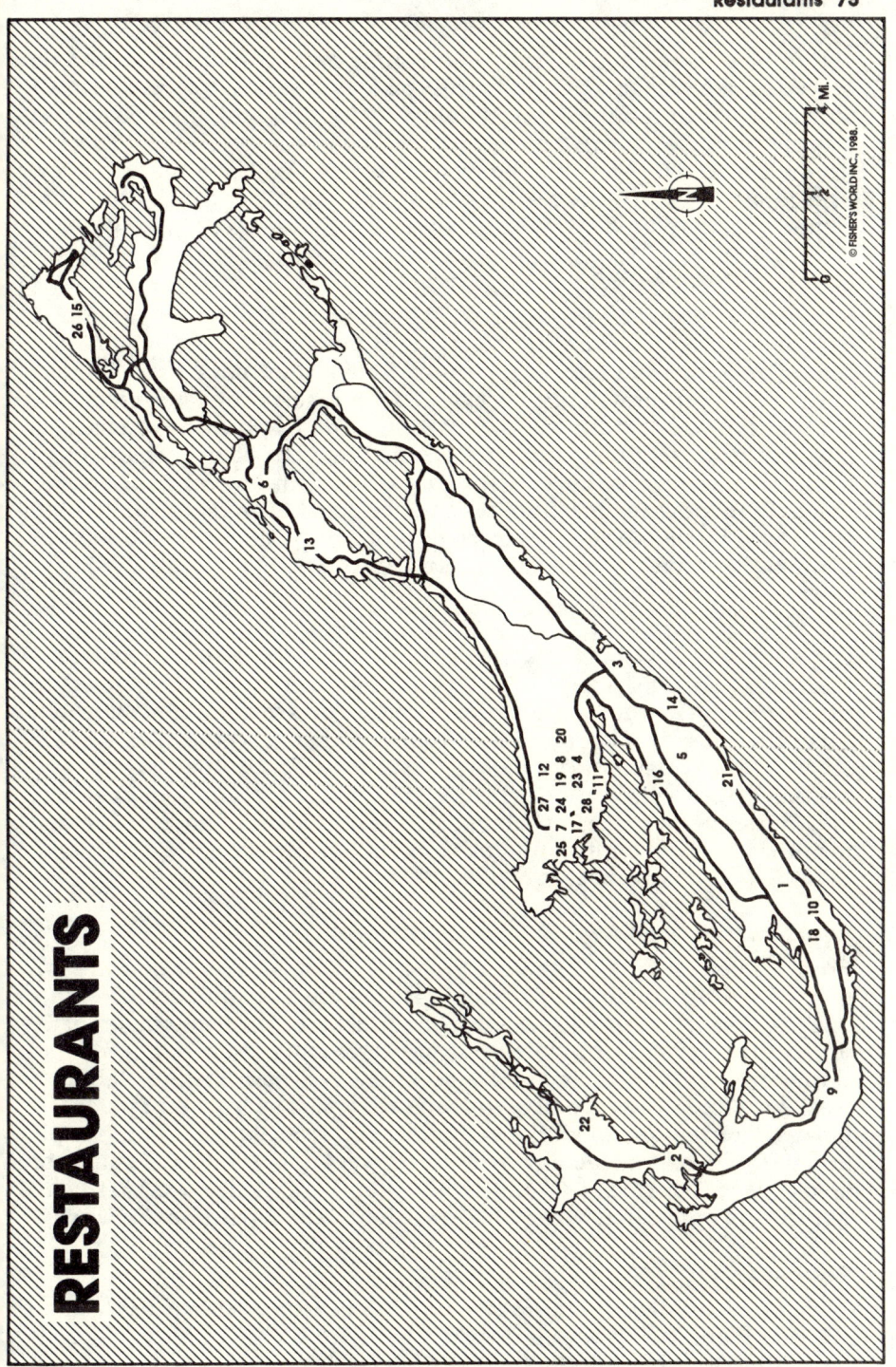

with a float of sevruga caviar. Main course options include Boudin de crevettes, a sausage of shrimps with pistachio sauce; mignon de veau with a caviar and butter sauce; salmon with dill; and lamb cutlets in a peppery sauce. All are served with steamed fresh vegetables. To keep its guests in sailing trim, the restaurant thoughtfully stars its low calorie offerings. The dress here is strictly jacket and tie, the mood romantic and refined. *Very expensive.*

Lantana Colony Club

Somerset Bridge. Phone 234-0141. This restaurant offers a sure hand with inventive fare skewing toward Continental, in a softly candlelit dining room and adjacent solarium. Since hotel guests are understandably given preference over outsiders, reservations are essential. (Dining hours are 7:30 to 8:45 nightly.) Though the menu changes frequently, possibilities include Bermuda fish chowder; medallions of lobster, in season; yellowfin tuna in a white wine sauce; sirloin steak in a light mustard sauce; and fresh panbroiled Bermuda rockfish. Plan to arrive a bit before your reserved dining hour to allow time to wander through Lantana's botanical sculpture gardens. *Expensive.*

Horizons

Paget. Phone 236-0048. A member of the international Relias et Chateaux, this cottage hotel takes its food seriously. Assembled to measure, whisk, knead, and bake to perfection are an English chef, an Austrian sous chef, and a French pastry chef. Together they create such fare as rockfish appealingly paired with chutney sauce and bananas; Bermuda wahoo grilled with a light herb and lemon sauce; and for dessert a white chocolate mousse that ends all hope of sticking to one's diet. Only limited outside reservations are accepted, so it's best to book well in advance. Prix fixe. *Expensive.*

Penthouse

Front Street, Hamilton. Phone 295-3410. While a location on the top floor of a two-story building doesn't necessarily a penthouse make, this one justifies its name with top-drawer fare, served to a maximum of 50 diners in a formal, intimate setting overlooking a twinkling view of Hamilton Harbour. The ambitious menu ranges from the elaborate (veal sweetbreads on a bed of spinach with port wine in puff pastry or lobster mousse served with a vermouth and basil sauce) to the simple (fresh grilled fish of the day or panfried veal chops with rosemary, or steak). Good service is an important plus here. A nice extra is complimentary admission to the Oasis nightclub for all patrons. *Expensive.*

Fourways Inn

1 Middle Road, Paget. Phone 236-6517. Relaxed, attentive service and the chef's deft touch with a diverse menu are the main drawing cards here (though occasionally the fare does falter). A bonus is the setting:

a restored 250-year-old coral and cedar house, originally occupied by the Harvey family for some two centuries. Drinks, champagne by the glass, and caviar are served in the bar, dominated by a massive fireplace once used to cook the Harveys' meals. Dinner is in a formal high beamed and chandeliered main room or in the garden courtyard (also the site for Sunday brunch). Accompanying the sipping and supping is a pianist whose repertoire ranges from well-performed classical pieces to lively show tunes. Dinner starters include a hot Bermuda fish mousse and chilled avocado soup, followed by such main course offerings as fresh Bermuda almaco jack (a local fish) panfried in lemon butter; pink filet of lamb in a raspberry vinegar sauce; fresh Bermuda fish served en tartare with ginger; and roast beef with Yorkshire pudding. Fourways has an extensive wine and dessert list. (Do save room for one of their chocolate, Grand Marnier, or strawberry souffles!) *Very expensive.*

Tom Moore's Tavern

Bailey's Bay, Hamilton Parish. Phone 293-8020. When Franco Bortoli reopened this 300-year-old tavern in 1986, it was an instant success. No wonder. It's been beautifully restored, right down to the stunning fireplace that cheerily blazes on cool nights. But fair warning, the food, though often first rate, does tend to be inconsistent. The specialty of the house is quail filled with goose liver, morels, and truffles and baked in puff pastry; other offerings include fresh baked swordfish, as well as crisp duckling; oysters poached in champagne; a trio of Bermuda fish, game fish, and lobster tail. An alternative to dinner is Sunday brunch on the terrace overlooking Walsingham Bay. Dinner is *Very expensive.*

Once Upon A Table

49 Serpentine Road, Hamilton. Phone 295-8585. Set in a turn-of-the-century cottage with lace curtains framing the windows and a Bermuda buggy parked outside, this is one of the few top restaurants serving traditional Bermuda fare. Appetizers include deep-fried Brie with raspberry preserves; marinated wahoo; and a seafood crepe. Main courses feature whatever local fishermen have caught that day, perhaps red hind, rainbow runner or dolphin (not the mammal) served with delicate sorrel and lemon sauces. Local vegetables, too, are menu staples, including green papaw, the bittersweet Bermuda orange and loquats (used in sorbets). Given 48-hour notice, owner Llew Harvey will provide a special all-Bermuda-recipe dinner. Other recommendations are rack of lamb, and medallions of pork in a light whisky and morel sauce. *Moderate.*

Romanoff

Church Street, Hamilton. Phone 295-0333. Your meal here will begin with vodka, chilled just so, and a dash of caviar, courtesy of the owner.

Next on the agenda might be a turtle soup or borscht, then perhaps owner Antun Duzavic's award-winning specialty, Tournaedos Flambe Alexandra. Other options on the lengthy menu include simple, and perfect, rockfish; a fine saddle of veal; crisp duckling; and steak tartare (also a house specialty). Though the deep burgundy decor, candlelight, and Wedgewood china create an elegant air, there's a lot of flambeing going on here (thanks to five of the more popular menu entrees) requiring much scurrying of waiters. On a calm night, the show is an amusing diversion; when the restaurant is busy, the fuss can be a bit distracting. *Very expensive.*

The Waterlot Inn

Middle Road (on the waterfront), Southampton. Phone 238-0510. This, one of our favorite restaurants in Bermuda, is set on a quiet cove in a rambling 300-year-old farmhouse. For decades, the Inn was run by Miss Claudia Darrell, one of Bermuda's favorite and most colorful daughters. In 1916, for instance, it was Claudia who rousted the menfolk out of the local bars during a hurricane and organized the rescue of a ship and crew caught on the reefs near Elbow Beach. When she died in 1949, flags all over the island flew at half mast. What has this to do with the Waterlot Inn of today? Nothing really, though we're convinced that Claudia's spirit still benignly lingers here. Dining is either inside or on a waterfront terrace. The dependably good fare includes a fresh tomato with goat cheese soup; panfried rockfish; veal medallions with spinach, pine nuts, and port sauce; rack of lamb with herb mustard; filet of beef with foie gras and truffles; and for dessert, a not-to-be-missed souffle. On Sundays, a jazz band comes to play for the brunch crowd. *Very expensive.*

The Greenhouse

Sonesta Beach Hotel, South Shore Road. Phone 238-8122. During the day a buffet luncheon is served, but in the evening a newly pruned and polished menu is offered. Wahoo Steak Meuniere is one of the specialties, as is a panfried catch of the day; other dishes include pork medallions roasted with Lady apples and served with spinach pasta and Calvados; and steak with a choice of sauces. For dessert we opt for a chocolate and truffle concoction, appropriately called Chocoholic's Delight. The fare is consistently good and the ocean view, from the Greenhouse's wraparound terrace setting, is soothing. *Expensive.*

The New Harbourfront

Front Street, Hamilton. Phone 295-4207/295-4527. Our favored spot is on the terrace overlooking Albouy's Point and the ocean liners tied up along Front Street, though there's also an indoor, larger restaurant. Both offer the same eclectic menu, which culls a dish or two from many of the world's major ethnic groups—a sort of melting pot menu that ranges from Caciucco Mediterranean (scampi, scallops, swordfish, and salmon trout in a balsamic sauce) to Chicken Cantonese to Veal Oscar to one of the house specialties, roast lamb with apricot sauce. Many of the dishes are topped with rather elaborate sauces, and for our taste, there's a bit of overkill here, but some of the lighter sauces are quite pleasing. Those who dine here gain free entry to The Club, a nearby nightspot. *Expensive.*

Fisherman's Reef

Burnaby Hill, Hamilton. Phone 292-1609. As you might suspect, the accent here is on both local seafood—rockfish, guinea chicks (small lobsters), shark, wahoo, and yellow tail tuna—and fish from farther asea, like Maine lobster, salmon, and scampi. A few steak and veal entrees are also available. This spot, with a second floor view of Front Street is just upstairs from Bermuda's oldest pub, the Hog Penny. On your way in or out of Fisherman's Reef, we suggest you glance at the pub's menu and perhaps plan a lunchtime return visit. The fish here is fresh and well prepared, there are burgers, chops, a steak and kidney pie, a quartet of spicy curry dishes (thanks to an Indian chef), and a Reuben sandwich. In season, a guitarist leads spirited sing-alongs. Fisherman's Reef is *Moderate;* the Hog Penny is *Inexpensive* at lunch. (The two are under the same ownership.)

Plantation Club

Bailey's Bay, Hamilton Parish. Phone 293-1188. Cozy and quiet, filled with plants and white wicker and the good-humored banter of the patrons who seem to know one another, this restaurant specializes in such Bermudian dishes as a spicy fish chowder laced with black rum; onion soup, with Bermuda onions and Gruyere cheese; panfried wahoo topped with almonds and bananas; charcoaled lamb served with a loquat chutney; and Bermuda lobster. In summer, owners Chris and Carol West move tables, chairs, and candles outside under the stars. *Moderate.*

The Norwood Room

Stonington Beach Hotel, Paget. Phone 236-5416. Stop first for a drink in the sunken bar near the pool, then head into the airy high-beamed dining room, where your hosts, waiters, chefs et al will be Bermuda College students. No, this is not amateur hour. They're all serious, well-trained budding restauranteurs enrolled in the college's hotel school. Their contagious smiles and enthusiasm help make this a memorable evening. An important plus is fine food (admittedly finer on some nights than others), much of it created from old Bermuda recipes, with a selection of international standards: duckling, rack of lamb, steak with herb butter. On Wednesday nights, the accent is on French fare, and twice a month there's a ten-course gourmet night ($32.95, including the service charge). If your dinner and service is all you'd hoped it would be, do pass around compliments; they're genuinely appreciated here. *Moderate.*

The Margaret Rose

St. George's Club, St. George's Parish. Phone 297-2100. There's a whisper of Paris here: elegant, stylish, and coy. There is also a rose motif, but you guessed that. Don't come expecting great subtlety or surprises, but you will find very well-prepared dishes and a setting artfully designed for romance. Hors d'oeuvres include salmon with horseradish cream, and blue point oysters; as a second course, there is a quartet of chilled soups, including cucumber and avocado. Among the entrees are a broth of shrimps, clams, mussels, scallops, and local Bermudian fish; lamb chops coated with an onion mousse; saddle of veal and lamb. *Expensive.*

Glencoe

Salt Kettle in Paget. Phone 236-5274. Glencoe has the only female head chef on the island: Roberta Williams, a graduate of the Culinary Institute of America. More relevant is that she delivers consistently inventive and top-notch fare. A sampling includes mussels in a delicate Pernod and cream sauce; a light fish casserole sauteed in vermouth; Louisiana-style blackened fish; and a filet mignon paired with an intriguing sherry raspberry sauce. As a bonus, this prix fixe ($32.50) dinner menu is served in one of the airiest and prettiest restaurants in Bermuda, set right on the edge of Salt Kettle Bay. On Saturdays, a buffet or beach barbecue, depending on the weather, is substituted for the formal menu. If dinner here doesn't fit into your schedule, suggest lunch instead. Although the menu is much more casual—burgers, fish cakes, omelettes and the like, the view of bobbing sailboats in the harbor makes a stop here well worthwhile. *Expensive* (dinner).

The Tiara Room

Princess Hotel, Hamilton. Phone 295-3000. While we doubt that this would make anyone's list of top ten restaurants in Bermuda, the decor is so grand that the Tiara Room simply can't be passed over. Huge crystal chandeliers, ornate table settings, and a smashing view of Hamilton Harbour do draw diners. Unfortunately, the crystal and cutlery are more impressive than the cuisine. Your best bet is to avoid some of the stickily oversauced entrees and opt for simple dishes: fresh rockfish, escalope of veal, steaks, crisp duckling, or rack of lamb. *Very expensive.*

Henry VIII Pub And Restaurant

South Shore Road (near the Sonesta), Southampton. Phone 238-1977. Scoff if you wish at the hokey Tudor decor, the concept of costumed serving wenches, and a menu that (in Olde English script) includes Steak Anne Boleyn and Fish Catherine Parr. But when in the mood for nonsense, this place is fun and the food is not bad at all! In addition to the aforementioned fare, there's fresh panfried local fish, an English mixed grill (steak, liver, lamb, bacon, sausage, and mushrooms), a steak and kidney pie, lamb chops with herb butter, and, of course, roast beef with Yorkshire pudding. A Sintraesque pianist presides in the Oak Room bar. *Expensive.*

Bombay Bicycle Club

Hamilton. Phone 292-0048. Not only is the name of this restaurant wonderful, but its Delhi food has won a loyal and enthusiastic Bermudian clientele. The longish menu ranges from the traditional: tandoori chicken, lamb kabob, and beef tikka; to a vegetable and fruit curry, lobster tandoori, and spiced shrimp cooked in a coconut sauce. With 24 hours notice, eight or more friends can sit down to a Badshami Feast offering tastes of all the house specialties ($34 per person). Plan to arrive hungry, sample a little of this, a bit of that, and between courses watch the glossy gathering of fellow diners doing the same. *Expensive.*

Chopsticks

Reid Street East, Hamilton. Phone 292-0791. A calm, sophisticated Chinese restaurant done in light woods, Chopsticks purveys Cantonese, Szechwan, Hunan, and Peking cuisines. If this sounds overly ambitious, not to worry. The menu has been pared down to entrees that the chef knows intimately and prepares with a sure hand. Selections include pork in plum sauce, sweet and sour Bermudian fish in a delicate batter, hot shrimp and beef dishes, Peking duck, and, a surprise, deep-dish dessert pies with ingenious fillings. *Moderate.*

The Golden Hind

South Shore Road, Warwick Parish. Phone 236-5555. In 1987, Andy Allan (a former owner of Henry VIII) bought the Bermudiana's Beach Club and poured a reported $3 million into renovation. What emerged was the flashy Golden Hind, named for Sir Francis Drake's trusty ship and themed (in decor and menu) around exotic ports of call. You'll find Za Xia, a hot and sour shrimp dish that the menu claims was served to Drake by Chinese sailors; Palau Islands Salad, with hearts of palm, bamboo shoots, bean sprouts, mushrooms and pineapple; Poo Cha, a Thai dish of hot stuffed crab and pork; A Lo Pobre Callo, sirloin steak with sauteed onions—supposedly a recipe "from the mountains of Peru"; Rack of Lamb Terra Australis, which despite the silly name is standard and good (though at $44 for two, not inexpensive). The restaurant's bar, called Jimmy's Pub, in honor of the mad, bawdy piano player who presides therein, is a lively place for an after-dinner brandy. Chances are that you'll eat well here and have fun—and it should be noted that the restaurant boasts a spectacular ocean view—but we suggest that you not put this at the top of your list of "must" Bermudian dining experiences. *Very expensive.*

LUNCHTIME RESTAURANTS

The Somerset Country Squire

Mangrove Bay, Somerset. Phone 234-0105. While this is not the place to come for haute cuisine, it is a very pleasant spot for a west end of the island lunch break. We suggest heading straight for the breezy patio dining area overlooking Mangrove Bay, rather than the darkish, tapestry-banquetted downstairs restaurant. Consistent with its English tavern trappings, the specialty of the house is steak and kidney pie served with a mug of ale. Other offerings include hamburgers, steaks, salads, veal sausages, and panfried local fish. Other fish, as in a seafood platter of shrimps and scallops, also appear on the menu, but with a laudable notation on its imported status. We wish more restaurants were this forthcoming. A children's menu is available. House wine is served by the litre, half litre, and glass. *Inexpensive to Moderate.*

Loquats

95 Front Street, Hamilton. Phone 292-4507. Despite the rather self-congratulatory menu (corn and pumpkin chowder is described as "absolutely delicious" and Cornish hen as "roasted to perfection"), Loquats does offer good (they say "mouthwatering") local fish, as well as baby back ribs, roasted chicken, shark fritters, burgers (five kinds, including a chickenburger), and salads. Dining is either inside, with the Bermuda shorts-clad businessmen crowd, or outside, on a balcony with a view of the boats in Hamilton Harbour. While there are better spots for dinner, lunch is fun and late night snackers are happily accommodated here until 1 A.M. *Inexpensive to Moderate.*

Other lunchtime restaurants well worth a stop include the very popular **M.R. Onions** on Par-la-ville Road in Hamilton, with an entire menu deliciously built around the Bermuda onion; the **Robin Hood Pub**, on Richmond Road in Pembroke, where young Bermudians congregate for pizzas and ale; the **White Horse Tavern** in St. George's, which when not overcrowded serves up a great tempura batter fish sandwich; the **Conch Shell** in the Emporium Building in Hamilton, with a well-conceived French/Asian menu, offering snacks to full course fare; and **The Red Carpet**, in the Armory Building on Hamilton's Reid Street, for wonderful fresh homemade pasta.

TEA

And since Bermuda is a member of the British Commonwealth, a post-lunch break for tea is both traditional and very pleasant indeed. Just a few of the many spots to stop for a sip and accompanying nibble are the **Waterloo House, Carriage House, Rosedon**, both **Princesses**, the **Fourways Inn**, and **Trimingham's.**

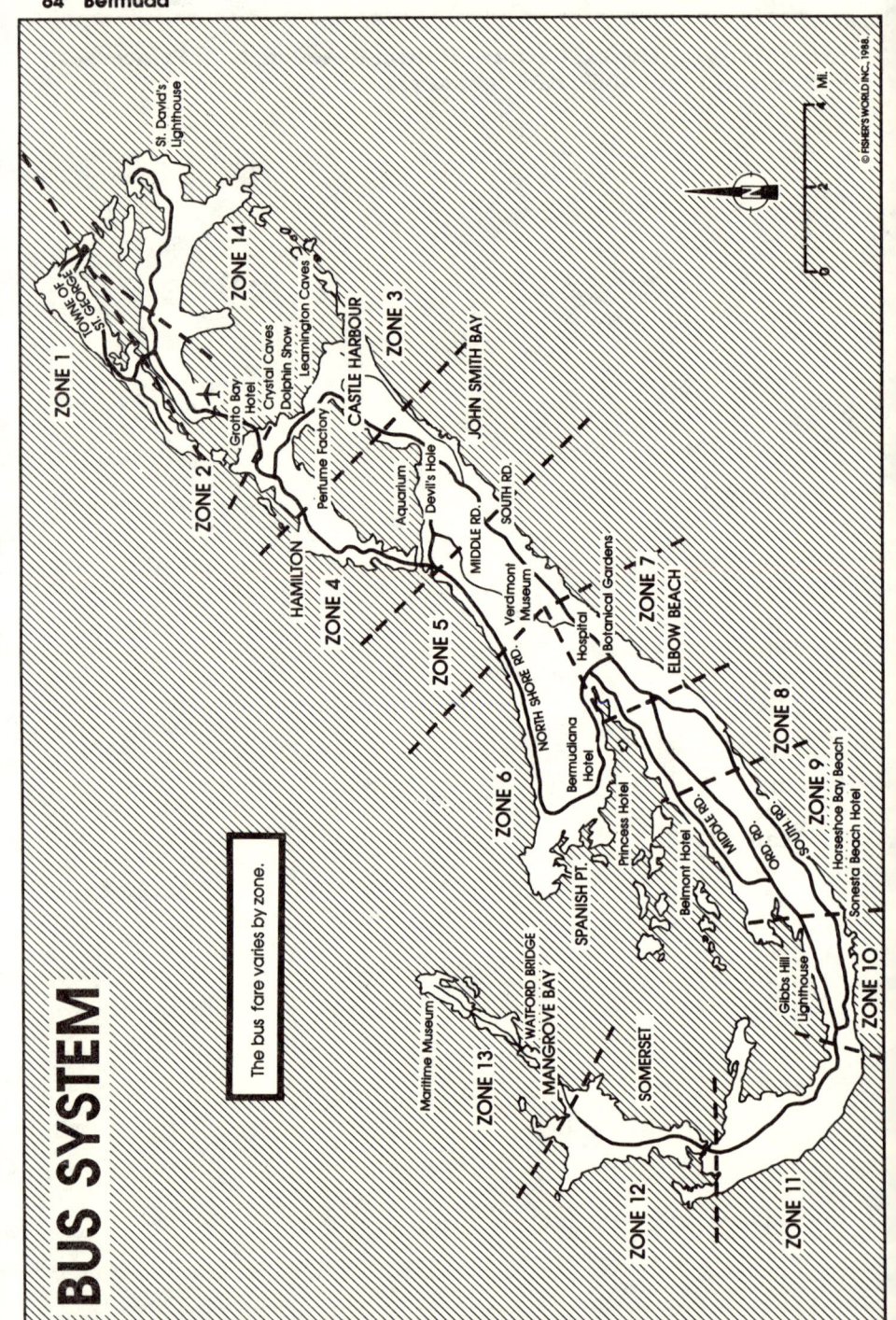

Nightlife/Entertainment

Major hotels all have some sort of entertainment usually nightly in season. The Peacock Room of the Elbow Beach, for instance, spotlights steel bands and limbo reviews, as does the Inverurie Hotel's Le Cabaret Night Club, which uses the calypso beat as a warm-up for its current headliner, usually either a singer or comedian. Lillian's, a supper club at the Sonesta, features a nightly trio to strum and hum through dinner, while the Southampton Princess' supper club, Windows On The Sound, brings in a dance band for between-courses turns around the floor; and apres dinner opens up The Touch Club, where the music turns disco. Big band sounds can be found at Cheek to Cheek, a night club located in Prosper's Cave at the Grotto Bay Beach Hotel.

But without contest, the two most dazzling hotel nightclub shows are staged at The Empire Room and The Gazebo Lounge. The former is located at the Southampton Princess, the latter at the Hamilton Princess. Both feature lavishly staged reviews with punch and pizzazz, long-legged showgirls, and zippy show tunes.

Away from the hotel scene, entertainment is divided primarily between sing-along spots and discos. In the first category is the Henry VIII Pub on the south shore, with its popular Oak Bar piano player; The Golden Hind, whose piano player Jimmy Keys leads lively renditions of romantic to ribald tunes; The Hog Penny in Hamilton, with a guitarist leading the flock; and Loquats, which usually features a singer/piano player. The entertainers generally enter around 9 P.M. and carry on until 1 A.M., and sometimes beyond.

Discos include the splashy Oasis atop The Emporium Building in Hamilton, heavy with tropical accents, salmon velveteen banquets, and a pounding beat. As a respite or alternative, Oasis also offers a quieter room, The Bambu Lounge, featuring live and often quite good jazz. The Club, located upstairs from Hamilton's Little Venice restaurant, draws a somewhat more sophisticated crowd. Done in reds and blacks, with a small dance floor and mirrors to reflect the action, it technically opens at 10 P.M., but doesn't really start moving for another hour, then continues until 3 A.M. Jacket and tie are requested at both Oasis and The Club.

Outside of Hamilton, on Middle Road in Riddell's Bay, is a casual, local hangout called Flavors. Though its light and sound aren't state of the art, its patrons can boogie with the best.

For those who love jazz, The Sparrow's Nest on Reid Street East in Hamilton has perhaps the most consistently good groups on the island, especially on Saturday nights, when improv is at its hottest, (the surroundings are a bit seedy). Another alternative to discos is found at the Clay House Inn on North Shore Road in Devonshire, where limbo troupes, calypso singers, and steel bands reign. And though strictly jukebox driven, The Swizzle Inn, on Middle Road near St. George's, is great fun, especially for the younger crowd. By all means bring your business card to add to the hundreds covering every inch of wall space. Then watch the Inn's peculiar roulette wheel, spun every half hour or so to determine the price of rum drinks.

While not necessarily nocturnal, entertainment of a different sort is available year round in conjunction with Bermuda's cultural calendar. A six-week-long Performing Arts Festival, held in January and February, for instance, attracts orchestras, ballet companies, such jazz institutions as The New Orleans Preservation Hall Jazz Band, folksingers, and opera companies.

Also, Gombey dancers in elaborate beribboned dress are part of the island's folklore tradition and may be seen at festive occasions throughout the year. The dances, complex series of leaps and pirouettes, are related to those in the Caribbean, but with a special beat unique to Bermuda.

For news on current cultural events and special performances, check local newspapers or ask your hotel for information. Don't bother to ask about gambling possibilities. There are no casinos, nor any interest in opening any.

Shopping

Speaking of cashmere, we're told by some of the island's top purveyors that proper care involves hand washing with Lux or Ivory soaps, with a drop of hair conditioner added to the rinse water for softness. If well cared for, quality cashmere will nicely weather decades of wear.Liquor, though truly duty-free, carries a catch-22. Bermuda law requires a minimum liquor purchase of two or five bottles, while U.S. law dictates that only one bottle per person can be brought in without duty. For those traveling in twos, this works out fine. If not, the duty on your extra bottle may mitigate the price advantage of a Bermuda purchase.While "duty-free" is a much ballyhooed advantage to setting off on a Bermuda shopping spree, we caution you to look closely at price and quality before leaping. That Waterford decanter may be less here than at your local department store, but is it less than at your neighborhood crystal outlet? And check cashmere carefully. One-ply cashmere in the States can be found (in some places) with tags in the $40 range. Two- and three-ply, on the other hand, soars into the hundreds of dollars here and in the U.S. and Canada. Nevertheless, some of Bermuda's best cashmere, though pricey, is less expensive than hometown equivalents. Also, you may well find some cashmere colors in Bermuda that are not available at home. (You may find, too, that some of the styling is a bit dowdy.)Bermuda's prime shopping attractions, in addition to crystal, liquor, and cashmere, are china, watches, cameras, perfumes, and English woolen goods (including tartans, which you'll find at every turn). For savvy shoppers who know the at-home prices of individual brands, there are good values to be found, especially during winter when sales proliferate.

By the way, you needn't steer away from the hotel boutiques on Bermuda. Unlike most places in the world, the prices in hotel shops are not marked up. And the sales help is often more cordial than that

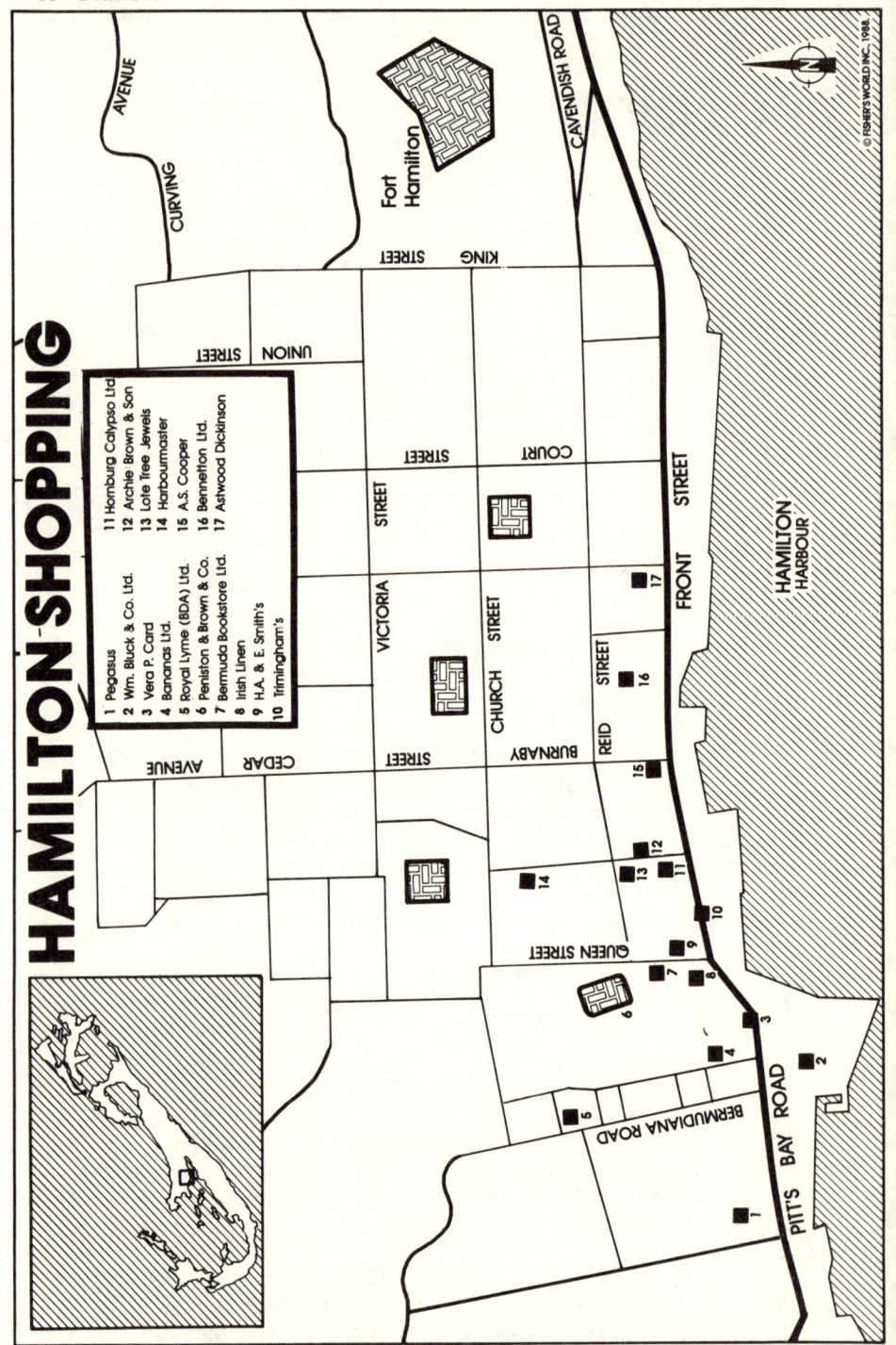

found in the Front Street shops where the deluge of cruise ship shoppers seems to have drained the smiles from the faces of many shopkeepers.

There are also a number of made-in-Bermuda products, identified by a Bermuda Product sticker, which make good gifts (for yourself, as well as others on your list). At the top of our list is Outerbridge's Sherry Peppers. Most department stores stock a four-pack of sauces (sherry peppers, hot mustard sauce, rum peppers, and Bloody Mary Fix), as well as individual bottles of barbecue sauces, ranging from mild to very hot, vinegar peppers, and a line of pepper jellies. The peppers find their way into many of the island's restaurant dishes and local cookbook recipes.

Local scents include Lili Perfumes, Royall Lyme fragrances with their distinctive bumpy glass bottles, and sachet bags filled with the fresh smell of cedar chips. (Cedar trees, which once flourished everywhere on the island, were all but wiped out in a devastating blight.)

There are a number of gifted artisans and artists on the islands. Some of the former are mentioned in the following Hamilton and St. George's shopping descriptions; a selection of the latter are included in the Galleries and Studios section.

A final note about shopping. I've included many of the island's best known stores, as well as my favorite haunts, and provided commentary that I hope will be helpful.

Hamilton

Of the four most famous Front Street establishments—Trimingham's, William Bluck, Archie Brown and Smith's—Trimingham's is usually a visitor's first stop. While this miniature department store is not a Herrod's or Bloomingdale's, it does offer a representative glance at Bermuda style—from the very correct private label blazers in the men's shop to the fine china, crystal, Hermes, jewelry, and leather goods collections serenely displayed elsewhere. The Trimingham family has lived in Bermuda for centuries, and their store has anchored Front Street shopping since the mid-1800s. They may not have invented classic Bermuda taste, but they cater to it with unerring precision.

William Bluck & Co., down the street apiece, is a favorite for fine crystal and china, from around the world. They are the exclusive purveyors of Herend, including some pieces designed expressly for Bluck. And as a real bonus, service here is both efficient and courteous.

Behind the flagged front of Archie Brown & Son are high quality (if a bit dowdy) cashmeres and English-classic Harris tweeds for men and women.

Smith's, another English goods emporium, offers a selection of more updated styles (including cashmeres in a range of luscious hues), along with ever-popular Burberrys, china, crystal, perfumes and children's clothes.

And speaking of emporiums, nearby is The Emporium, which houses a covey of specialty shops including Mirage Designs, with mostly Bermuda hand-crafted items: boxes, jewelry, pillows, pottery, etc., and one of our favorite shops, Kamla, where India-born Kamla Wakefield offers antique jewelry from India and Europe, beautiful beaded sweaters (most under $100), swimwear, sandals of her own design, hand-embroidered dresses and well-crafted games (backgammon, etc.). Here too is Portobello, with antique European jewelry, stamps and coins, as well as Esprit, with its kooky collection of toys.

The English Sports Shop is notable for its fine English men's clothes and woolens and summer weight woven silk sports jackets, while The Irish Linen Shop (on the corner of Front and Queen streets) is a mecca for exquisite, top quality linens, from Souleiado French cotton to Irish damasks. There's little that's inexpensive, nor are the goods overpriced—you get what you pay for. But because there are only a few items here that can be considered "easy care," it's helpful to have a maid to handwash, iron, and care for whatever you carry home.

Calypso, owned by Polly Hornburg and her daughters, Lisa and Susannah, is set in a two-story shop painted a suitable bright yellow—suitable, because the casual clothes within, many designed by Mrs. Hornburg, boast vibrant colors in chic, wearable styles. In addition to cotton, silk, and knitwear dresses, pants and separates, you'll find the island's largest selection of bathing suits (Gottex, Jantzen, etc.), a sizable array of fragrances and a Calypso exclusive: Louis Vuitton luggage and accessories.

For the teen set, a stop at one of the three Front Street Bananas shops is mandatory. Clear, tropical colors on sweatshirts, jeans, T-shirts, sunglasses, hatbands, whatever, make these happily jumbled and reasonably priced stores a popular alternative to Bermuda's more staid offerings.

Jewelry stores abound, both on Front Street and in adjoining cul-de-sacs, and this is perhaps the place to mention that jewelry (like watches, china, glassware, and woolen goods) is given a preferential import duty rate of 8.5 percent, which means that prices are competitive with, and sometimes lower than, stateside equivalents. Many shops offer excellent selections and we suggest you pop into any that catch your fancy. One that I am especially fond of is Solomon's Jewellers, which deals exclusively with fine jewelry, with many special pieces designed in owner Alan Porter's own workshops. Other well-established shops include Astwood Dickinson, a resident of Front Street for over 80 years; Crisson, which specializes in watches and timepieces and handles some—including Rolex, Piaget, Cartier, and Dupont—exclusively; and Lote Tree Jewels (in Walker Arcade, off Front Street) the place to find 14k-gold beads in any length you desire.

Perfume, too, can be found everywhere. But Peniston Brown and its sister shop, Guerlain have perhaps the most extensive collections, with over 125 lines of Italian and French perfumes, as well as English soaps by Chelsea of London, and boxed selections of mini-bottles or vials. Good for experimenting with different scents, they also make nifty stocking stuffers. For those a bit overwhelmed by the selection, but wishing to experiment with a new scent, there are tester bottles (for many perfumes) and a somewhat helpful printed description of the most popular brands.

Other notable Front Street shops include the ubiquitous Benetton, the Italian "McSweater" chain, which seems to have outposts everywhere we look; Vera P. Card, if your tastes run to Hummel and Lladro figurines; and A. S. Cooper & Sons, one of my favorites, for china, glassware and—on the main floor—spiffy displays of little take-home gifts, such as a jar of spices for mulled wine.

Shopping, of course, is not limited to Front Street. There are chic alleyways off the main drag for additional browsing, as well as good shops sprinkled here and there throughout Hamilton.

Stefanel, in Walker Arcade, off Reid Street, for instance, offers Italian imports, including wool and cotton knit sweaters, as well as cotton and linen suits for men and cotton dresses for women. Nearby is Sisley, with unisex togs akin to, but dressier than those found in its Benetton sister shop. Mexicale Rose, Chancery Lane off Front Street, is devoted to things Mexican: earrings and belt buckles of malachite and turquoise; old coins. For bargains, check out St. Michael, the brand name for London's famous Marks & Spencer stores. It's on Reid Street, across from Trimingham's back door. Sometimes there are lots of high quality goods; other times the selection can most kindly be called uninspired. But since the stock changes frequently, the store is worth a look.

The Harbourmaster, in Washington Mall, stocks the largest collection of luggage in Bermuda; W. J. Boyle & Sons, on Queen and Reid streets, is a good place to head for casual and dress (though not elegant), shoes; the Bermuda Coin & Stamp Company, on Cellar Lane, as you've guessed, sells stamps and coins, from the souvenir variety to the very rare; Pegasus Prints and Maps, on Pitts Bay Road across from the Hamilton Princess, carries 18th and 19th century maps of Bermuda, the Americas and elsewhere around the world, as well as delicately hand-colored English botanical prints, assorted sporting and riding-to-the-hounds prints and inexpensive current maps of Bermuda; and Timeless Antiques, on Church Street, specializes in wonderful old grandfather clocks as well as English oak pieces.

Finally, I suggest you seek out one of the local book shops, The Book Mart or The Book Rack, for instance, for special books on Bermuda's history, landscape, cooking, etc, that can only be purchased on the island.

St. George's

When you visit St. George's, sooner or later you'll find yourself at the doors of Frangipani, an irresistible shop on Water Street stocked with warm-weather clothing gathered from around the world and displayed with imagination and humor. You'll find light-as-air Greek cotton

92 Bermuda

ST. GEORGE'S SHOPPING

1. Frangipani
2. Taylors
3. Which Craft
4. The Cow Polly
5. The Bridge House Art Gallery and Craft Shop
6. Benetton
7. English Sports Shop
8. Irish Linen
9. Frith's Liquors
10. Triminghams
11. Tokaram's Ltd.

© FISHER'S WORLD INC., 1988.

dresses and drawstring pants, a rainbow of cotton sweaters, lacy fashions from Hawaii, batik from Bali, shell jewelry from the Pacific, silks from Manhattan. And you'll be waited on by a very pleasant sales staff.

Farther down the street, behind a sign proclaiming "Tartan By the Yard," is Taylors, which also offers tartan already made up into kilts, skirts and scarves for men, women, children, and even babies. They also stock a large, if not terribly interesting, collection of cashmere, lambswool and Shetland sweaters and some soft and wonderful blankets.

Down on Somers Wharf, in a cool, pale yellow complex of shops, is Which Craft, which offers all sorts of craftwork created by Bermudians, including Gombey dolls rendered by Marion MacPherson, needlepoint pillows, crocheted tea cozies, knitted animals, wooden toys, and on one wall, a selection of items specifically designed for the lefthanded: scissors, ladles, can openers, rulers, even boxer shorts.

A little farther on, also on Somers Wharf and definitely worth a stop, is The Cow Polly, which has little to do with dairy products, but much to do with the sea, including sea scene needlepoints (the store began as a needlepoint specialist shop), wooden, hand-painted napkin rings in fish shapes, and scrimshaw carvings. Also on display are good-looking wicker baskets, photo frames, embroidered baby frocks, aprons, placemats, and in time for Christmas, handmade tree ornaments.

The Bridge House Art Gallery and Craft Shop on King's Square offers a potpourri of enticements: prints and watercolors by local artists in cedar frames, and needlepoint designs of Bermuda, creations by Jill Amos Raine, including dolls that range from $150 to around $300, and intriguing watch montages by Joy Blackburne, featuring the ever-popular map of Bermuda, as well as sailboats, Bermuda scenes, etc. (from $30 to $100).

Elsewhere On The Island

Branches of many of the aforementioned shops can be found in the chic shopping arcades of the island's major hotels.

My favorite Icelandic sweater shop, for instance, has its base on South Shore Road in Paget, but also has boutiques at the Sonesta Beach, Elbow Beach, Bermudiana and the Hamilton Princess. The Chameleon Sweater Shop offers many familiar Icelandic designs (found too at Constables of Bermuda, on Front Street), but owner Robert Trott also stocks exclusively the Alafoss line with richer colors and more interesting styling. Though these sweaters and sweatercoats are often too warm for city wear, they're perfect for Bermuda's brisk winter season or for at-home country living.

Collections of a different kind are found at the Thistle Gallery, on Park Road on the outskirts of Hamilton. Owner Hugh Davidson carries some Bermuda reproduction pieces (since true made-in-Bermuda antiques, including the famed Bermuda chest, are now very rare), as well as fine antiques from England, Europe and the Far East. Many of his finds are strikingly handsome and for antique lovers, the gallery is well worth a special detour.

Out on Harbour Road in Paget is Foxie Cooper's The Bamboo Gate, home of some very chic—and pricey—wardrobe additions; on Middle Road in Southampton is The Rising Sun, a jumble of gadgets, gourmet cookery accessories and, because owner Anne Powell is a dedicated horsewoman, a selection of tack.

Shopping isn't one of Somerset Village's big draws, but if meandering there, look for a folksy little store called The Old Market. Inside is a scramble of merchandise—from the obligatory rack of T-shirts to jams and marmalades, well-crafted wooden games, botanical placemats, old coins, and a case of antique silver pieces, containing such absolute necessities as delicate Victorian grape shears.

Galleries & Studios

The best known, and I think, the best gallery on the island, is The Windjammer Gallery, on the corner of Reid and King streets in Hamilton. Owner Susan Curtis handles all of Bermuda's top artists, as well as a selection of works from America and Europe. Set in a typical Bermuda house, each of the smallish rooms is devoted to either an individual artist or a group of artists with complementary styles or subjects. The backyard garden is the province of Desmond Fountain's sculptures.

As long as the gallery isn't thronged, Ms. Curtis or her assistant are happy to talk at length to visitors with a genuine interest in Bermudian art. And both are extremely knowledgeable and helpful.

A number of the Windjammer artists also open their own studios, by appointment, to those with a real interest in purchasing a piece of Bermuda artwork. (There is, by the way, no duty on fine art taken home to the U.S., Canada, or the U.K.)

Desmond Fountain, for instance, a local sculptor with an international following, can be phoned at 292-3955 or by writing ahead to P.O. Box 317, Flatts 3, Bermuda. His lifelike bronzes, many life sized, are created by the ancient "lost wax" process. Lantana Colony Club has two of his bronzes in its gardens and Alwin Gallery, one of London's top sculpture galleries, features Mr. Fountain's work on a regular basis. In keeping with his reputation, his works sell in the $15,000 to $30,000 range.

Diana and Eric Amos likewise will open their Warwick studio to guests who call them at 236-9056. Diana works in oils and watercolors to capture soft luminescent Bermuda landscapes, while husband Eric's focus is birds, painted in their natural habitat. Indisputably the island's premier bird painter, his work is in the British royal family's collection and has been featured at leading London galleries.

Those who love the sea and ships, as Captain Stephen Card does, are likely to be entranced by his nautical scenes, especially his mighty ocean liner portraits. For a close-up view of his work, call him at 234-2353.

Alfred Birdsey, a Bermuda institution now in his mid-seventies, works in watercolors and oils, in dashes and pastels, impressionistically summing up seascapes, country scenes, and village life. Twelve of his large watercolors grace the Bank of Bermuda, and by special commission he's created work that hangs in offices and homes around the world. At his studio, one can select a watercolor from around $35 to $300, a limited edition print ($30-$500), an oil (beginning at $100), or carry off a box of his Christmas card designs for a mere $10. Phone 236-6658. (Mr. Birdsey himself may not be available for a chat, but one of his daughters, who are also artists, usually acts as host.)

Close by, also in Paget, is Mary Zuill, a sparkling silver-haired lady whose watercolors capture whimsical flowers, pastel cottages, and flowering landscapes. The paintings leaning against the walls of her small studio run from $50 up to around $200, and like Mr. Birdsey, she'll do special commissions on request. She welcomes visitors from April through November on Tuesdays through Fridays. Phone 236-2439.

Photographer Graeme Outerbridge offers his own view of Bermuda via a discerning eye that disdains the obvious and instead sums up the island's form and substance in striking, definitely non-postcardlike photos. A regular contributor to major magazines, he was among the photographers commissioned to participate in three of the world's most ambitious pictoral projects, A Day in the Life Of. . . The Soviet Union, America, and Japan. When not off on assignment, he can be reached at his Southampton studio at 238-2411.

And, finally, art of a different sort is embodied in the Bermuda costume dolls created by Kathleen Kensley Bell. Each doll takes weeks to sculpt before it is ready to be painted and dressed, and many are specially commissioned, as are more traditional busts or portraits to immortalize an individual. Costs range from $150 to $400. To view the current collection at her home in Paget, phone 236-3366.

By the way, all the artists who open their studios to the public ask that visitors plan to phone and drop by during traditional business hours, which means in most cases, Monday through Friday, from around 10 A.M. to 5 P.M.

In addition to the Bridger House gallery mentioned in the St. George's Shopping section, another small gallery is The Art House, on South Shore Road in Paget. It features medium-priced decorative art, mostly created by Bermudians (but is closed January and February). Other art centers include the Hamilton City Hall Art Gallery (in Hamilton) and the Bermuda Arts Centre at the Dockyard near Somerset (part of the Maritime Museum), where crafts mingle with art (though there's little fine art).

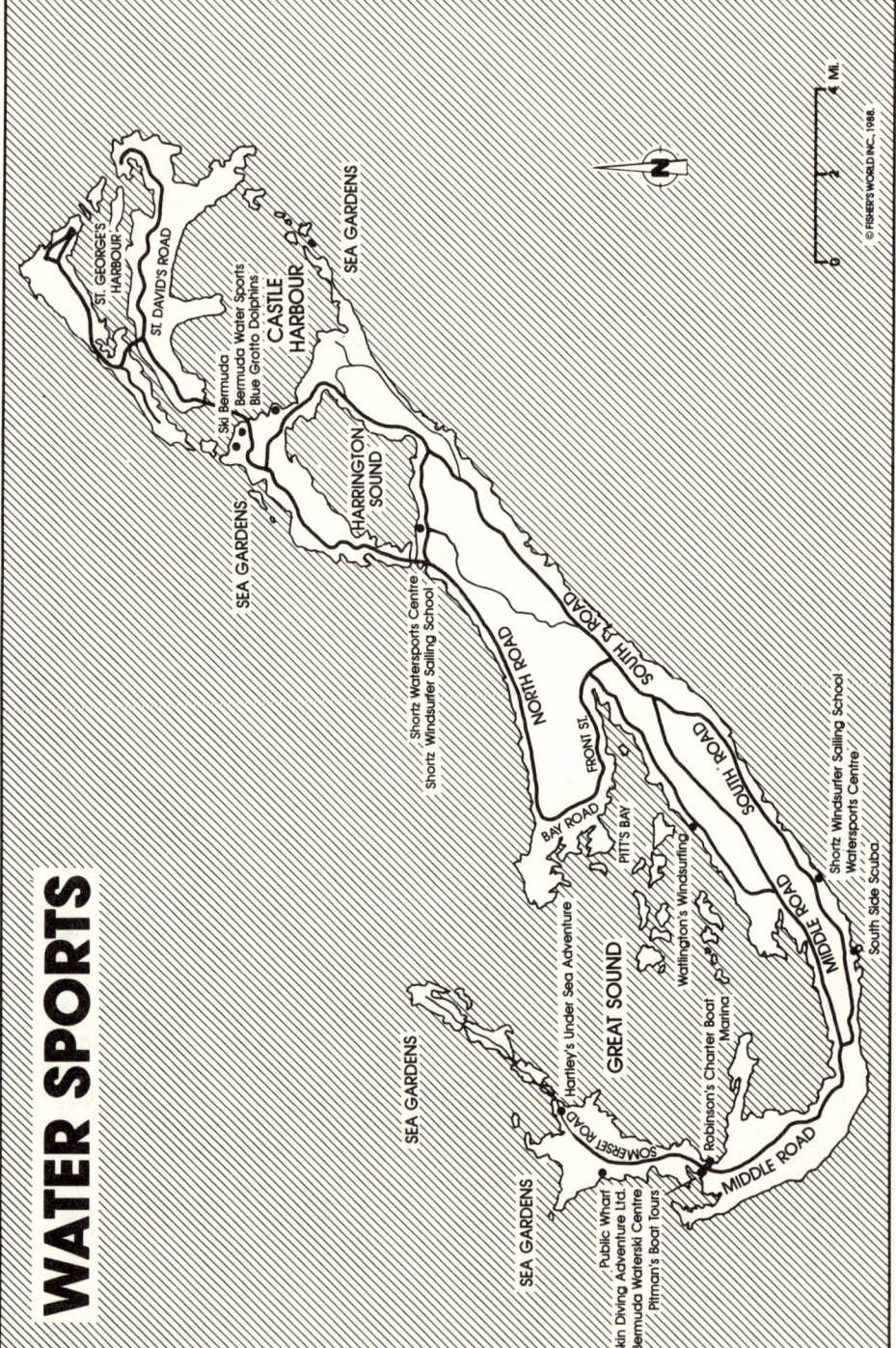

SPORTS

For those who enjoy sports best from a shady vantage point, Bermuda offers soccer from October to April, cricket from May to September, as well as rugby, field hockey, golf and tennis tournaments, sail, motor, and dinghy races, and even an occasional table tennis match.

Hands-on sports enthusiasts have even more from which to choose. Following is a roundup thereof.

Boating and Sailing

The sea has always been a seducer, and the special aquamarine of Bermuda's waters sooner or later draws most visitors from firm footing into, or onto, some manner of boat. Towboats and kayaks can be rented for around $10 an hour, sunfish or Boston whalers for about $25, sailboard and waterbikes for $15. A two-hour sailing lesson averages $70, and if the instructions don't bring mastery, the 56-foot sloop Chicane can be chartered, with skipper, for $240 for three hours.

Many of the major hotels launch boat or sail excursions, of either the protected water or far asea varieties, from their own docks. On request, these facilities are usually open to unregistered guests. And all hotels can arrange boat rentals.

Grotto Bay Hotel (293-2640) offers Boston whalers to yak boards; Salt Kettle Boat Rentals (236-4863) rents sunfish to sailboard to daysailers to a 35-foot Flybridge Cruiser, as well as a captained ketch, sloop or yawl. (This is also the place to inquire about sailing lessons.)

Captain John Shirley Boat Rentals (234-0914) handles sunfish, widgeons, windsurfers, and a Boston whaler with a sun roof as well as rods, reels, and tackle. Robinson's Charter Boat Marina (238-9408) offers sunfish, rowboats, whalers, and a 15-foot Glasspar V-bottom ($45 for two hours).

The best bets for windsurfing are the Glencoe-based Windsurfing School (236-6218), which provides boards and if needed an instructor and a wet suit; the Shortz Windsurfing Schools at the Palmetto Hotel (293-2323); and the Sonesta (238-8122). The Bermuda Waterski Centre (234-3354) offers waterskiing as well as lessons in trick skiing, knee boarding, and skurfer.

Bermuda Water Tours (295-3727) rents a 40-foot ketch to parties of up to 15; Bermuda Caribbean Yacht Charters (234-0497) has a 52-foot ketch that holds up to 25 people; and Ocean Yacht Charters (295-1180) has two 41-foot OutIsland Morgans, each holding no more than 18 people; and Mayflower Charters (295-8291) has a dandy 51-foot schooner, named Beluga II. Other possibilities include Salt Kettle Boat Rentals' two 41-foot sailboats, Somerset Bridge Cruises (234-0235) 44-foot CSY; and Starlight Sailing Cruises (292-1834) 31-foot sloop. All of the preceding come with a captain, most with snorkeling gear. A few will pack a picnic lunch. Prices average around $200 for three hours (except for Starlight's sloop, which runs about $200 for a full day). But the prices vary according to the size of your party, the itinerary you choose, and fluctuating fuel prices. Check out too, the new submarine plying Bermuda's water. At presstime, rates were not yet set but thought to be in the $50 per person range. Your hotel will have details.

Of course, many of Bermuda's visitors neither need nor want a professional captain at the helm. Most of this breed arrive on their own boats and use Bermuda as the base for further sea excursions. William F. Buckley Jr., for instance, returns regularly as a participant in the every other year Newport-to-Bermuda Race which attracts some 180 of the world's finest yachts.

This race, held in June and co-sponsored by the Royal Bermuda Yacht Club, is definitely not for Sunday sailors. Torn spinnakers, storm-snapped masts or days of hot, becalmed seas are not unusual. One writer described the trip as "sailing to Bermuda on the rhumb line and the rum line." Once the sailors reach port, they tend to celebrate nightly and mightily.

Other regularly scheduled races include the mid-June Bermuda Ocean Race from Annapolis, Maryland, to Bermuda, and the late-April Bermuda Invitational Week, in which six to seven classes of yachts from Bermuda, the U.S., the U.K., and Canada compete in the Great Sound. There are races, too, for powerboats, including a July Around the Island race which draws top drivers from around the world.

On a smaller scale is the every other Sunday (during spring, summer, and fall) Bermuda Fitted Dinghies race series. The race sites alternate between St. George's Harbour, Hamilton Harbour, the Great Sound, and Mangrove Bay, and they're great fun to watch. The 14-foot boats carry as much sail as many ocean-going yachts and unless kept moving by a crew of six or seven (one designated as a bailer) will, in a twinkling, dunk all hands.

Perhaps the most spectacular sailing sight in Bermuda's recent history took place in 1986 when Bermuda became the rendezvous port for European yachts and tall ships heading for the July 4th celebration of the 100th birthday of the Statue of Liberty. More than one awed onlooker wept openly at the beauty of the fleet, a reaction those who love ships and sailing and the sea can well appreciate.

Diving And Snorkeling

Helmet Diving. Helmet diving is a bit of misnomer. While there is a helmet large enough to go on over eyeglassess and so waterproof that one's hair stays dry, no dive is required. Rather, participants are dropped about 10 to 12 feet below the water's surface. There they are met by a guide who conducts a tour of reef life, provides food to feed the fish, points out sponges breathing freely without a helmet, and so on. It's safe for nonswimmers and children over eight.

The Hartley Helmet Diving Cruise (292-4434) in Flatt's Village and Hartley's Under Sea Adventure (234-2861) at the Village Inn Dock in Somerset, take visitors out to distant reefs. Both of the Hartley trips take about 3 1/2 hours and include a drink and, for an extra charge, underwater portraits. The price per person is $28 (without portrait).

Scuba Diving. The four scuba centers in Bermuda will tell you, quite accurately, that on a calm day, underwater visibility extends a startling 200 feet. All offer scuba courses and, for certified divers, a choice of diving spots. Experienced divers have the option of participating in night dives. A one-hour scuba lesson runs around $25; half day $60. A two-tank dive runs from $50-$60.

The four are: Grotto Diving (293-2915 or 292-2592 after 5 P.M.) at the Grotto Bay Hotel; Nautilus Diving (238-2332 or 238-8000) at the Southampton Princess; Skin Diving Adventures (234-1034 or 238-0779 after 5 P.M.) in Somerset Bridge; and South Side Scuba (238-1833 or 236-0394 after 5 P.M.) at the Sonesta Beach Hotel.

By the way, should you run into trouble, there is a recompression chamber at the King Edward Memorial Hospital, Finger Point Road, in Paget.

Snorkeling. In addition to all the hotels that rent or loan snorkeling equipment, there are also five snorkeling cruises. If a complimentary rum swizzle is important to you, ask about its availability. Otherwise the cruise particulars are very similar: bring your own bathing suit and towel; they'll provide snorkel gear, buoyancy aids, flippers, and some of the world's choicest shallow-water wreck diving spots.

The companies are: Bermuda Cruises (292-7094) in Hamilton; Bermuda Water Sports (293-2640) at the Grotto Bay Hotel; Hayward's Explorer Snorkeling and Glass-Bottom Boat Cruises (292-8652), Front Street, Hamilton; Pittman's Boat Tours (234-0700), Somerset Bridge Hotel; and Salt Kettle Boat Rentals (236-4863) in Salt Kettle.

BEACHES

HOTEL BEACH CLUBS

ELBOW BEACH SURF CLUB
SOUTH SHORE BEACH CLUB

Charge for non-house guests, reservations required.

St. Catherine Beach
John Smith's Bay
Gravelly Bay
Church Bay
Devonshire Bay
Grape Bay
Elbow Beach
Elbow Beach Surf Club
Coral Beach
South Shore Beach Club
Marley Beach
Warwick Long Bay
Shelly Bay Beach
Clarence Cove
Chaplin Bay
Horseshoe Bay
East Whale Bay
Stinky Bay
Boat Bay
West Whale Bay
Whitney Bay
Spring Benny's Bay
Somerset Long Bay

© FISHER'S WORLD INC., 1988.

WATERSKIING

This sport is permitted in the protected waters of Hamilton Harbour, Great Sound, Castle Harbour, Mangrove Bay, Spanish Point, Ferry Reach, Ely's Harbour, Riddell's Bay and Harrington Sound. May through September is ideal for water skiing. Bermuda law requires water skiers be under direct supervision of a licensed boat captain. Most top-drawer hotels have such skippers available.

Grotto Bay Hotel, for instance, has an excellent water skiing program (293-2640). A nonhotel water skiing option is the @IBermuda Waterski Centre (234-3354), located at Robinson's Marina in Somerset Bridge. They've boats specially developed for water skiing, as well as instructors.

FISHING

The estimated 650 species of fish found in local Bermuda waters draw anglers from around the world—particularly from May to November when the fish are at their feistiest. No license is required, nor is there a fee to enter one's prize catch in the Annual Game Fishing Tournament (January 1-December 31). The Tournament, open to visitors, presents awards for top catches in 26 classes of game fish. Check with the Bermuda Department of Tourism, Global House, 43 Church Street, Hamilton or write to Bermuda Game Fishing Association, P.O. Box HM1306, Hamilton HM FX, Bermuda, for the rules of the game.

Some of the species a visitor might reasonably expect to lure are:

Deep-sea (offshore) Fishing: wahoo, greater amberjack, almaco jack, rainbow runner, great barracuda, dolphin, blue marlin, white marlin, blackfin tuna, yellowfin (Allison) tuna, little tunny, skipjack tuna.

Reef Fishing: greater amberjack (school size), almaco jack (school size), great barracuda, little tunny, bermuda chub, gray snapper, yellowtail snapper, assorted bottom fish.

Shore Fishing: bonefish, palometa (pompano), gray snapper, great barracuda.

Protected marine life includes marine turtles, whales, porpoises and dolphins, plus all corals, queen and harbor conch, helmet shells, bonnet shells, netted olive shells, Bermuda cone shells, scallops, and the Atlantic pearl oyster. In addition, lobsters are strictly off-limits to visiting fishermen.

Bermuda also prohibits spearfishing and spearguns and limits the catch of nonprotected species to no more than two within any 24-hour period.

Shore Fishing Equipment Rentals. Rods, reels, and tackles for shore fishing can be rented from Fly Bridge Tackle, on Church Street, Hamilton (295-1845); Four Winds Fishing Tackle, Par-la-Ville Road, Hamilton (292-7466); Salt Kettle Boat Rentals, Salt Kettle (236-4863); and Captain John Shirley Boat Rentals, Mangrove Bay (234-0914).

Daily rentals average $10 with a $20 deposit; weekly rentals run around $35.

Chartered Boats for Deep-sea Fishing. All chartered boats must be inspected and relicensed every year. Do ask to see the current license when boarding. If it's up to date, you're in good hands. All the licensed boats carry experienced captains and are well equipped with outriggers, sturdy fighting chairs, medical supplies, communications equipment, and the necessary tackle and bait. Visitors are expected to bring along their own lunch and refreshments.

When you book a charter, ask about the skipper's policy on caught fish. Some skippers keep all or most of the catch; others allow renters to take home their pick of the catch.

Following is a selection of the boats available for half- and full-day charter. For additional options and information, contact Mrs. Margaret DeSilva at the Bermuda Sport Fishing Association Booking Office, Creek View House, 8 Tulo Lane, Pembroke HM 02, Bermuda. Phone 295-2370 or 295-5535.

Boat	Captain	Phone
Challenger 45' Sportsfisherman	Alan Card	234-0872
Ellen B 28' Down East Type	Michael Baxter	234-2963 (reef fishing)
Linda Too 37' Sportsfisherman	Dendrick Taylor	297-1115
Lady Clare 35' Sportsfisherman	David Adcock	234-2605
Lady Gina 42' Hans Peterson	Allan Virgil	238-2655
Tango 36' Hattaras	David DeSilva	295-2370
Mako 3 43' Sportsfisherman	Allen DeSilva	295-2036/ 295-0835
Marlin Too 35' Down East Sports	Milton Pitman	234-1086
Lobster Reef 42' Bruno Stillman	Eddie Dawson, Sr.	292-6898
Sea Wolf 43' Sportsfisherman	Russell Young	234-1832
Traveler 41' D&D Downeaster	Ricky Richards	234-2378
Troubadour 42' Double Ender	Blake West	293-0813

Rates vary widely depending on the size of the boat and the number of people in your party.

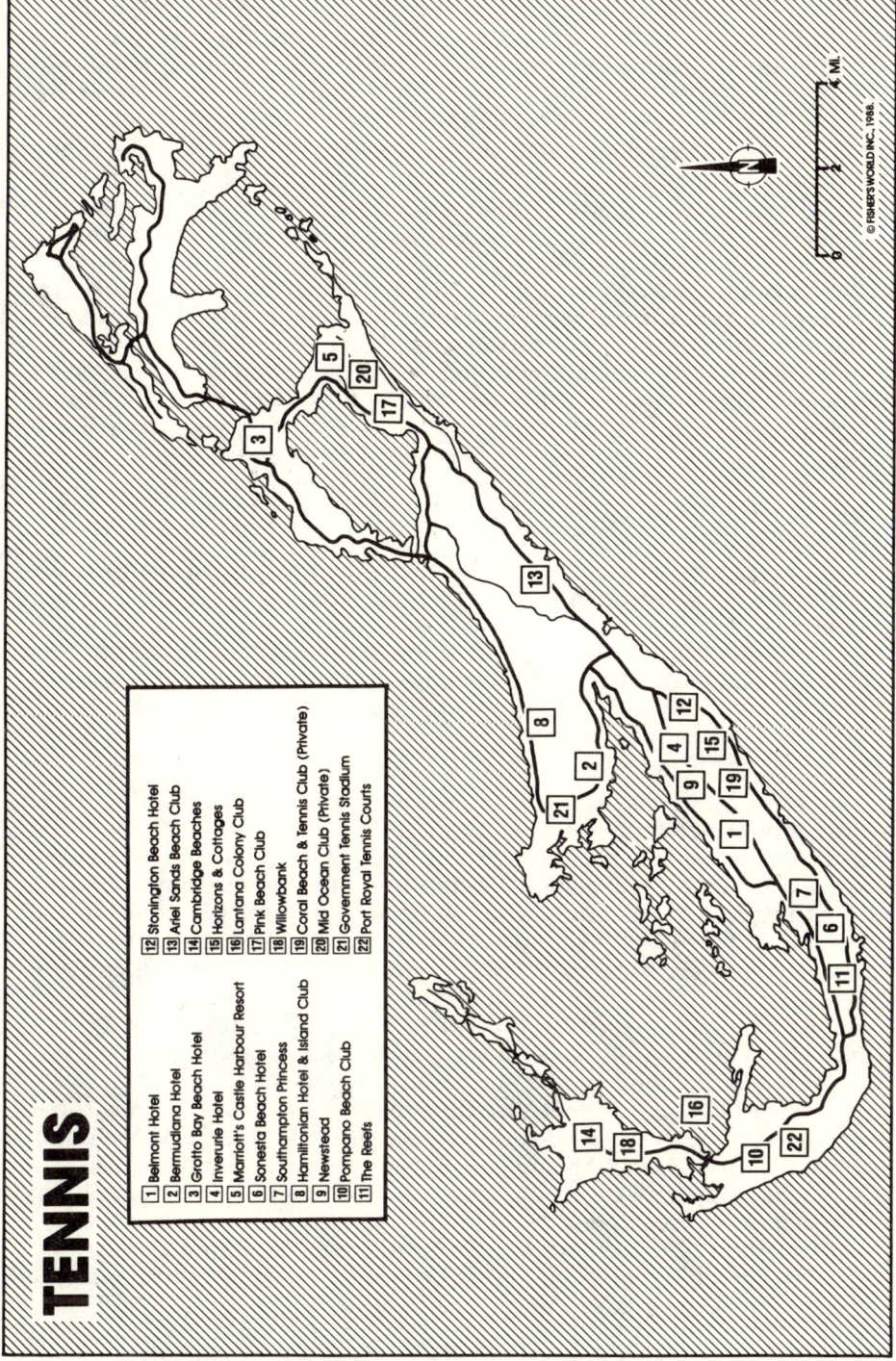

Tennis

Bermuda claims the honor of having introduced tennis to Americans in Staten Island, New York, in 1874. Most courts prefer proper tennis attire; a few demand it (noted below). Some hotels allow only their registered guests to play; some hotels (not always the same) even charge their guests. All hotels charge unregistered guests from $5-$12 per hour. Among the hotels allowing outsiders to play are the Belmont, Bermudiana, Elbow Beach, Grotto Bay, Hamiltonian, Horizons and Cottages, Marriott's Castle Harbour, Newstead, Sonesta Beach, Southampton Princess, Stonington Beach and Willowbank. The public courts at the Government Tennis Stadium demand tennis attire. The Port Royal Tennis Courts does not. Most hotels have racquets for rent and balls for sale. Many major hotels have resident professionals whose hourly instruction fees are in the $20-$40 range. All leading hotels have some lighted courts for evening play (extra charge in some cases). In total, there are some 100 courts from which to choose. For tournament schedules write the Bermuda Department of Tourism or the Bermuda Lawn Tennis Association, P.O. Box HM341, Hamilton HM BX, Bermuda.

There is platform tennis (paddle tennis) on two lighted courts at the White Heron Country Inn, but you should reserve a day in advance (238-1655).

Squash may be played at the Bermuda Squash Racquets Club on Middle Road in Devonshire, next to the National Sports Club. Open 10 A.M. to 4 P.M. by reservation (292-6881).

Golf

It's not unusual for a golf foursome to land in Bermuda with the goal of playing all the courses, known as "collecting" courses, much as a numismatist collects coins. For those so inclined, plan on seven rounds—or nine if the island's 9-hole and "mashie" are included.

Bermuda's courses are among the world's most picturesque... and quirky. At Port Royal's notorious sixteenth, for instance, both the tee and hole are set high on cliff edges, with glistening sand, a circle of reef, and rich blue water one hundred dizzying feet below. Add to this drama, an ever-present wind swirling unpredictably, and it's not surprising that errant balls and ragged tempers are the norm.

The most famous course on the island belongs to the ultraprivate Mid Ocean Club. President Eisenhower—no slouch with a four-iron—arranged conferences (and rounds) here with world leaders, including Churchill and Harold Macmillan; President Truman and the Duke of Windsor also came to play (not together). Serious golfers can obtain the necessary members' introduction to play its wide fairways on visitors' days: Wednesdays and Fridays. Just ask at your hotel.

Considered by most experts to be one of the top 50 courses in the world, Mid Ocean is known as a test of driving skill. The fifth hole, called Cape, is reportedly where Babe Ruth lost some dozen balls trying to hit a tee shot over Mangrove Lake to the green. He failed. Everyone

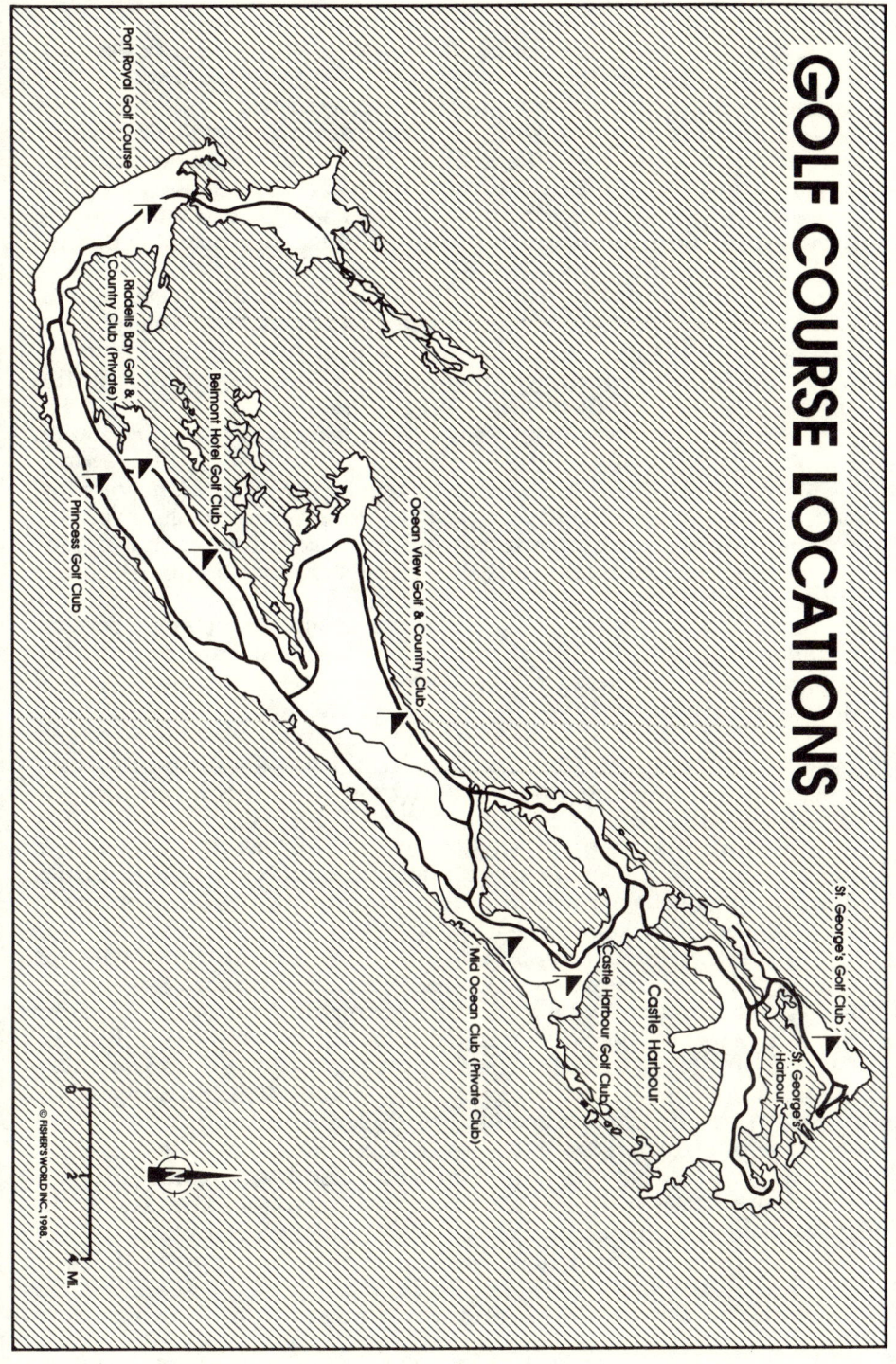

does. Carts here are for members' use only— only if they're over 65, with a medical certificate! The club does have some caddies on hand, but your best bet is to plan to pull or carry your bag.

Port Royal is the second major golf course on Bermuda. Created by Robert Trent Jones in 1970 and owned by the Bermuda government, it easily handles some fifty thousand rounds a year, making it one of the world's busiest public courses. The terrain here is hilly and the feeling rural. Look for the partially restored ruins of Whale Bay Battery near the fifteenth fairway.

Riddell's Bay, dating back to 1922, is Bermuda's oldest course. Relatively short (5,414 yards), it features lots of water views and a few over-water challenges. A considerate member has created a hole-by-hole guide to playing here, with special tips on how to deal with the wind that sweeps off the nearby Great Sound.

There are also three hotel links on the island: at Marriott's Castle Harbor, the Belmont, and the Southampton Princess.

Marriott's entry is a killer for those who opt to walk it (and very few do). Referred to as a "mountain goat" course, it features deep valleys, correspondingly steep hills and requires close to five hours of concentration. One the bright side, the course is in top condition and the views are ravishing.

In somewhat poorer condition is the cramped Belmont course, which demands precision shots to keep the ball out of roughs or adjoining fairways. Here too (as at Riddell's Bay) a helpful member has penned advice on the how-to's of playing each hole.

The par-3 executive 18-hole at the Southampton Princess—which meanders around bougainvillea and oleander bushes, up and down gentle hillsides and past the hotel's myriad other sports activities—is surprisingly challenging, partly because of its small greens. But this is also the place to try for a hole-in-one. In fact, the club has a hole-in-one competition open to all players. Simply drop 50 cents in a designated bowl before heading out to play, and if your tee shot is very true, the pot (worth at least $1,000) is yours.

Two other island courses are the 9-hole Ocean View Golf and Country Club and the 18-hole St. George's Golf Club, both government owned. The former is smack in the center of the island. No water hazards here, but there are a number of ocean views from elevated tees. Compared to other Bermuda courses, it's relatively tame, though there are a few surprises. St. George's, opened in mid-1985 and designed by Robert Trent Jones, is still settling in. Called "sneaky," partly because of the capricious winds that whip in from the Atlantic, it is a short course (par 64), but with time should be suitably competitive.

Finally, there's the 9-hole "mashie" (pitch-and-putt) course at Horizons and Cottages. Started by a previous managing director, it's well groomed but not challenging, not hilly, and not particularly frustrating. In short, it's a respite from some of the island's more grueling golf opportunities. And it can be rewarding. For guests of

Horizons, the management often organizes mini-tournaments, with bottles of wine or champagne as prizes.

The more official tournaments are listed on The Bermuda Golf Association's (P.O. Box HM433, Hamilton HM BX) calendar. There are dozens of them, but the most famous is the Bermuda Goodwill Tournament, held just before Christmas. Begun in 1953, its aim is to promote international friendship among golfers—and each year it attracts nearly one hundred clubs, from the U.S., Canada, and the U.K. Played on four courses, it's a 72-hole best-ball-stroke competition among teams of four, consisting of a club professional and three amateur club members. The program also includes a ladies' tournament and a bevy of social activities. Trophies are given out for low gross, low net, longest drive, etc.

Although golf can be played year round in Bermuda, many players prefer the winter season (November to March), when prices are lower, the weather is brisk but not cold, and the grass is at its best. (Reseeding usually takes place in late September to early November.)

One last bit of trivia: Bermuda has more golf courses per square mile than any other country in the world. Of more practical interest: hand cart rentals average around $3; gas cart rentals range from $15 to $25 for 18 holes; a dozen golf balls cost from $25 to $30; club rentals average around $12; an hour lesson runs from $30 to $40. Greens fees range from a high $50 at Mid Ocean and Castle Harbour to $15 to $25 at other courses.

Swimming, Riding, Running & Pedaling

Swimming. Since the island has a maximum width of only two miles, the visitor is no more than a mile from water at any given time, so there are plenty of swimming opportunities.

Riding. Those who like to canter off on their own will be disappointed to learn that horses cannot be hired and ridden without supervision. Nevertheless, if you've brought along some long pants and hard-heeled shoes and don't mind the companionship of probably no more than a dozen fellow riders, there are two stables waiting to plunk you on horseback. Both provide riding lessons ($20 to $35 per hour) and hour-long trail rides ($20 to $25).

The two are: Lee Bow Riding Centre in Devonshire (229-4181) and Spicelands Riding Centre on Middle Road in Warwick (238-8212 or 238-8246). The latter offers a special eye-opening breakfast jaunt (at 7 A.M.), somewhat prettier trails, and short stretches of beach riding. (Bermuda, understandably, doesn't allow much riding on its pristine public beaches.)

Running. You can pick up the "Bermuda Handy Reference Map" from your hotel or the tourist office for the location of the some 700 acres of public parklands and the gently winding Railway Trail, or just jog along the nearest beach or roadway. You won't be alone. In fact, running has become so popular in Bermuda that there's a two-mile "fun run," organized by the Mid Atlantic Athletic Club and held once a

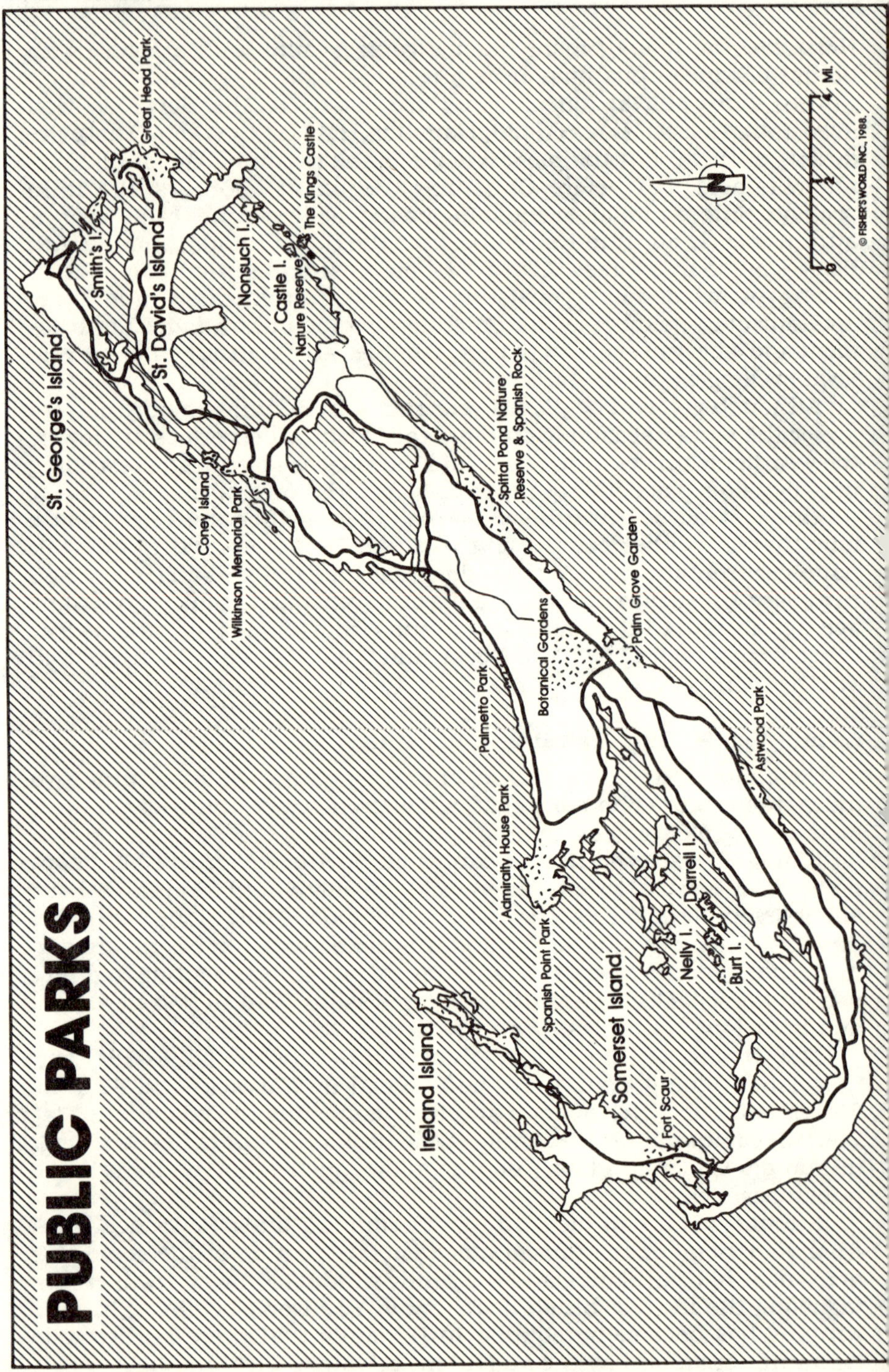
PUBLIC PARKS
St. George's Island
Smith's I.
St. David's Island
Great Head Park
Nonsuch I.
Castle I.
Nature Reserve
The Kings Castle
Coney Island
Wilkinson Memorial Park
Spittal Pond Nature
Reserve & Spanish Rock
Palm Grove Garden
Botanical Gardens
Palmetto Park
Astwood Park
Admiralty House Park
Spanish Point Park
Darrell I.
Nelly I.
Burt I.
Somerset Island
Ireland Island
Fort Scaur
N
0
2
4 Mi.
© FISHER'S WORLD INC., 1988.

week, every week. During daylight savings time, it's on Tuesday evenings at 6 P.M.; other months it begins at 10 A.M. on Sundays. Runners meet in front of Camden House on Berry Hill Road in Paget. (No admission fee.) Even international runner Grete Waitz, who trains in Bermuda, participates occasionally.

For those who plan to be in Bermuda in January, there's also an annual 10k mini-marathon. Information and entry forms can be requested from the Bermuda Track & Field Association, P.O. Box DV397, Devonshire DB BX, Bermuda.

Pedaling. Given the dearth of cars in Bermuda, it's not surprising that bicycling is popular. However, though there are plenty of mopeds for rent on the island, there are relatively few decent bicycles for rent. We can only suggest that you call around and hope for the best. If you do manage to snag one, you can join in the Sunday morning "fun ride" sponsored by the Bermuda Bicycle Association, which leaves from the Botanical Gardens in Paget at 8:30 A.M. The route changes from week to week and you can drop out to follow your own inclinations at any time.

OTHER RECREATION

The island's Department of Agriculture and Fisheries has published an excellent Guide to Bermuda's Public Parks and Beaches by J. Hubert Jones, which includes regulations for use. It notes that there are 744 acres of land within the colony's parks system, of which 597 are managed by the Department of Agriculture and Fisheries, while 147 acres are privately owned parks and gardens open to the public.

The island's largest reserve is Spittal Pond Nature Reserve in Smith's Parish (walking and horse trails, as well as bird-watching opportunities). Here one also finds the historic marker FT 1543, known as Spanish Rock.

One of the prettiest recreational areas is Somers Gardens in St. George's Parish with its tall palms, exquisite flowers, and flowering hedges. Not to be missed either are the Botanical Gardens in Paget Parish. Coney Island, next to Grotto Bay in Hamilton Parish, offers walking and horse trails in addition to its swimming, boating, and fishing facilities.

GOLF COURSES I

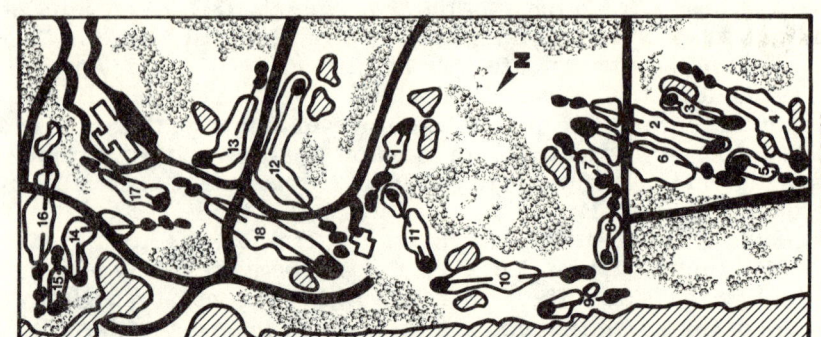

ST. GEORGE'S

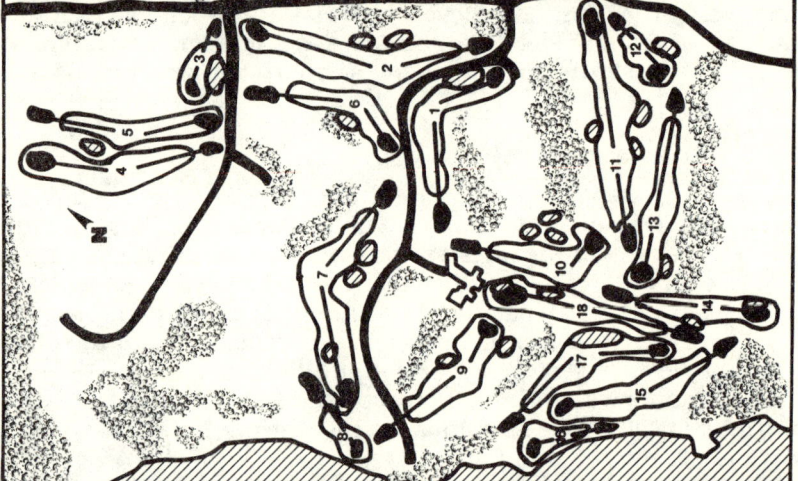

PORT ROYAL

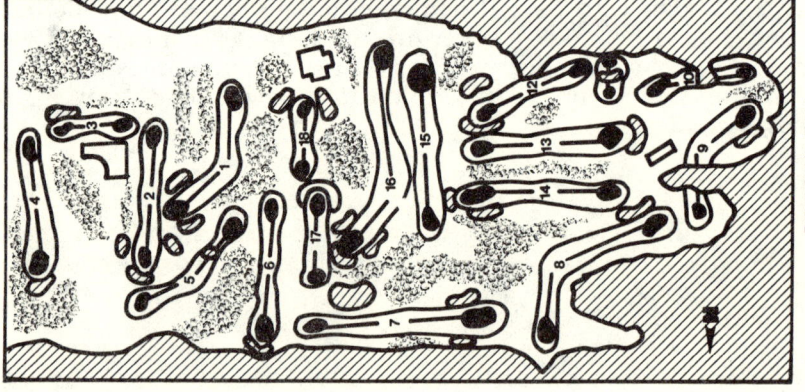

RIDDELL'S BAY

Sights Around The Island

ST. GEORGE'S

    The Bermuda Journey. 25-minute synopsis of Bermuda's history. Town Hall. Adults $3.50; Children under twelve $2.00.
    Deliverance. Replica open to visitors. Ordnance Island. Adults $2.00; Children under twelve .50 cnets.
    Historical Society. Duke to Kent St. Open 10 A.M. to 4 P.M., Mondays-Saturdays. Adults $2.00, Children under sixteen .50 cents.
    St. George's Library, Stuart Hall, Aunt Peggy's Lane. Open 9 A.M. to 5 P.M., Monday, Wednesday, Saturday. Closed one hour for lunch. Admission free.
    Tucker House. Water Street. Open daily, except Sundays and holidays. Admission charge.
    Carriage Museum. Water Street. Open daily, except Sundays and holidays. Admission free, but donations welcome.
    Confederate Museum. Corner of King's Square at Duke of York Street.

NEARBY ST. GEORGE'S

    Gates Fort.
    Fort St. Catherine. Open daily 10 A.M. to 4:30 P.M. Admission fee.
    St. David's Lighthouse and Carter House. St. David's Island. Get pass from Naval Air Station to visit Carter House. Phone Lydell O'Dey, 297-1150.
    Tucker's Town.

SANDY'S PARISH

    Maritime Museum. North Ireland Island. Open 10 A.M. to 5 P.M. daily except Christmas. Admission fee.

112 Bermuda

GOLF COURSES II

OCEAN VIEW

MID-OCEAN

CASTLE HARBOUR

Old Cooperage. Across from museum. *The Attack on Washington* hour-long multimedia show. Continuous showings begin on the half hour, all day long. Admission fee.

Gladys Morell Nature Reserve. East Shore Rd. near Cavello Bay, Somerset. Open daily.

The Springfield Museum and Gilbert Nature Preserve, Somerset Rd., contains the Somerset Library (open Monday, Wednesday and Fridays). Nature preserve open every day, year round.

SOUTHAMPTON PARISH

Gibbs Hill Lighthouse. Lighthouse Rd. Open 9 A.M. to 4:30 P.M. daily. Admission fee.

PAGET PARISH

Paget Marsh. Twenty-six acres owned by National Trust & Audubon Society. For permission to enter, phone the Trust Office at 236-6483.

Botanical Gardens. Guided tours of grounds and greenhouses Tuesday, Wednesday, Friday at 10:30 A.M. Free.

Camden House. In the center of the gardens. Open Tuesdays and Wednesdays, noon to 2 P.M. Free.

HAMILTON PARISH

Aquarium Museum and Children's Zoo. Open 9 A.M. to 4:30 P.M. daily. Admission fee.

Blue Grotto Dolphin Show. Performance five times daily (closed January 11 - February 15). Admission fee.

Crystal Caves. Open 9:30 A.M. to 4:30 P.M. daily. Adults $2.00; Children $1.00.

Leamington Caves. Open 9:30 A.M. to 4:30 P.M. Monday-Saturday (closed part of the winter season). Adults $2.50; Children $1.00.

DEVONSHIRE PARISH

Palm Grove Gardens. Open daily, except Sunday.

Palmetto House. Three rooms open for viewing on Thursdays only, from 10 A.M. to 5 P.M. Admission is free, but donations are welcome.

SMITH'S PARISH

Verdmont. Collector's Hill, off South Shore Rd. Open 10 A.M. to 5 P.M. weekdays. Admission charge.

Spittal Pond Nature Reserve. South Shore Rd. Open daily. Free admission.

Winterhaven Farm Cottage. East of Spittal Pond. Open Monday and Thursdays afternoons.

North Nature Reserve. Mangrove Lake.

PEMBROKE PARISH

Sessions House. Hamilton. For timing of court sessions phone 292-1350. House meets on Fridays. Phone 292-7408 for time.

The Cabinet Building. Hamilton. Senate convenes on Wednesdays at 10:00 A.M. for information phone 292-7408.
Fort Hamilton. Near Cavendish Road and Crow Lane on way to Paget Parish. Free.
Spanish Point. At top of Permbroke Parish.

WHAT TO DO WHEN YOU LOSE YOUR WALLET: 11 TIPS

by
Frances Sheridan Goulart

Leaving home without your wallet is bad enough. Leaving your home away from home without it is worse. Nevertheless, lots of travelers do. If your bulging billfold is like most, here's an inventory of what you've kissed goodbye, says the Traveler's Aid Society: a driver's license, credit cards, automatic check-approval card, secret cash-credit number (which you were instructed to memorize and destroy), social security card, John Hancock card, Blue Cross-Blue Shield and State Farm cards, the key card to the office parking lot, and that grim organ-donor notice plus a blank check or two, appointment cards, and a few phone numbers and family snapshots.

Here's What to Do:

1. Not to worry. A first-class crook can use your credit cards and it needn't cost you a dime. Fifty dollars a card is the most you have to worry about — and if you remember to advise credit card companies, you won't have to pay that.

2. Surprisingly enough, you're not responsible for forged checks with your name on them. If a felon has your blank checks and your check-approval card in areas where automatic check-approval machines are used, he can add up cash as fast as points on a pinball machine. But he'll collect the bank's cash, not yours. It's a bank's responsibility to cover forged checks.

3. If you remember where the loss or theft occurred, get on the phone and get a search started. Also, leave your name with the post office and police station. It's not uncommon for a thief to take only the cash and drop the wallet in a mailbox or mail it back to police headquarters.

To Prevent Loss — Here are 8 Tips:

1. Empty your billfold. Get rid of useless memos and outdated receipts. Put back only what's really important. For instance, take out your title and registration, and parking-lot key card. Keep them, or facsimiles, in your car. Keep your traveler's checks and their serial numbers separate. Never keep a plane ticket in your wallet. If you lose it, you may wait months to get your money back. And if a thief uses it, your aren't protected. Keep secret phone numbers in your head, in a pocket, or at home.

2. Xerox everything in your billfold. This gives you instant knowledge of what's lost and records all the numbers of everything.

3. Look in the phone directory or on the cards themselves for the numbers you'll have to use if your wallet is lost. Write them on the Xerox sheet. This is useful if you're traveling and have to call long distance. (Many credit cards put toll-free numbers on their cards.)

4. Make a second Xerox of the Xerox. Keep on at home and take one on trips. When you travel, keep the copy anywhere except your billfold.

5. When the wallet is lost get out the Xeroxes and start calling. It takes awhile to get new cards but having the numbers will help keep you going. Replacing your driver's license is harder. So is getting a new social

security card because of increasing fraudulent use by illegal aliens and others who want to work and don't have cards. You have to show proof of identity to get a new card — a problem if you've lost all those proofs.

6. If you sign up with a Credit Card Service Bureau, they'll replace many things for you for just one phone call and a fee. You can even insure your cash as part of a package deal with some home owner's or renter's insurance. And if you're extra cautious, you can keep all vital statistics in a safe deposit box.

7. Don't delay. If you're tempted to put off this wallet safeguarding procedure, just ask yourself which side of the finders-keepers-losers-weepers equation you'd rather be on — then do your duty.

8. Want something better and safer than an old-fashioned wallet? Consider a new fangled Chester — a strap-on-vest that holds keys, money, credit cards, passports, and sells for $10. Write: D.D. and D. Traders, 4559 N.W. 7th Street, Dept. 84449, Miami, Fl 33126.

What We Leave Behind: 10 Most-Frequently Lost Or Forgotten Traveler Items

A wallet isn't the only essential American travelers head for home without. You wouldn't be human if you didn't forget something coming or going. Here are 10 other essentials we leave behind, according to American Express Travel Service and the International Traveler's Aid Society:

1. Your toothbrush.
2. Prescription glasses or sunglasses.
3. Collapsible umbrella/pocket-sized raincoat or poncho.
4. Pocket camera, travel iron, hair dryer.
5. Vitamins and prescription drugs.
6. Road maps, travel guides.
7. Emergency sneakers, an extra sweater.
8. Beach books and vacation reading.
9. Traveler's checks.
10. Rolls of change (for tips, phone calls and miscellaneous emergencies).
11. Losers weepers: Every day 1,000 American travelers have their wallets snatched. (The average take — $250.)

Frances Sheridan Goulart's work has appeared in Travel and Leisure, Yankee Magazine, *and others. She is author of more than a dozen books on health and fitness.*

GOLF COURSES III

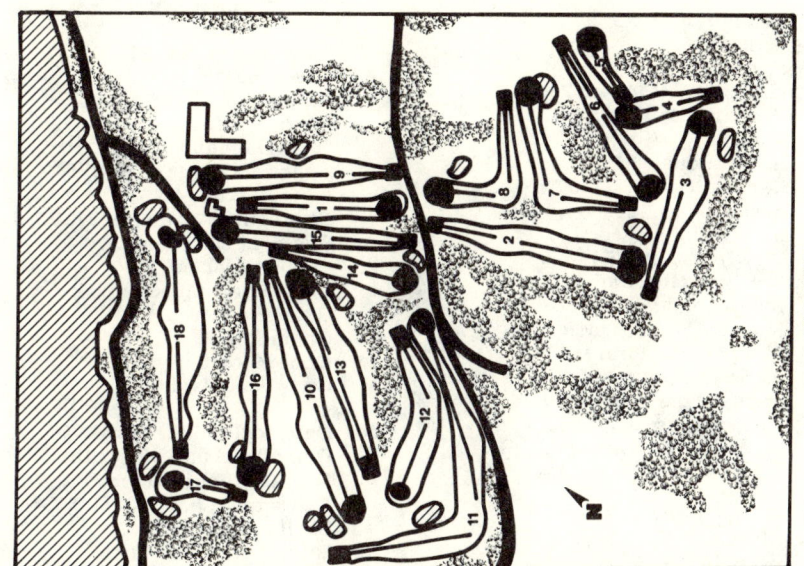

BELMONT

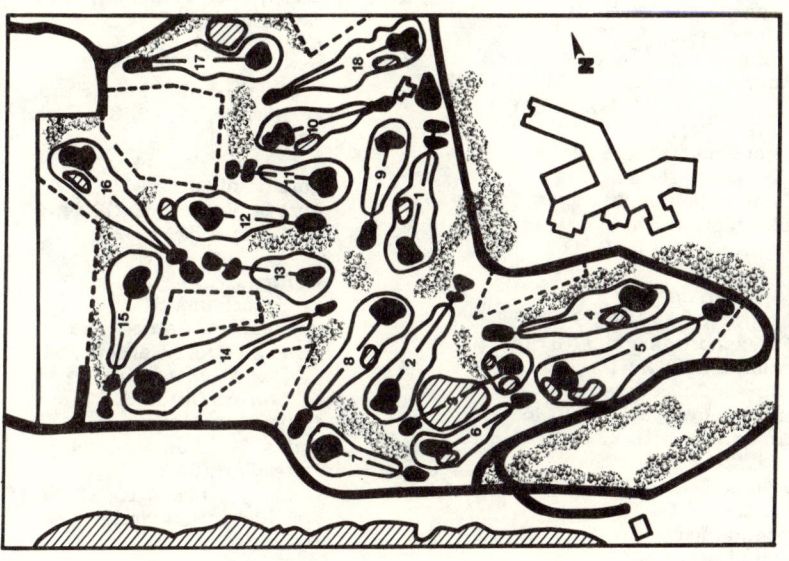

PRINCESS GOLF

INDEX

Admiralty House, 22
Agriculture, 6, 51
Albouy's Point, 17
Aquarium Museum and Zoo, 56
Architecture, 2, 15, 47, 54, 57, 58
    Bridge House, 30
    Camden House, 53, 57
    Carter House, 36
    Chapel, Unfinished, 31
    Clay House Inn, 54
    Maritime Museum, 47, 49
    Old Statehouse, 29, 30
    St. David's Lighthouse, 36
    St. George's Library, 32
    St. Peter's Church, 31, 57
    Springfield Museum, 49
    Tucker House, 32-4, 59
    Verdmont, 54, 58
Artists & Artisans, 18, 30, 49, 89, 90, 93, 94-5
Automobiles, 7-8

Bermuda
    birds, 29, 49, 52, 54, 56
    building in, 39-40
    colonization of, 3-10
    division of, 18, 43
    English on, 1, 4-10, 15, 27-8
    fauna of, 29, 52, 53, 54
    government of, 1-2, 5, 6, 8-10, 19, 21, 30-2
    houshold income, 39
    libraries, 18, 32
    population of, 39
    Portuguese on, 3, 6
    queen's visit to, 9, 41
    size, 39
    Spanish on, 3-4
    tourism, 1, 7, 9, 39-41
    transportation on, 7-8, 43
Bermuda blinds, 51
Bermuda Collection, 63
Bermuda Company, 5, 15, 52
Bermuda Gazette, 32
Bermuda Journey, 29
Bermuda National Trust, 31, 34, 49, 53, 54
Bermuda Regiment Band, 41, 52
Bermuda shorts, 41
Bermudez, Juan de, 3, 27
Black Watch Well, 21
Blue Grotto Dolphin Show, 56
Boilers, the, 51
Butler, Governor Nathaniel, 30

Cabinet Building, 20

Camden House Museum, 53-4, 57
Carriage Museum, 34
Carter, Christopher, 36
Carter House, 36
Cathedral Rocks, 51
Caves, 56
Churches
    in Devonshire, 54
    in Hamilton, 19, 21
    in St. George's, 31-2, 57
    in Sandys, 49
Churchill, Winston, 9, 21, 72, 104
Clermont House, 53
Cobbler's Island, 22
Confederate Museum, 34
Cottage colonies, 63
Coward, Noel, 57
Craft Market,
Crown Jewels, 34

Dale, Richard S., 31, 57
Darrell's Island, 52
Day, Governor Samuel, 32
Deliverance, 5, 18, 27, 30, 34
Devil's Hole, 56
Dunroissil, Lord, 41

Edwin, 5
Eisenhower, President, 9, 72, 104
Ely's Harbour, 51
Espionage, 8, 52

Featherbed Alley Print Shop, 31
Ferries, 15, 17, 52, 61
Fishing, 56
Fort Alexandra, 34
Fort Hamilton, 20-1
Fort St. Catherine, 27, 34, 40
Fort Scaur, 51

Gardens
    Arboretum, 54
    Botanical Gardens, 53, 57
    Palm Grove Gardens, 54
    Palmetto Park, 54
    Somers Gardens, 31
Galleries & Studios, 94-5
Gates, Sir Thomas, 4, 34
Gates Fort, 34
Gombey dancers, 10, 22, 86
Goodrich, "Honourable," 30
Green, John, 58

Hamilton
    city of, 15-20
    made capital, 15
    theatre, 18
Hamilton Hotel, 7
HMS *Irresistible*, 49

Index

Historical Societies, 4, 18, 31
Horseshoe Bay, 51
hurricanes, 29, 52, 53

Ireland Island,

Jamestown, Virginia, 27, 29, 30, 34
Kings Square, 30

La Garza, 3
Laniel, Premier Joseph, 9, 72
Lighthouses
    Gibbs Hill, 51
    St. David's, 36

Macmillan, Harold, 104
Man Called Intrepid, A, 52
Mandrake the Magician, 52
Maritime Museum, 47, 49
Moore, Governor Richard, 34
Moore, Tom, 30, 32, 56

Natural Arches, 36
Nature Reserves
    Edmund Gibbons, 54
    Gilbert, 49
    Gladys Morell, 49
    North, 56
    Paget Marsh, 52
    Spittal Pond, 54, 57
Norwood, Richard, 17, 18

O'Neill, Eugene, 57
Ordnance Island, 30
Outerbridge, Mary, 21
Oviedo, Fernandez de, 3

Palmetto House, 54
Parks, 17, 18, 31, 36, 45, 49, 52, 53-4, 56, 57, 109
Patience, 5, 18, 27, 30
Peppercorn Ceremony, 29, 31
Performing Arts Festival, 86
Perot Post Office, 18
Plough, 5, 27
Princess Hotel, 7, 17, 66, 70, 80, 83, 85
Princess Louise, 7
Princess Margaret, 41
Printer's Alley, 32
Privateers, 1, 5, 7, 30, 51, 58

Railway Trail, 43
Rainey, Joseph, 7, 32
Ramirez, Capt. Diego, 3, 4, 22
Rendezvous Time, 22
Rise and Fall of the Third Reich, The, 8

Rolfe, John, 4
Royal Bermuda Yacht Club, 17, 56
Royal Gazette, 7, 8
Royal Hamilton Amateur Dinghy Club, 53
Ruth, Babe, 104

St. David's Island, 36
St. George's
    capital, 29, 31
    forts, 34-5
    founding, 27
    history, 27-9
    museums, 34
    town crier, 41
    walking tour, 29
St. George's Island, 29
Salt Kettle Bay, 53
Sayers, Capt. Hugh, 31
Sayle, Capt. William, 54, 58
Scaur Lodge, 51
Sea Venture, 4, 5, 18, 27, 34, 36
Sessions House, 19-20
Shark hash, 36
Sharples, Governor Sir Richard, 21, 31
Shopping, 17, 22, 23-5, 87-95
Slavery, 5, 6, 7, 9, 31, 32, 34
Somers, Admiral Sir George, 4-5, 18, 27, 30, 31
Somers, Matthew, 5
Somers Isle, 27
Somerset Bridge, 51
Somerset Village, 47, 49
Spanish Point, 4, 22
Spanish Rock, 3-4, 56
Springfield Museum, 49
Stephenson, John, 31
    Stockdale, Joseph, 32
Swan, Premier John, 39

Tribe roads, 43
Truman, President, 104
Tucker, Daniel, 5
Tucker, Henry, 32, 59
Tucker, "Nea," 32
Tucker, Sir George, 59
Tucker House, 32-4, 59
Tucker's Town, 36
Twain, Mark, 7, 57

Unfinished Chapel, 31
U.S. Consulate, 7
U.S. Naval Air Station, 1, 36

Verdmont, 54, 58
Visitors' Service Bureaus, 17, 24, 29

Washington, George, 6, 7, 18
Waterville House, 53
Wellington, Duke of, 20, 51
Whaling, 1, 49
William, Lord Cavendish, 54
Wilson, Woodrow, 7, 57
Windsor, Duke of, 8, 20, 104
Winterhaven Farm Cottage, 56
Witchcraft, 30

Zoo, 56

BERMUDA
By Susan Irwin-Wiener

TRAVEL PLANNER

INCLUDES —
- **TRAVELERS ADVISORY SECTION**
  - General Trip Planning Information
  - Specific Info On Bermuda

- **ABSTRACT OF AUTHOR'S CHOICES**
  - Where To Stay
  - Recommended Restaurants
  - Things To Do

- **COMPLETE SET OF MAPS**

World of Travel PUBLISHING

1989

About the Author

Susan Irwin-Wiener is a New York public relations executive who has visited the island many times on business and pleasure trips.

Publisher: Frank A. Marshall
Senior Editor: Emily R. Grusky
Cover Design & Illustration: Eric Walker
Map Design: Marit Jaeger-Kanney

All prices are based on those available at time of writing. It is inevitable that changes will have taken place by the time that this book is published. Please double check so as to be sure of latest figures. We will be delighted to hear from you, whether it be a recommendation or complaint at World of Travel Publishing, 106 South Front Street, Suite 2E, Philadelphia, PA 19106.

© 1989 by Fisher's World Inc.   ISBN 1-55707-040-7

All rights reserved. No part of this book may be reproduced or utilized in any form or by any means, electronic or mechanical, including photocopying, recording or by any information storage and retrieval system, without permission in writing from the publisher. All inquiries should be addressed to World of Travel, 106 S. Front Street,

Table of Contents

Traveler's Advisory/Planning Ahead
   Travel Agents & Tour Operators 1
   Travel Bargins Too Good to be True 1
   Travel Insurance 3
   Emergency Telephone Numbers 3
   General Airport Tips 3
   Complaints Against Airlines 5
   General Health Hints 5
   Senior Citizens 5
   Traveling with Children 5
   American Embassies & Consular Services 5
   Detailed Customs Information 7
   A Travel Glossary 13

Traveler's Advisory/Bermuda
   Costs 15
   Documentation 15
   Pets 15
   Climate 17
   Packing 17
   Handicapped Traveler 19
   Holidays & Special Events 19
   Sources of Information 31
   Getting There-By Air 31
   Getting There-By Sea 31
   Formalities on Arrival 33
      Customs 33
      Getting into Town 33

   Settling Down 33
      Money 33
      Purchases of Property 33
      Investments in Local Companies 35
      Banking 35
      Tipping 35
      Business Hours 35
      Electricity 35
      Drinking Water 35
      Communications 37
      Cables 37
      Telephones 37

Time	37
Press, Radio, Television	37
Medical Assistance	37
Getting Around	**40**
Motorbikes & Bicycles	41
Carriages	41
Hotels	**41**
Restaurants	**45**
Nightlife & Entertainment	**47**
Sights Around the Island	**47**
Churches & Synagogues	**51**
Shopping	**53**
Sports	**57**
Going Home	**59**

LIST OF MAPS

Beaches	48
Bermuda, general map	2
Bermuda Railway Trail - Key to Railway Trail	26-27
Bus System	22
Ferry Schedule	24
Golf Course Locations	54
Golf Course I	56
Golf Course II	58
Golf Course III	60
Hamilton	28
Hamilton area	16
Hamilton Bike & Hike Tour	30
Hamilton Shopping	32
Ireland Island	12
Parishes of Bermuda	4
Public Parks	50
Restaurants and Restaurant Key	42-43
Resorts & Hotels	40
St. David's Island	10
St. George's	6
St. George's Bike or Hike Tour	36
St. George's Island	34
St. George's Shopping	38
Somerset Island	8
Tennis	52
Tucker's Town Area	18
Water Sports	46
West End	20

TRAVEL ADVISORY- PLANNING AHEAD

TRAVEL AGENTS AND TOUR OPERATORS

You'll save a lot of time if you use an agent or tour operator, even if you plan an independent trip. If you don't know of a reliable agent, get in touch with the American Society of Travel Agents (ASTA), PO Box 23992, Washington, D.C. 20026-3992 or phone (703)739-2782, and ask for the name of an agent near you. ASTA has a Consumer Protection Plan in case a tour operator goes bust on you, among other things.

As for the tour operator, the company should be a member of the United States Tour Operators Association (USTOA). The latter's Financial Security Plan for Consumer Protection insures your payments against loss in case of some financial trouble by the firm. Information at USTOA, 211 E. 51st St., New York City, NY 10022; phone (212)944-5727.

You may wish to enquire whether your travel agent is a Certified Travel Counselor (CTC).

TRAVEL BARGAINS TOO GOOD TO BE TRUE

There are some warning signs an alert consumer will look for when checking out travel bargains advertised by companies whose names are unfamiliar at first. The American Society of Travel Agents says to watch out for:

1. Does the price seem unreasonably low compared to similar offers?
2. Do they ask for your credit card number over the phone or say they will send a messenger to collect your check when the information you seek is being delivered?
3. Will the firm give you its name, address, phone number, and name of their bank?
4. Do they press you to make an immediate decision?
5. Does the firm have a prepared brochure? Will they send you definite information, including total cost, in writing, before you have to commit any money?
6. Do they tell you which airline you'll be flying and which hotel you'll be staying at? ("Major" isn't a good enough description.)
7. Do they quote one price, then ask you to provide additional deposit or join a club?

Most scams involve oral misrepresentation, high pressure tactics, and offers in the $50 to $400 range, determined to be the "affordable" range almost anyone can pay.

BERMUDA

TRAVEL INSURANCE

Check your own policies to see if you are covered for medical expenses while traveling, for loss of luggage or other personal belongings, for liability in case of an accident while you're driving a car, rented or otherwise, and see what they provide.

Some coverage, such as trip cancellation, is bound not to be in any insurance policy you have for save normal routine.

Some outstanding firms and the coverage they provide:

Access America, 600 Third Ave., New York, NY 10163; phone toll free (800)851-2800. A subsidiary of Blue Cross and Blue Shield of the National Capital Area (Washington, D.C.) and Empire Blue Cross and Blue Shield (New York). Has two programs, one for North American travel (USA, Canada, Caribbean, Mexico), and another for travel overseas (Europe, Asia, Africa, South America, Australia).

Acess America operates a hotline: call collect (202)822-3948 in Washington, D.C. for overseas emergencies. Inside U.S., Canada, Puerto Rico and USVI call collect (800)654-1908. (Telex 706305 ACCESS WSH in Washington, D.C.)

Travel Guard International, 1100 Center Point Drive, Stevens Point, WI 54481-2849; phone (800)782-5151 (Wisconsin (800)634-0644).

Underwritten by CIGNA Insurance Company, with offices worldwide.

International SOS Assistance, Inc., POBox 11568, Philadelphia, PA 19116; phone toll free (800)523-8930 (PA or outside USA (215)244-1500).

Health Care Abroad, 1511 K St. N.W., Washington, D.C., 20037; phone (202)393-5500. Health insurance and medical assistance directory.

World Access, 2115 Connecticut Ave. N.W., Washington, D.C. 20036; phone (202)822-3978. Long-term health coverage overseas.

EMERGENCY TELEPHONE NUMBERS

U.S. Government: State Department Overseas Citizen's Emergency Center, Washington, D.C. 20520, phone (202)632-5225 or 634-3600. Staffed 24-hours for illness or accident abroad.

Bureau of Consular Affairs publications: *Tips for Travelers for (Blank) Country*, a general *Travel Tips for Senior Citizens*, or *Your Trip Abroad*. Write: Bureau of Consular Affairs, Public Affairs Office, State Department, Washington, D.C. 20520. For nonemergency calls, telephone during normal business hours.

GENERAL AIRPORT TIPS

☐ Check in early at airport
☐ Don't check bags at the curb (harder to trace if lost).

PARISHES OF BERMUDA

COMPLAINTS AGAINST AIRLINES

Department of Transportation of the U.S. Government likes phone calls rather than letters. Phone (202)366-2220. But you can write them for a copy of *Fly Rights: A Guide to Air Travel in the U.S.*, at Consumer Affairs Division, Room 10405, Intergovernmental and Consumer Affairs, Dept. of Transportation, 400 Seventh St. S.W., Washington, D.C. 20590.

The Aviation Consumer Project, P.O. Box 19029, Washington, D.C. 20036, has a book called *Facts and Advice for Airline Passengers* for $2, which you can carry with you as your travel.

GENERAL HEALTH HINTS

Have a dental check-up before your vacation or business trip.
Take extra pair of eyeglasses or dental bridge/plates with you.
Take copy of important prescriptions with generic names of medicine.
Carry a good supply of needed medications.
If you have serious allergy, this should be on an ID bracelet or necklace.
Make sure you have right vaccinations if going to non-industrial nations.
Review your medical insurance coverage or get some.
If you are really concerned, carry a summary of your medical history with you, and possibly a copy of your latest EKG.

SENIOR CITIZENS

There are hundreds of programs for senior citizens, and even the term has been defined many different ways. You can join the AARP (American Association of Retired Persons) from the age of 50, and even if you aren't retired. For only $5 a year, you get a whole raft of benefits, many of which will assist you in traveling. Call (202)872-4700 or write AARP at 1909 K St. N.W., Washington, D.C. 20049.

National Association for Mature People, Box 26792, Oklahoma City, OK 73118, tel. (405)523-5060.

National Council of Senior Citizens, 1151 K St. N.W., Washington, D.C., tel. (202)347-8800.

TRAVELING WITH CHILDREN

Most travel industry people refer to children under 2 as infants, between 3 and 12 as children, and over 12 as adults, at least so far as fares are concerned. Special facilities for children are available on airplanes (but notify them in advance). There are even special menus, often with several choices, for infants and kids.

AMERICAN EMBASSIES AND CONSULAR SERVICES

1. Register with the nearest U.S. embassy or consulate if you plan to stay in one country for "some time." This will help in

St. George's Island

replacing a lost or stolen passport or to help evacuate you in an emergency.
2. Don't expect an embassy or consulate to help you as a traveler unless you are in serious legal, medical, or financial difficulties. "Please do not," they say, "expect them to find work, get residence or driving permits, act as travel agents or interpreters, search for missing luggage, or settle disputes with hotel managers."

A free list of embassy addresses, etc. can be obtained by asking the Superintendent of Documents, U.S. Government Printing Office, Washington, D.C. 20402, for a copy of *Key Officers of Foreign Service Posts.*

Before leaving home: You may wish to contact the Office of Citizens Consular Services in Washington if you have questions about the following: Acquisition and loss of citizenship, passport and registration services abroad, claims, child custody disputes, estates, judicial services abroad, federal agencies benefit program abroad, report of birth abroad, third country representation.

Office of Citizens Consular Services itself: (202)632-3666.

If you want a Travel Advisory on a certain country, phone the State Department's Bureau of Consular Affairs, Program Planning and Coordination Staff, at (202)632-3816 or 3732.

Detailed Customs Information

In addition to basic information on the $400 exemption described later, some niceties about the system include:

Additional duty. After you get $400 worth of goods free, and pay a flat 10 percent on the next $1,000 worth, you go to the Tariff Schedules of the United States, available at any Customs office or better libraries. There are individual rates on specific items. The Customs officials say the average tourist purchase is dutiable at about 12 percent.

Duty rates for liquor above your exempt limit are generally 10 percent of their value. The Internal Revenue tax is $10.50 per gallon on distilled spirits, from 17 cents to $10.50 on wine, and 29 cents per gallon on beer. The Customs agents enforce the law of the state where you arrive concerning importation of liquor, and some states don't allow any, even if you pay additional tax or duty. (New York allows anything in, providing you pay.)

Personal belongings. If you're worried about foreign-made possessions you intend to take abroad, such as a camera, you may register them (if they have serial numbers) with a Customs office before leaving the U.S.

If you mail home your belongings and they're American made, mark the package "American Goods Returned."

Vehicles. If you take your car into Mexico or even overseas, you must present proof of U.S. origin when you return, such as vehicle (state) registration, or aircraft FAA Certificate, or boat's yacht license

8 Bermuda–Travel Planner

SOMERSET ISLAND

© FISHER'S WORLD INC., 1988.

or motorboat ID. You could also register with Customs before departure if you like, but that is not mandatory.

GSP (Generalized System of Preferences). Goods from certain developing countries are given preference and may enter the U.S. duty-free or at a lower rate of duty than is presently accorded other nations. There is a leaflet available from the Customs people (see addresses below) called GSP and the Traveler, outlining all of these countries and articles so exempted.

Paying the Duty. You can pay in U.S. currency, but not foreign, by personal check (U.S. bank), by money order, travelers checks or government check, provided the amount does not exceed the duty by more than $50.

Duty Free Shops. When you buy at one of these abroad, the phrase means the seller hasn't paid duty to his country on the item, so the price is lower to you. You still have to pay duty to your country on returning home.

Gifts mailed from abroad. You can't send a gift to yourself, so it must be addressed to another person. Liquor, tobacco, and perfume containing alcohol that are worth over $5 retail, can't be counted in the $50 gift exemption. You can't send more than one of these $50 gift packages per day to the same person. Mark the package "Unsolicited Gift" and indicate contents and retail value.

Antiques. To be considered an antique an object must over 100 years of age. To import oject(s) duty free requires documentation of age.

Prohibited Articles:
1. Narcotics and dangerous drugs.
2. Toxic substances.
3. Liquor-filled candy and absinthe.
4. Obscene articles and publications.
5. Seditious and treasonable material.
6. Lottery tickets.
7. Products made by forced labor.
8. Endangered species or their byproducts (tortoise shell, leopard skins, etc.).
9. Monkeys and other primates.
10. Most agricultural products (because of disease or pests).

Restricted:
1. Agricultural items. Contact APHIS, Department of Agriculture, 6505 Belcrest Rd., Hyattsville, MD 20792, tel. (301)436-8411, for leaflets and advice.
2. Money. More than $5,000 in U.S. or foreign currency or coins, travelers' checks, money orders, or negotiable instruments or investment securities in bearer form must be reported to Customs on departure and on arrival. It is not illegal to take amounts in excess of $5,000 out of the country into it, but it must be reported at all ports of entry. Automobiles. Must pass safety and air pollution control standards. Contact En-

ST. DAVID'S ISLAND

vironmental Protection Agency, Washington, D.C. 20406, phone (202)472-9413. or Department of Transportation, Washington, D.C. 20590, phone (202)426-1693. Or ask Customs for leaflet, *Importing a Car*.
4. Cultural treasures, art, or artifacts, especially pre-Columbian. Check with Customs and the country of export for special requirements.
5. Firearms and ammunition. Contact Bureau of Alcohol, Tobacco and Firearms, Department of the Treasury, Washington, D.C. 20226, phone (202)566-7135.
6. Medicines containing narcotics. If you use them, have a prescription or written statement from your personal physician that the medicine is being used under a doctor's direction and is necessary for your physical well being while traveling, and carry the drugs in their original containers.
7. Wildlife and fish are subject to certain restrictions. Contact the U.S. Fish and Wildlife Service, Department of the Interior, Washington, D.C. 20240, phone (202)343-9242, or state authorities. Check with Customs for designated ports of entry, and ask for their leaflet on *Pets, Wildlife and Customs*.
8. Merchandise originating in North Korea, Vietnam, Cambodia and Cuba. Contact Office of Foreign Assets Control, Department of the Treasury, Washington, D.C. 20220, phone (202)376-0443, and ask for FAC Regulations and Cuban Assets Control Regulations.
9. Research materials, like disease organisms, etc. Contact Foreign Quarantine Program, U.S. Public Health Service, Center for Disease Control, Atlanta, GA 30333, phone (404)329-3496.
10. Foreign-made articles. Some may be restricted by trademark owner, especially in the field of perfumes and watches. Ask for the Customs leaflet, *Trademark Information for Travelers*.

Military and other Government personnel may have special exemptions if they are traveling under permanent change of station orders, and should check with their personnel office for details.

Custom Addresses

For Customs leaflets, write U.S. Customs, P.O. Box 7407, Washington, D.C. 20044, or call (202)566-8195.

If you have any questions about your Customs clearance, write the Assistant Commissioner, Office of Inspection and Control, U.S. Customs Service, Washington, D.C. 20229.

Customs regulations and procedures are outlined in a free publication, *Know Before You Go*, available from P.O. Box 7118, Washington, D.C. 20044.

Travelers' Tips on Bringing Food, Plant, and Animal Products Into the United States is the name of a free booklet (in English, Spanish,

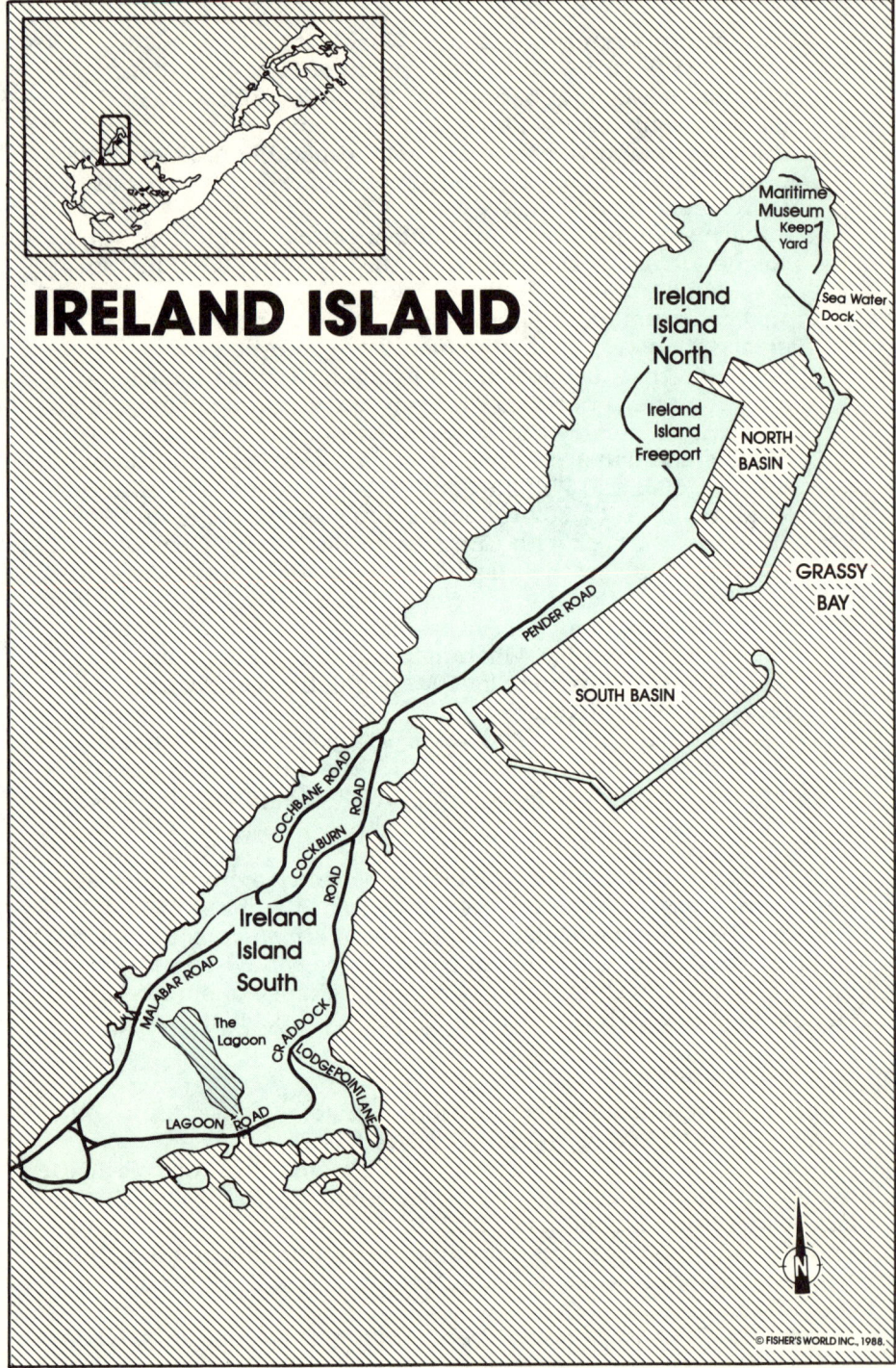

Italian or Japanese) available from the Animal and Plant Health Inspection Service, U.S. Department of Agriculture, 732 Federal Bldg., 6505 Belcrest Rd., Hyattsville, MD 20782.

A TRAVEL GLOSSARY

Most travelers know what terms like charter, bumping or transfer mean, but there are a few terms that remain somewhat obscure. Here they are, with English translation:

Add-On. A supplement, perhaps to a tour package.

Adjoining rooms does not necessarily mean connecting.

Aft. The rear of the ship, or in that direction.

AP. American Plan, hotel rate which includes three meals a day, almost always breakfast, lunch and dinner. Also called pension plan.

APEX. Advance Purchase Excursion Fare on an airline.

Bareboat charter. Chartering a boat without crew or provisions.

B and B. Bed and Breakfast. Sleeping room in private home or guesthouse, which includes full breakfast. Some hotels call this BP, the Bermuda Plan.

Bow. The front of the ship.

BP. See B and B.

Bulk fare. A bunch of seats acquired by a tour operator, for example, who must then seek to fill them.

Continental Breakfast usually means coffee, roll, butter, and sometimes, juice.

Courier. European term for tour escort.

CP. Continental Plan, hotel rate which includes continental breakfast.

Double can also mean twin-bedded room, as often it means only that room can accommodate two people. Specify double bed if you want one.

Demi-Pension. See MAP.

Direct flight does not always mean nonstop, nor does it always mean on the same aircraft. It only means the same flight number.

Efficiency. Term describing hotel, motel or condominium room with housekeeping facilities, such as stove, refrigerator, sink.

EP. European Plan, hotel rate which excludes meals.

FIT. Foreign Independent Travel. Custom-designed tour for an individual and/or his party.

Forward. At or near the front of the ship.

Interchange flight. A through flight which requires passengers to changes planes on route. Sometimes the old rail term, "change of gauge," is used.

ITX means Independent Tour Excursion Airfare. A fare which includes prepaid land package at destination, but passengers may travel separately.

Joint fare. A special through fare for travel on two or more airlines.

Lanai. A room with a patio or balcony which is close to or overlooks water or a garden.

Lido. A swimming pool and the area surrounding it, unless you're speaking of Venice, where an entire island is called the Lido.

MAP. Modified American Plan. Hotel rate includes two meals, usually breakfast and dinner. Also called demi-pension.

Open Jaw. Essentially a roundtrip, but passenger departs for return trip from a point other than the original destination, or returns to a different point from the point of origin.

Parlor Car most often is on a train, but could be a bus, with individual seats that swivel, and food and bar service.

Pitch. In the plane, the distance between rows of seats, front to back. On a boat, the rise and fall of the ship's bow at sea.

Pension. See AP.

Pool route. Most common in Europe, where airlines flying same routes share equally their total revenues, borrow planes and crews from each other and share check-in counters.

Rack rate. Usually in hotels, the offical posted rate for each room. Can often be discounted, if you but ask, "What is the rack rate?"

Share Fare/Rate. Cost to single person willing to share accommodations with person of same sex, if one can be found by tour operator.

*Shoul*der. The season between the high (or peak) and low (or off-peak) seasons.

Starboard. Right side of the ship as you face front (bow).

Stern. Very rear of ship.

Tender. When boat can't dock, a tender takes passengers from ship to shore.

Tour Escort/Leader. Often used interchangeably, but a leader is really the expert lecturer or specialist whose reputation attracts tour participants, and an escort is the person who accompanies the tour throughout, making everything run smoothly. The escort is sometimes called Tour Manager.

Value Season. Any season other than peak. Prices are lower.

(Most of the definitions above thanks to the Institute of Certified Travel Agents, Box 56, Wellesley, MA 02181, tel. (617)237-0280. The institute awards the CTC (Certified Travel Counselor) diploma to agents with five years' minimum experience who have completed a two-year travel management course.)

TRAVELER'S ADVISORY- BERMUDA

COSTS

The British colony of Bermuda is a self-governing member of the Commonwealth, and a prime tourist destination for North Americans. It is now moderately expensive for U.S. and Canadian visitors, but there is virtually no difference between prices in or near Hamilton, the capital, or at resorts out on the island. Fortunately, despite cost increases parallel with our own over the past decade, Bermuda is still a buy for the money, and the experienced traveler may be assured that he will get his money's worth, whether he seeks relaxation, sports and sightseeing activity, or just a resort area where there are few if any slums and where gentility, courtesy, and elegance are everywhere.

In general, prices in Bermuda are comparable to those in such prime mainland U.S. vacation areas as Florida and California. Most places, except many hotels, take credit cards.

DOCUMENTATION

Bermuda requires a return (round trip) or onward-bound air or sea passage ticket of all visitors. Passports and visas are not required by Bermuda immigration. All visitors are required, however, to present valid identification such as a passport (valid or expired), birth certificate (bearing a raised seal-hospital birth registration not acceptable), voter's registration card if it bears a signature, U.S. alien registration card (Green Card), U.S. naturalization certificate or Canadian certificate of citizenship. (A driver's license or baptismal certificate does not pass muster as proof of citizenship.) Visitors may remain for three weeks after which time they must apply to the Chief Immigration Officer for permission to stay longer.

No vaccinations are required, except for smallpox for those who have visited a country where any part thereof is infected.

PETS

Most airlines will allow pets, either in cargo or on the plane if your pet will fit into a carrier that can go under the seat. There is usually a fee and you must have proof from your veterinarian of current vaccinations. If your pet travels cargo, be certain the area is temperature controlled—some cargo holds are unheated.

Cruise ships do not allow pets. Some hotels and guest houses will permit pets if you request permission in advance of your visit. Before your trip you must obtain a permit from the Bermuda Department of Agriculture, Box HM 834, Hamilton 5, Bermuda.

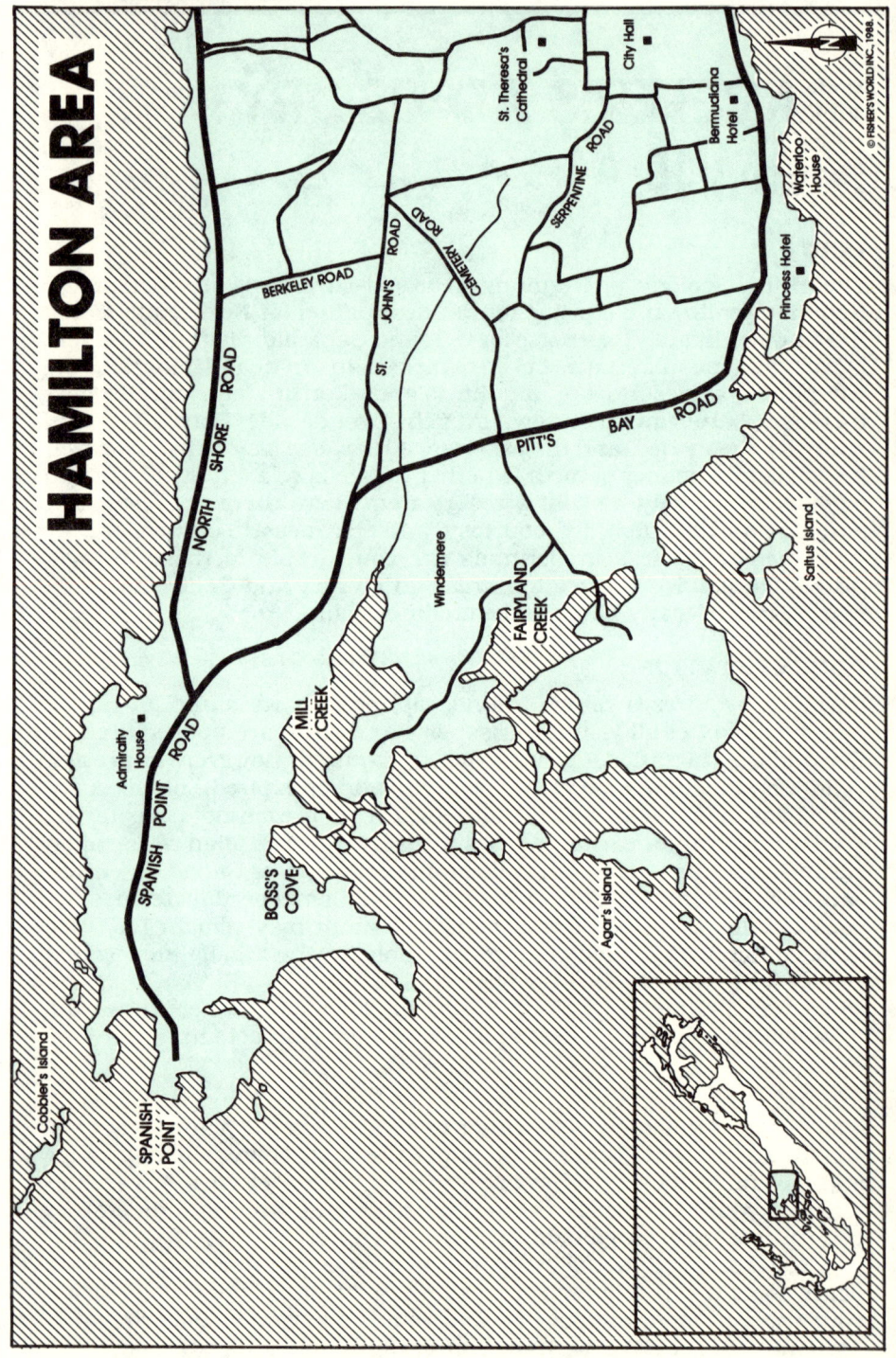

CLIMATE

When meteorologists talk about a "Bermuda high," denoting clear, sunny weather, they are in earnest. Bermuda's climate, while not tropical, has a well-deserved reputation for moderation. The island is well sheltered from frigid mainland blasts by the Gulf Stream passing due north and west, protecting the area from snow and frost. Hay fever sufferers have long found special relief in Bermuda.

For over half a century the average temperatures during April, for example, have hovered around the 66 F. mark with a daily range of 11.2 F. The number of hours of bright sunshine daily averaged 7.2; rainfall, 4.21 inches for the month.

The island really has only two seasons, spring and summer. Spring temperatures, from mid-November through mid-April, range from the 60s to the low 70s. Summer temperatures prevail the rest of the year and range through the 70s and 90s. Evening temperatures are generally 10 degrees lower than daytime.

The following table shows Bermuda's monthly average daytime temperatures.

	F°	C°		F°	C°
Jan.	68	20	July	85	29
Feb.	67	19	Aug.	86	30
Mar.	68	20	Sept.	84	29
Apr.	71	22	Oct.	79	26
May	75	24	Nov.	74	23
June	80	27	Dec.	70	21

PACKING

Bermuda used to be known as a stuffy and even snobbish travel destination for Americans. All this has changed within the past decade. One need not pack a monocle or sport a title to feel at home in the poshest of Bermudian gathering places. But there is still a basic conservatism abroad in the island, so the mainland visitor should be aware of what to pack and what to leave out.

Bathing attire, bikinis, short shorts and abbreviated tops for women are not for the public or dining rooms of hotels. Nor are men permitted to appear in the same places shirtless. Beachwear is strictly for the beach, while smart tennis, golfing, and biking togs are acceptable for sports occasions. For street wear, bare feet are out; sandals, loafers, tennis shoes are acceptable.

Many hotels, restaurants, and even discos request (and a number require) jacket and tie in the evening, and correspondingly suitable garb for women.

Visitors who expect to use motorbikes extensively for getting around in Bermuda should bring along practical attire for that activity. So should those who expect to go sailing, horseback riding, etc.

18 Bermuda–Travel Planner

TUCKER'S TOWN AREA

- CASTLE POINT
- HOWARD BAY
- Caliban
- Blue Horizons
- CASTLE HARBOUR
- TUCKER'S TOWN BAY
- TUCKER'S TOWN
- Mid-Ocean Club
- Natural Arches
- Mid-Ocean Golf Course
- SOUTH ROAD
- PAYNTER'S ROAD
- Castle Harbour Golf Course
- Marriott's Castle Harbour Hotel

© FISHER'S WORLD INC., 1988.

During the winter, autumn-weight clothes are appropriate for both men and women, including a light topcoat. It's not a bad idea to throw in a few sweaters, too (especially if motorbiking is on your agenda). Some days are very brisk.

Any articles of clothing forgotten at home may be replaced in Bermuda's fine shops. Electronic and optical goods such as tape-recorders, tape, cameras, film and lenses should be brought with you, since prices are higher there for these items than in most mainland cities. Also do make sure you pack whatever prescription drugs you'll need.

HANDICAPPED TRAVELERS

The Society for Advancement of Travel for the Handicapped has a branch in Bermuda. For detailed information write: Mr. Richard M. Kitson, President, Society for the Advancement of Travel for the Handicapped, P.O. Box 449, Hamilton 5, Bermuda. Phone (809)292-3595. Telex: 3240 KITCO, BA.

For a complimentary copoy of the guide *Access Guide to Bermuda for the Handicapped Traveler* write SATH International, 26 Court Street, Brooklyn, NY 11242. Phone (718)858-5483.

It is generally assumed that handicapped visitors will be accompanied by one or more persons able to assist them. Handicapped persons and senior citizens who are not fully active are advised to notify the hotel of their choice well in advance of their arrival regarding their condition and the need for any special assistance.

Facilities for handicapped persons confined to wheelchairs are not extensive in Bermuda. The Department of Tourism lists the following hotels as those best suited for visitors confined to wheelchairs:

Bermudiana (Hamilton); Marriott's Castle Harbour (Tucker's Town); Elbow Beach Hotel (Paget); The Princess (outskirts of Hamilton); Sonesta Beach (Southampton); Southampton Princess (Southampton); Stonington Beach Hotel.

All of these establishments have elevators large enough for wheelchairs to enter, door widths range from 28 inches to 39 inches. Bathrooms are generally large enough to accommodate a wheelchair. Main entrances are flat and in most cases the recreational areas including pools, beaches, and gardens are also accessible. All have wheelchairs available and sufficient staff to assist guests anywhere within the hotel precincts.

HOLIDAYS & SPECIAL EVENTS

As dates vary slightly from year to year, check exact days with the tourist bureau before making your plans.

Public Holidays

New Year's Day (January 1); Good Friday and Easter (variable); Bermuda Day (May 24); the Queen's Birthday (mid-June); Remem-

WEST END

berance Day (November 11); Christmas Day (December 25); Boxing Day (December 26); plus Cup Match and Somers Day (the Thursday and Friday before the first Monday in August) and Labour Day (first Monday in September).

January

New Year's Day. January 1. Public holiday.

Bermuda Rendezvous Time. Program of activities continues throughout the month.

Annual Bermuda Square and Round Dance Festival. Open to visitors and residents alike. Featuring internationally renowned staff callers. For further information write: Bermuda Square Dance Convention, P.O. Box 145, Avon, MA 02322, USA.

Bermuda Festival. A six week International Arts Festival under the auspices of H.E., the Governor. It includes classical, popular, and jazz concerts, modern ballet and theatrical presentations. For a new calendar of events and reservations, write: Bermuda Festivals, Ltd., P.O. Box HM AX, Bermuda. Phone (809)295-1291.

Bermuda International Marathon and Ten Kilometer Race. Held under I.A.A.F. Rules, sponsored by the Bermuda Track and Field Association. For additional information and entry forms, write: Bermuda Track & Field Association, P.O. Box DV 397, Devonshire DV BX, Bermuda.

Annual Regional Bridge Tournament. January-February, at the Southampton Princess Hotel, sponsored by the Bermuda Unit of American Contract Bridge League.

February

Bermuda Festival. Continues.

Bermuda Rendezvous Time. Weekly program of activities continues throughout the month.

Annual International Chess Tournament. Elbow Beach Hotel. Bermuda Chess Association, P. O. Box HM 1705, Hamilton 5, Bermuda.

Bermuda Valentine's Mixed Foursomes. Golf tournament (February 12-18) at the St. George's Golf Club and Port Royal Golf course.

Annual Sandys Rotary Club International Golf Classic. Late February. Hosted by Southampton Princess Hotel. Golfing at Port Royal, Belmont, Riddell's Bay and Southampton Princess courses. Contact: The Secretary, Sandys Rotary Club, P.O. Box SN 416, Southampton 8, Bermuda.

March

Bermuda Rendezvous Time. Throughout March.

Bermuda College Weeks. For thirty-five years this uniquely Bermudian festival has drawn thousands of college students from the U.S. and Canada. College Weeks derived from earlier Rugby Weeks. Today this youthful festive holiday includes beach and limbo parties, boat

22 Bermuda–Travel Planner

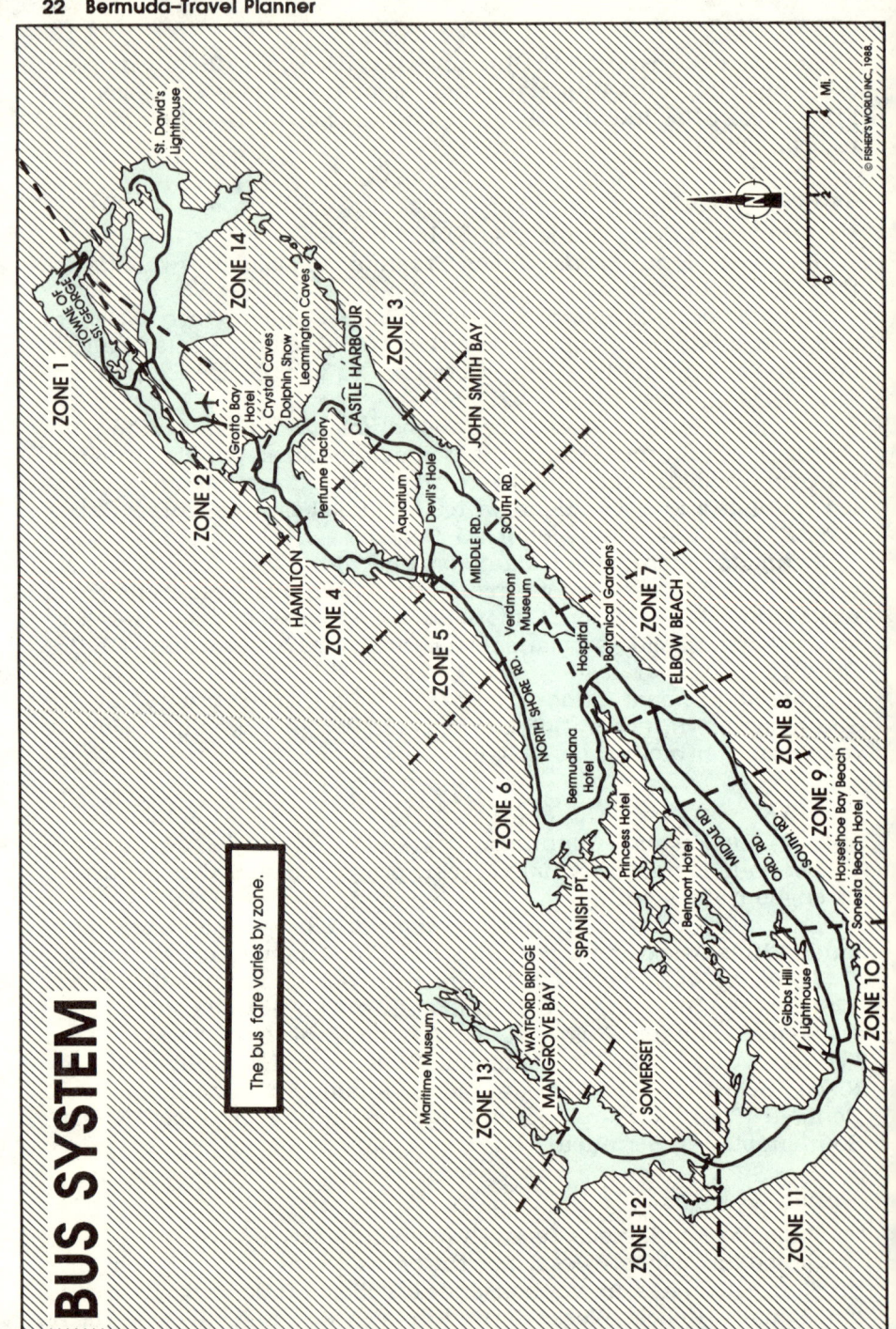

cruises and entertainment plus get acquainted dances and steel band concerts. The host in Bermuda is the Department of Tourism.

Bermuda Dog Shows International. Early March. All breeds, unbenched. Obedience trials. Held in the Botanical Gardens, Paget.

Bermuda Amateur Golf Championship for Men. Limited to 64 players with handicaps of 18 or less. Singles match play at scratch in flights of 16. Finals of all flights followed by presentation of prizes. Mid Ocean Club.

Open Houses and Garden Tours. Late March to early May. Sponsored by Garden Club.

April

Bermuda College Weeks. Continue into April.

Bermuda Ladies' Amateur Golf Championship. Mid-April. Port Royal Golf Course. Handicap limit 24. Singles match play at scratch in flights of 16. Limited to 96 competitors.

Palm Sunday Walk. Scenic walk organized annually by the Bermuda National Trust.

Good Friday. Public Holiday. Traditionally the day for flying kites in Bermuda. Young and old, resident and visitor, everyone does it.

Easter Sunday. Public Holiday. Check the daily newspaper for times and locations of outdoor Easter sunrise services for all denominations. Visitors welcome.

Annual Peppercorn Ceremony. Celebrates the Masonic Lodge of Bermuda's payment of one peppercorn in rent to the government. Bermuda Regiment parades in King's Square, St. George's and there are general festivities.

Agricultural Exhibition. Annual event, held in the Botanical Gardens, Paget East. A variety of ring events are offered, including horse shows, as well as culinary exhibits, displays of Bermuda crafts, school displays, and also displays of Bermuda-grown flowers, vegetables, fruit, and livestock.

Open Houses and Garden Tours. Continues.

May

International Race Week. Yachtsmen from around the world compete with Bermudians in six yacht classes. Sponsored by the Royal Bermuda Yacht Club.

Bermuda Game Fishing Tournament Fleet Parade. Charter fishing boats leave Hamilton Harbour and parade out through Great Sound to the sea to open the fishing season. Boats leave Albuoy's Point in Hamilton at 7 A.M.

Bermuda Mixed Golf Foursome Championship. A 36-hole stroke competition, partners better ball event. Bermuda Mixed Foursome Trophy to low gross winners and Sir George Somers Trophy to low new winners. Course to be announced.

Bermuda Heritage Month. Cultural and sporting activities to commemorate Bermuda's heritage, culminating on Bermuda Day, May 24

FERRY SCHEDULE

Hamilton → Paget → Warwick

Monday through Friday
(Saturday's first ferry leaves Hamilton at 8:45 am)

Hinson's Island Stops only on request

Leave Hamilton	Hinson's	Belmont	Darrell's Wharf	Salt Kettle	Hodson's	Lower Ferry	Arrive Hamilton
7:15am	7:25am	—	7:30am	—	—	—	7:40am
7:45	—	7:55	8:00	8:05	—	—	8:10
8:15	—	8:25	8:30	—	—	—	8:40
8:45	—	8:55	9:00	—	—	—	9:10
9:20	—	9:30	9:40	—	—	—	9:50
10:00	—	10:20	10:10	—	—	—	10:30
10:40	—	10:50	11:00	—	—	—	11:10
11:20	—	11:40	11:30	—	—	—	11:50
12 Noon	—	12:10pm	12:20pm	—	—	—	12:30pm
12:40pm	—	1:00	12:50	—	—	—	1:10
1:20	—	1:30	1:40	—	—	—	1:50
2:00	—	2:20	2:10	—	—	—	2:30
2:40	—	3:00	2:50	—	—	—	3:10
3:20	—	3:30	3:35	—	—	—	3:45
4:10	—	4:30	4:20	—	—	—	4:40
5:10	—	5:20	5:25	—	—	—	5:35
5:40	—	6:00	5:50	5:45	—	—	6:10
6:15	—	6:25	6:35	6:45	—	—	6:50
7:00	—	7:10	7:15	7:20	7:25	7:30	7:35
7:50	—	8:10	8:00	7:55	—	—	8:20
8:36	—	8:45	8:55	9:00	—	—	9:05
9:20	—	9:40	9:30	9:25	—	—	9:50
10:05	—	10:15	10:20	10:25	10:30	10:35	10:40
10:45	—	11:05	10:55	10:50	—	—	11:15
11:20	—	11:30	11:35	11:40	—	—	11:45

Sundays and Public Holidays

Leave Hamilton	Hinson's	Belmont	Darrell's Wharf	Salt Kettle	Hodson's	Lower Ferry	Arrive Hamilton
10:10am	—	10:20am	10:25am	10:30am	10:35am	10:40am	10:45am
11:00	—	11:20	11:10	11:05	—	—	11:30
11:45	—	11:55	12:05pm	12:10pm	—	—	12:15pm
12:30pm	—	12:50pm	12:40	12:35	—	—	1:00
1:15	—	1:25	1:35	1:40	1:45	1:50	1:55
2:30	—	2:50	2:40	2:35	—	—	3:00
3:15	—	3:25	3:35	3:40	—	—	3:45
4:00	—	4:20	4:10	4:05	—	—	4:30
4:45	—	4:55	5:00	5:05	5:10	5:20	5:25
5:40	—	6:00	5:50	5:45	—	—	6:10
6:25	—	6:35	6:45	6:50	—	—	6:55
7:10	—	7:35	7:30	7:25	7:20	7:15	7:45

Hamilton → Paget

Monday through Friday
(Saturday's first ferry leaves Hamilton at 8:45 am)

*Does not return to Hamilton Terminal

NOTE: See Hamilton - Paget - Warwick Ferry Schedule for ferry schedule to Paget stops after 5:45 pm Monday through Friday, Saturdays, and Sundays

Leave Hamilton	Lower Ferry	Hodson's	Salt Kettle	Arrive Hamilton
7:45am	—	—	8:05am	8:10am
8:15	8:20	8:25	8:30	8:35
8:45	8:50	8:55	9:00	9:05
9:15	9:20	9:25	9:30	9:35
9:45	9:50	9:55	10:00	10:05
10:15	10:20	10:25	10:30	10:35
10:45	10:50	10:55	11:00	11:05
11:15	11:20	11:25	11:30	11:35
11:45	11:50	11:55	12:00pm	12:05pm
12:15pm	12:20pm	12:25pm	12:30pm	12:35
12:45	12:50	12:55	1:00	1:05
1:15	1:20	1:25	1:30	1:35
1:45	1:50	1:55	2:00	2:05
2:45	2:50	2:55	3:00	3:05
3:15	3:20	3:25	3:30	3:35
3:45	3:50	3:55	4:00	4:05
4:15	4:20	4:25	4:30	4:35
4:45	4:50	4:55	5:00	5:05
5:15	5:20	5:25	5:30	5:35
5:45*	5:50	5:55	—	—

Hamilton → Somerset → Dockyard

Monday through Friday

Leave Hamilton	Dockyard	Watford Bridge	Cavello Bay	Somerset Bridge	Arrive Hamilton
6:15am	—	7:00am	—	6:45am	7:30am
6:25	6:55	7:15	7:25	7:40	8:10
7:35	8:05	8:15	8:25	—	8:50
9:00	9:30	9:50	10:00	10:15	10:45
10:00	11:15	10:55	10:45	10:30	11:45
11:00	11:30	11:50	12:00pm	12:15pm	12:45pm
12Noon	1:15pm	12:55pm	12:45pm	12:30pm	1:45pm
1:00	1:30	1:50	2:00	2:15	2:45
2:00	3:15	2:55	2:45	2:30	3:45
3:00	3:30	3:50	4:00	4:15	4:45
4:00	5:15	4:55	4:45	4:30	5:45
5:20	6:35	6:15	6:05	5:50	7:05
6:00	7:05	6:55	6:45	6:30	7:35

Saturday

Leave Hamilton	Dockyard	Watford Bridge	Cavello Bay	Somerset Bridge	Arrive Hamilton
7:00am	7:30am	7:50am	8:00am	8:15am	8:45am
9:00	9:30	9:50	10:00	10:15	10:45
10:00	11:15	10:55	10:45	10:30	11:45
11:00	11:30	11:50	12:00pm	12:15pm	12:45pm
12Noon	1:15pm	12:55pm	12:45pm	12:30pm	1:45pm
1:00	1:30	1:50	2:00	2:15	2:45
2:00	3:15	2:55	2:45	2:30	3:45
3:00	3:30	3:50	4:00	4:15	4:45
4:00	5:15	4:55	4:45	4:30	5:45
5:20	6:35	6:15	6:05	5:50	7:05
6:00	7:05	6:55	6:45	6:30	7:35

Sunday and Public Holidays

Leave Hamilton	Dockyard	Watford Bridge	Cavello Bay	Somerset Bridge	Arrive Hamilton
9:00am	9:30am	9:50am	10:00am	10:15am	10:45am
11:00am	12:15pm	11:55	11:45am	11:30am	12:45pm
1:00pm	1:30pm	1:50pm	2:00pm	2:15pm	2:45pm
3:00	4:15	3:55	3:45	3:30	4:45
5:00	5:30	5:50	6:00	6:15	6:45

(a public holiday), when activities include a festival parade, the first Bermuda dinghy race of the season, and the annual half marathon for Bermudian competitors.

June

3rd Annual International Triathlon Championship. Limited to 400 triathletes from around the world. $100,000 purse.

Jackson School of Performing Arts Music Recital. Featuring woodwinds, drums, and piano. Held at Hamilton City Hall.

H.M. The Queen's Birthday. Bermuda celebrates (usually the second Monday) via a public holiday and a military parade on Front Street, Hamilton.

July

Somers Day. Special event in St. George's honoring founding father Sir George Somers, Sea Venture and oldest English settlement on the island.

Cup Match Cricket Festival. Late July or early August. Public holidays. A spectacular two-day cricket match between east and west ends of the island. A day of picnicking, gambling (the only day it's legal), and parading of finery.

September

Labour Day. First Monday in September. Public Holiday. Festivities.

October

International Bermuda Open Golf Championship. Open to male professionals and amateurs with handicaps of 12 and better. Port Royal Golf Course.

Bermuda Horse & Pony Fall Show. Exhibitions in flat classes, driving, jumping and Western, held at the Botanical Gardens.

November

Remembrance Day. November 11. Public holiday. The day is marked with a parade of Bermudian, British and U.S. military units, Bermuda police, and veterans organizations in honor of the men who died in service for their countries. Front Street in Hamilton.

Bermuda Four Ball Golf Championships for Ladies. Best ball stroke play in teams of two and over 36 holes. Handicap limit 35. Prizes for gross and net winners. Port Royal Golf Course.

Bermuda Four Ball Golf Championship for Men. Best Ball Stroke Play in teams of two and over 72 holes. Handicap limit 23. Prizes awarded to gross and net winners. Port Royal Golf Course.

KEY TO BERMUDA RAILWAY TRAIL

1. Somerset Bus Terminal
   The original railway building
2. Springfield & Gilbert Nature Reserve
3. Harman's Bay
   Rich Woodland of Fiddlewood
4. Heydon Trust Estate
5. The Bermuda Cedar
   View over the Great Sound
6. Fort Scaur
7. Somerset Bridge
   Smallest drawbridge in the world
8. Evans Pond
   Stands of native flora
9. Old Bermuda houses
10. Franks Bay
11. Relaxing view of Little Sound
12. Geological history
13. Dunes
    One of the largest
14. Black Bay
15. Gibbs Hill Lighthouse
16. Jews Bay
17. Princess Park
18. South Shore Beach Parklands
19. Tall Allspice Woodland
20. Khyber Pass, huge quarry
21. Warwick Pond, a bird sanctuary
22. Belmont Golf Course
23. Old Bermuda houses
24. Elbow Beach
25. Surinam Cherry
26. Superb view of the City of Hamilton
27. Paget Marsh Nature Reserve
28. Old Railway Tunnel, 450 feet long
29. Palmetto Park
30. Palmetto Hotel, 18th Century
31. Panoramic Views
    of the North Channel
32. Penhurst Park
33. Gibbet Island,
    where witches were burned
34. Lovely Flatts Inlet
35. Coney Island Park, Cricket Pitch
36. Bailey's Bay
37. Shelly Bay Park and Nature Reserve
38. Flatts Inlet, Harrington Sound
39. Aquarium
40. Tiger Bay Gardens
41. Mullet Bay Park
42. Rock Hill Park
43. Sugarloaf Hill
44. Lover's Lake Nature Reserve
45. At Ferry Point Park

Travel Advisory–Bermuda 27

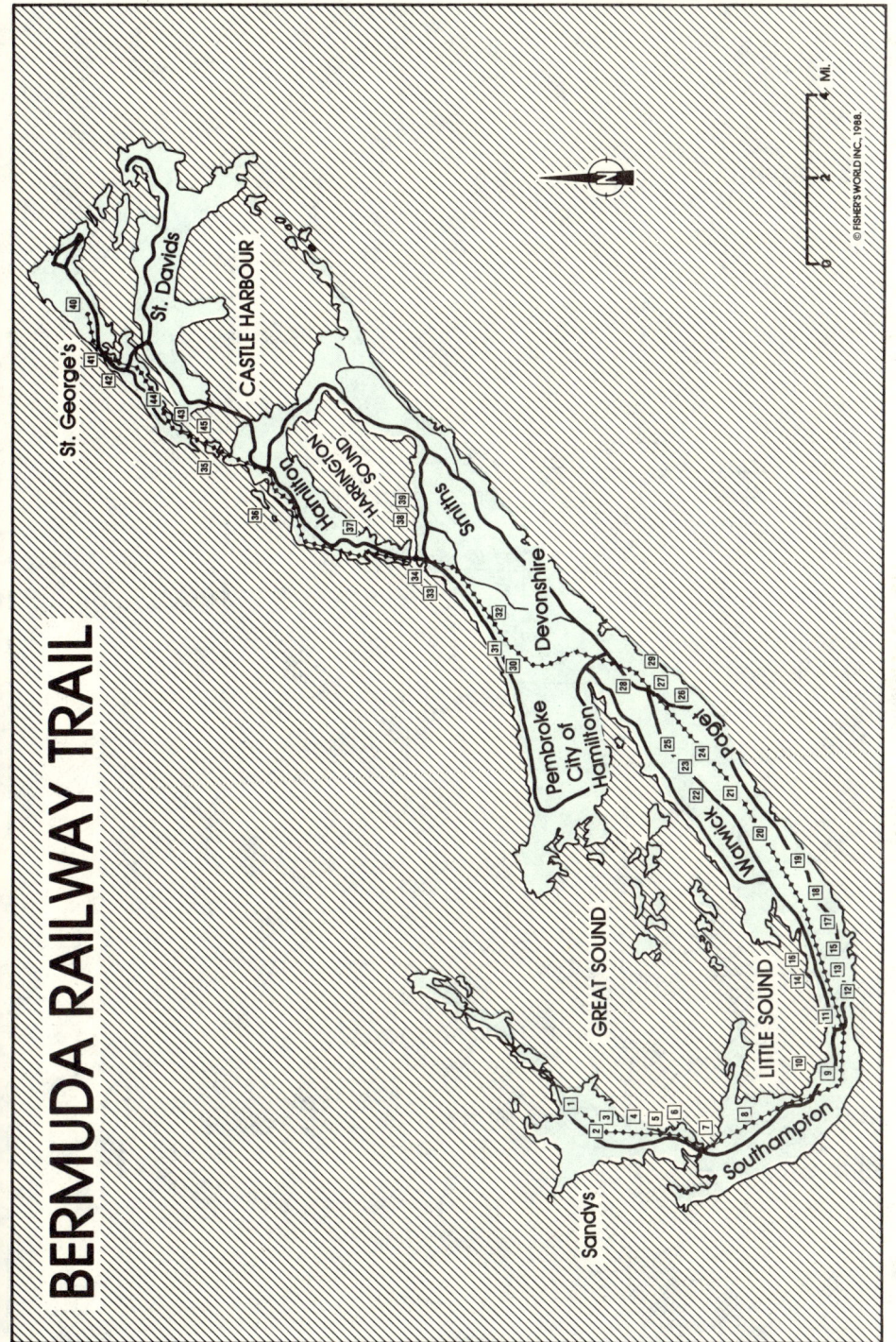

28 Bermuda–Travel Planner

HAMILTON

December

Golf. Seven 18-hole courses are available to visitors. Early in December is the *Annual Bermuda Goodwill Golf Tournament* for men. In late December the *Winter Junior Championships*, open to juniors twenty years of age and under.

Bermuda Goodwill Tournament for Men. Mid Ocean Club, Castle Harbour Golf Club, Belmont Golf and Country Club, and Port Royal Golf Course. Professional, invitation only. Spectators welcome.

Annual Belmont Invitation Tournament. Belmont Golf and Country Club. 72-hole stroke play. Open to professionals and amateurs. International team championship play for Bermuda Trophy.

Christmas Day and Boxing Day. December 25 and 26. Public holidays. Christmas Day is traditionally a family day in Bermuda. For times and locations of Christmas Eve midnight candlelight church services, and all Christmas Day services, consult the daily newspaper. Boxing Day is traditionally a day to go visiting, or to receive guests, in addition to a variety of sporting activities, which provide excellent spectator participation. Also a day to see Bermuda's Gombey dancers who may appear anywhere anytime—just follow the sound of their drums.

Bermuda College Weeks

Every spring since 1950, Bermuda has extended a special invitation to collegians. The tradition began some 40 years ago with the competition in rugby between U.S. Ivy League teams and counterparts from Britain during spring vacations.

For four or five weeks over Easter holiday time, the host, the Bermuda Department of Tourism, organizes and oversees activities calculated to appeal to college students everywhere. A College Week Courtesy Card serves as a passport to a week of beach parties, lunches, boat cruises, dances, and entertainment. The Courtesy Card is issued on presentation of a valid college student identification card.

A typical six-day week's activities include the following:

Sunday: Get acquainted dances at hotels and discos. Some cooperating places offer discounts to College Week guests. Jackets for gentlemen are generally de rigueur.

Monday: College day at the beach, Elbow Beach Surf Club. Entertainment and a complimentary lunch.

Tuesday: Limbo Party at Horseshoe Bay with complimentary buffet luncheon, swimming, and entertainment by the Bermuda Strollers. Student limbo contest.

Wednesday: College Week cruises. Morning or afternoon through the islands of Hamilton Harbour and Great Sound. Entertainment by the Bermuda Strollers on board. Complimentary lunch.

Thursday: Free day or second day of cruises, morning or afternoon.

Friday: Steel band concert, Cross Bay Beach at Sonesta Beach Hotel. Free lunch. Sand and surf.

HAMILTON BIKE OR HIKE TOUR

1. Ferry Terminal
2. Albuoys Point
3. Coin Collection
4. Barr's Bay Park
5. Par-La-Ville Park
6. Perot's Post Office
7. Bermuda Library
8. City Hall
9. Victoria Park
10. Holy Trinity Cathedral
11. Sessions House
12. Cabinet Building
13. The Cenotaph
14. Front Street
15. Botanical Gardens
16. Camden
17. Fort Hamilton
18. St. Theresa's Cathedral
19. Black Wath Pass & Well

© FISHER'S WORLD INC. 1988.

SOURCES OF INFORMATION

Tourist affairs including information for the traveling public are administered by a Ministry of Tourism, headed by a minister of Tourism.

Tourist Information Headquarters:

Hamilton: Global House, 43 Church Street, Hamilton HM BX. United States: Suite 201, 310 Madison Avenue, NYC 10017; Suite 1070, Randolph-Wacker Bldg., 150 North Wacker Drive, Chicago, Ill 60606; Suite 2008, 235 Peachtree Street, NE., Atlanta, GA 30303.

Canada: Suite 1004, 1200 Bay Street, Toronto, Ontario, Canada M5R 2A5.

Major tour operators serving Bermuda and firms handling hotel representation for major Bermuda hotels have reliable, well-informed executives who can supply first-hand information to potential visitors. Also, airlines serving the territory from the U.S. and Canadian mainland can supply up-to-date information.

In Bermuda, the larger hotels have full-time public relations personnel or social directors who know the island well and can make reliable recommendations to visitors seeking information.

GETTING THERE

By Air

Only about three hours from New York, Bermuda is served daily from JFK by Pan Am, American and Eastern. There are also direct flights from Boston via American, Delta and Pan Am; from Toronto courtesy of Air Canada; from Washington, D.C. and Baltimore via Eastern; from Washington D.C. is United (nonstop) and Pan Am (with a touchdown at JFK, but no plane change); from Atlanta by Delta and Eastern; and from St. Petersburg/Tampa via British Airways. In addition, there are convenient one-day connecting flights from most other major American cities including Chicago, Los Angeles, San Francisco and Dallas. In total, close to 400,000 visitors from the U.S. arrive by air every year. Another 32,000 jet in from Canada, some 15,000 fly in from the U.K., another 15,000 or so arrive at Bermuda's airport from other lands.

By Sea

While most visitors opt for airline transport, over 150,000 arrive each year via the ocean liners that nudge into port some 190 times during the April through mid-November cruise season.

HAMILTON-SHOPPING

1. Pegasus
2. Wm. Bluck & Co. Ltd.
3. Vera P. Card
4. Bananas Ltd.
5. Royal Lyme (BDA) Ltd.
6. Peniston & Brown & Co.
7. Bermuda Bookstore Ltd.
8. Irish Linen
9. H.A. & E. Smith's
10. Trimingham's
11. Hamburg Calypso Ltd
12. Archie Brown & Son
13. Lote Tree Jewels
14. Harbourmaster
15. A.S. Cooper
16. Benetton Ltd.
17. Astwood Dickinson

FORMALITIES ON ARRIVAL

Customs

Upon entering the country, visitors who qualify for entry may bring in with them duty free their own clothing and effects. This includes personal items such as sports equipment, cameras, hair dryers or heated rollers, small portable television sets or radios, traveling irons and so on. They are also permitted duty-free entry of one quart of wine and one quart of spirits, 200 cigarettes, 1 pound of tobacco and 50 cigars.

In Bermuda, anyone caught bringing in drugs or firearms (including a speargun) will be subject to a heavy fine or jail, or both. Drugs and medications prescribed by a doctor must be declared to Bermuda customs on entry.

The importation of firearms, parts, or ammunition is forbidden except with permission granted by means of a license issued by the commissioner of Bermuda police.

Getting into Town

There is bus transport from the airport, which is located at the extreme northeast tip of the island, to the major resort hotels of Bermuda as well as to the capital, Hamilton. There is a sliding scale of tariffs for these buses as well as for taxis. Fares are posted at the airport

SETTLING DOWN

Money

The Bermudian dollar, divided into 100 cents, exchanges at par with the U.S. dollar. Canadian currency is also accepted, but discounted at the exchange rate quoted for the U.S. dollar. British pounds and other currencies must be exchanged for local money at banks and official exchanges. All U.S. dollar traveler's checks are accepted and cashed everywhere, while major credit cards are accepted in most shops and restaurants and many hotels.

Various issues of commemorative coins have been made in denominations of $100, $50, $25, and $1. The Bermuda sterling notes which were in circulation before February 7, 1970, are no longer legal tender.

Commemorative coins may be purchased from reputable local coin dealers in Hamilton.

Purchases of Property for Residential Purposes

So far as exchange control is concerned, aliens who have the necessary government consents to purchase property in Bermuda are normally required to provide the whole of the purchase price in foreign currency. On the sale of such property, permission is given for the repatriation of the full sales proceeds after meeting local liabilities.

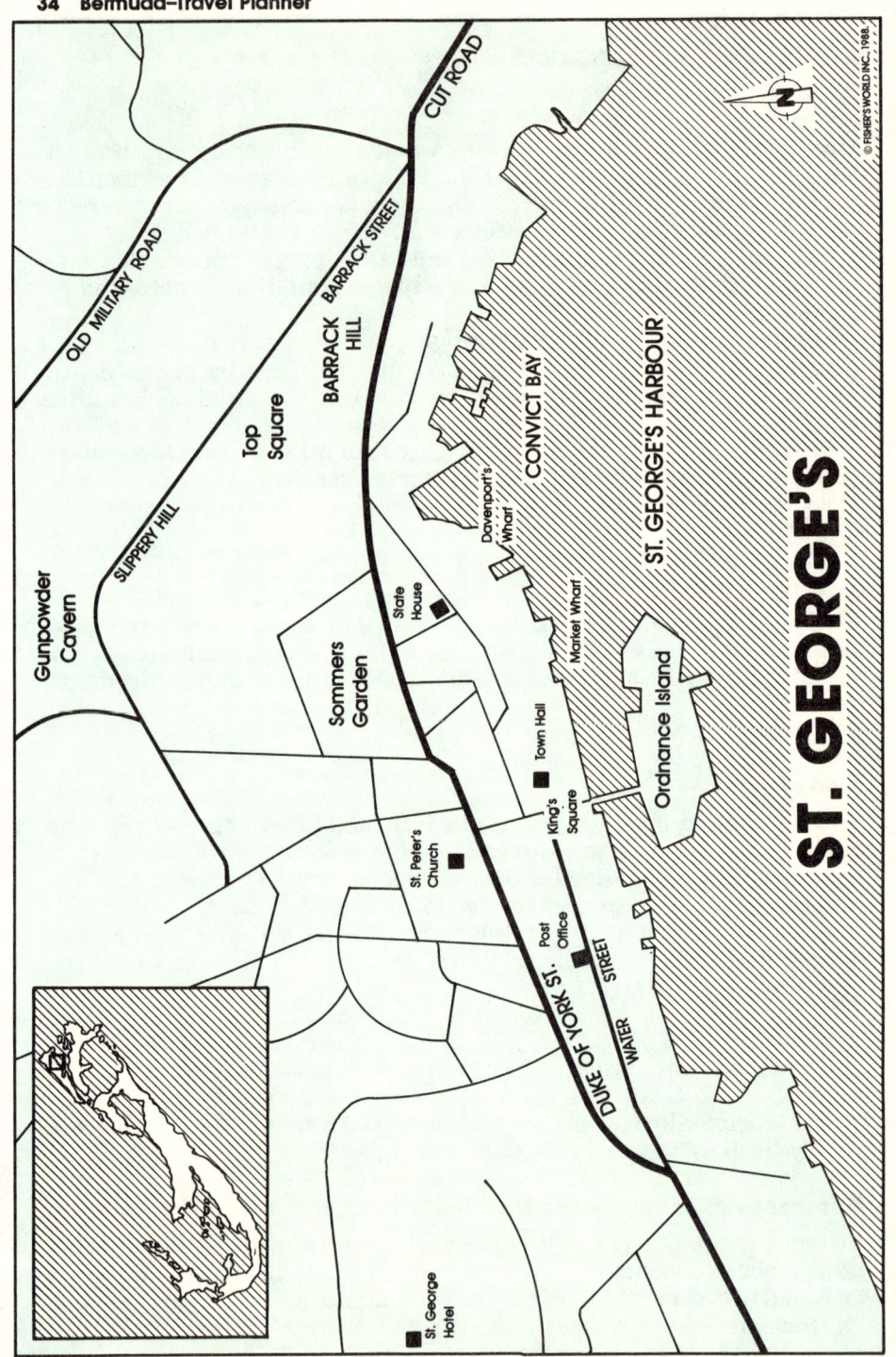

Investments in Local Companies/Mortgages

Exchange control consent is required for such investments by nonresidents. Permission, if given, carries repatriation rights. Under Bermuda law, local companies must normally be at least 60 percent Bermudian owned, and investors in local companies may be required to provide bank references.

Banking

There are three banks in Bermuda. The banking hours are 9:30 to 3:00, Monday through Friday, with an additional opening hour on Friday evenings from 4:30 to 5:30.

The Bank of Bermuda Limited: Front Street, Hamilton 5-31. Branches at Church Street, Hamilton; the Civil Air Terminal; Somerset; St. George's.

Bank of N.T. Butterfield Limited: Front Street, Hamilton 5-24. Branches in Somerset and St. George's.

Bermuda Commercial Bank: Church Street, Barclay's International Bldg., Hamilton.

Tipping

Where tips are not included in hotel or restaurant bills, add 10 to 15 percent for service. Some guest houses as well as hotels add a percentage or set amount per person, per day to the bill for accommodations. There is also a 6 percent government occupancy tax added to hotel bills.

Business Hours

Shops are generally open from 9 A.M. to 5 or 5:30 P.M. except on Sundays and holidays (although a few of the Front Street shops have begun opening up on Sundays in season). Some shops close Thursday afternoons. Most are open Saturday.

Electricity

Throughout the island electrical current is 110 volts, 60 cycles, alternating current. Appliances brought from North America do not need adaptors. Appliances brought from Europe and the U.K. do.

Drinking Water

Drinking water in Bermuda is filtered and so tap water is safe to drink. The island depends almost entirely upon rain for its water supply, which is caught on white roofs and water catches and stored in underground tanks. Although there may be a shortage of water in hotels and restaurants, it is fresh and pure and there are seldom any ill effects caused by drinking it. It is untreated in any way and does not require boiling. There are no factories to create smoke or water

36　Bermuda–Travel Planner

ST. GEORGE'S BIKE OR HIKE TOUR

Legend:
1. Visitors Information Centre
2. Deliverance Ship
3. Town Hall
4. Bridge House
5. State House
6. Somers Garden
7. Unfinished Church
8. St. George's Historical Society Museum
9. Featherbed Alley Printery
10. The Old Rectory
11. St. Peter's Church
12. Tucker House
13. Carriage Museum
14. Confederate Museum

Map labels: Club Med, Fort St. Catherine, Slippery Hill, Shinbone Alley, Blockage Alley, Duke of Kent St., St. George Somer's Statue, Princess St., Pound Alley, Kings Square, Ordnance Island, King St., Featherbed Alley, Duke of Clarence St., Church St., Duke of York St., Queen St., Printer's Alley, Barber's Alley, Water St., St. George's Golf Course, St. George's Club

© FISHER'S WORLD INC. 1988.

pollution, and, since the island is small, prevailing winds carry dust and impurities out to sea.

Communications

Bermuda is linked to a worldwide cable and overseas telephone service. Charges may be reversed. Direct dialing is possible to the U.S., Canada, Hawaii, Alaska, Bahamas, part of the Caribbean, U.K., Australia, Brazil, Denmark, Greece, Hong Kong, Italy, Luxembourg, Netherlands, Singapore, Sweden, and South Africa. Airmail arrives and leaves daily for North America and Europe. All mail received at the general post office in Hamilton by 9:30 A.M. is dispatched the same day.

Time

Standard time in Bermuda is Greenwich Mean Time minus four hours. Daylight Saving Time is in effect from the last Sunday in April to the last Sunday in October.

Cables

The Cable and Wireless office is situated on Church Street, Hamilton. It is open from 8 A.M. to 7 P.M., Monday to Friday, and 9 A.M. to 5 P.M. on weekends. Cables can, of course, be placed at any time by telephoning 295-1815.

Telephones

Bermuda has direct long-distance dialing (station to station) and rates are lower if dialing direct after certain times. Call operator for further information. If you require directory assistance, you may call 902. There is, of course, a 24-hour service, and reverse charges and credit cards will be accepted for the US, Canada, and Britain.

Press, Radio, Television

For such a small country, Bermuda is indeed well endowed with media. There is a daily newspaper, The Royal Gazette, as well as two weekend papers, Mid Ocean News and The Bermuda Sun. The Royal Gazette does not publish on Sundays. The *Bermudian Magazine* is published monthly. Tourist publications include *Welcome to Bermuda*, a guidebook; *Preview of Bermuda*, a guide for visitors; *This Week in Bermuda*; *Bermuda Weekly*, a guide to shopping, sightseeing, entertainment.

All radio and television broadcasting in Bermuda is commercial. Both are in the hands of one company, the Bermuda Broadcasting Company.

Medical Assistance

There is no national health scheme in Bermuda. All medical and dental practitioners are private and fees are about the same as those

ST. GEORGE'S SHOPPING

1. Frangipani
2. Taylors
3. Which Craft
4. The Cow Polly
5. The Bridge House Art Gallery and Craft Shop
6. Benetton
7. English Sports Shop
8. Irish Linen
9. Frith's Liquors
10. Trimminghams
11. Tolaram's Ltd.

in North America. There are many medical and dental practitioners, and visitors who require a doctor or dentist may generally obtain one through their hotel or guest house.

Pharmacists will fill only prescriptions signed by Bermudian doctors.

There is no ragweed in Bermuda, and timothy grass and other weeds and grasses causing hay fever are either lacking or sufficiently rare as to be of little importance.

King Edward VII Hospital is the only general hospital on the island. It has 237 beds in private and semiprivate rooms and in the public wards, which have four beds each. It is fully air-conditioned and equipped with modern, up-to-date facilities. There are specialists and consultants in anaesthesiology, gynecology, internal medicine, orthopedics, pediatrics, ophthalmology, pathology, psychiatry, radiology, and surgery plus well-equipped laboratories and physiotherapy departments. Four ambulances are stationed at the hospital with one more at St. George's, and there is a round-the-clock emergency receiving facility.

All visitors are required to pay in advance of a stay in the hospital or after treatment in the emergency department. Visitors should retain receipts and make claims on their insurance companies upon returning home.

Note: For nonresidents of Bermuda, a 50 percent surcharge is added to the hospital bill.

GETTING AROUND IN BERMUDA

Taxis, public buses, motorbikes, and bicycles are the four favored methods of getting around in Bermuda.

For many years, private cars were banned and, even now, there is a strict limit of one car per household. There are no rental car agencies. The speed limit for all vehicles is 20 mph (32 km) in the countryside and 15 mph (24 km) in town limits and public areas.

Ferryboats operate on regular schedules across Great Sound between Hamilton and Ireland Island on the extreme northwestern "hook" end of the Island and between Hamilton and the southern end of Sandys and the northern extremity of Southampton Parish.

Taxis are metered and have their tariffs fixed by law. As mentioned elsewhere, Bermuda's taxi drivers are among the very best in the world. They're friendly, intelligent, and helpful—and a font of information on the island's attractions and history.

Bermuda is served from end to end with modern, clean, efficient buses running on regular schedules throughout the day. The main bus terminal is on Washington Street just off Church east of City Hall in downtown Hamilton. Bus schedules can be picked up at the terminal's information booth or at your hotel.

Two-lane highways, where traffic must keep to the left, as in Britain, form an excellent backbone to the colony's physical configuration. They extend from Ireland Island on the northwest, through Sandys and

RESORTS & HOTELS

Bermuda–Travel Planner

- Club Med, St. George's Cove
- The St. George's Club
- Grotto Bay Hotel
- Marriott's Castle Harbour Resort
- Mid Ocean Club
- Pink Beach Club & Cottage
- Bermudiana Hotel
- The Princess
- Waterloo Hotel
- Stonington Beach Hotel
- Rosedon
- Harmony Club
- Elbow Beach Hotel
- Glencoe
- Belmont Hotel
- Coral Beach & Tennis Club
- Fourways Inn
- Pretty Penny
- Horizons & Cottages
- Lantana Colony Club
- Southampton Princess
- The Reefs
- Sonesta Beach Hotel
- Cambridge Beaches
- Pompano Beach Club

© FISHER'S WORLD INC. 1988.

Southampton parishes, curve to the east through Warwick Parish, where there are coastal roads along the shores of the sound and the Atlantic Ocean shoreline as well as through the widening bulk of the island as it separates into two parishes, with Paget to the south and the Pembroke Parish peninsula jutting into the sound on the north.

Motorbikes and Bicycles

There is probably no other resort area in the world where motorbikes and bicycles are more popular than in Bermuda. There are numerous agencies from which to rent motorbikes and bicycles throughout the island. There are several rules and guidelines regarding motorbikes including the following:

1. In Bermuda all street and road traffic moves on the left.
2. A license is not required to ride hired motorcycles, but visitors may not ride privately owned cycles unless they have a Bermuda driver's license.
3. Persons under 16 are not permitted to ride motorcycles.
4. All riders are required by law to wear a safety helmet. Cycle liveries are required to provide a helmet for each rider.
5. Cyclists must keep eyes on the road ahead and not look behind.
6. Cyclists should wear tight-fitting shoes instead of floppy sandals and long slacks should be rolled above the knee to avoid having clothing tangle in the engine.
7. Always lock cycles when parked.
8. Handbags and valuables in bags or parcels should be locked in basket with cycle lock.
9. Hours vary for gas stations. Many are closed on Sunday and all are closed on public holidays.
10. Deposits are required for compulsory safety helmet rentals, repair waivers, and locks and keys.

Carriages

The horse-drawn carriages of Bermuda are dwindling in number, but there are still enough. Honeymooners tend to monopolize them with good reason, as an evening drive amid the fragrance of the flowers in the gentle glow of moonlight is what dreams should be all about. Hire through your hotel or pick one up on Hamilton's Front Street near the flag pole.

HOTELS

Hamilton Parish

THE PRINCESS. Hamilton. Phone toll free (800)223-1818. *Expensive.*

MARRIOTT'S CASTLE HARBOUR RESORT. Phone toll free (800)223-5388. *Very expensive.*

KEY TO RESTAURANTS

SANDYS PARISH
- 2 Lantana Colony Club
- 22 The Somerset Country Squire

SOUTHAMPTON PARISH
- 9 The Waterlot Inn

WARWICK PARISH
- 1 Newport Room
- 10 The Greenhouse
- 16 Glencoe
- 18 Henry VIII Pub and Restaurant
- 21 The Gold Hind

PAGET PARISH
- 3 Horizons
- 5 Fourways Inn
- 14 The Norwood Room

PEMBROKE PARISH
- 4 Penthouse
- 7 Once Upon A Table
- 8 Romanoff
- 11 The New Harbour Front
- 12 Fisherman's Reef
- 17 The Tiara Room
- 19 Bombay Bicycle Club
- 20 Chopsticks
- 23 Loquats
- 24 M.R. Onions
- 25 Rolan Hood Pub
- 27 Conch Shell
- 28 The Red Carpet

HAMILTON PARISH
- 6 Tom Moore's Tavern
- 13 Plantation Club

ST. GEORGE'S PARISH
- 15 The Margaret Rose
- 26 White Horse Tavern

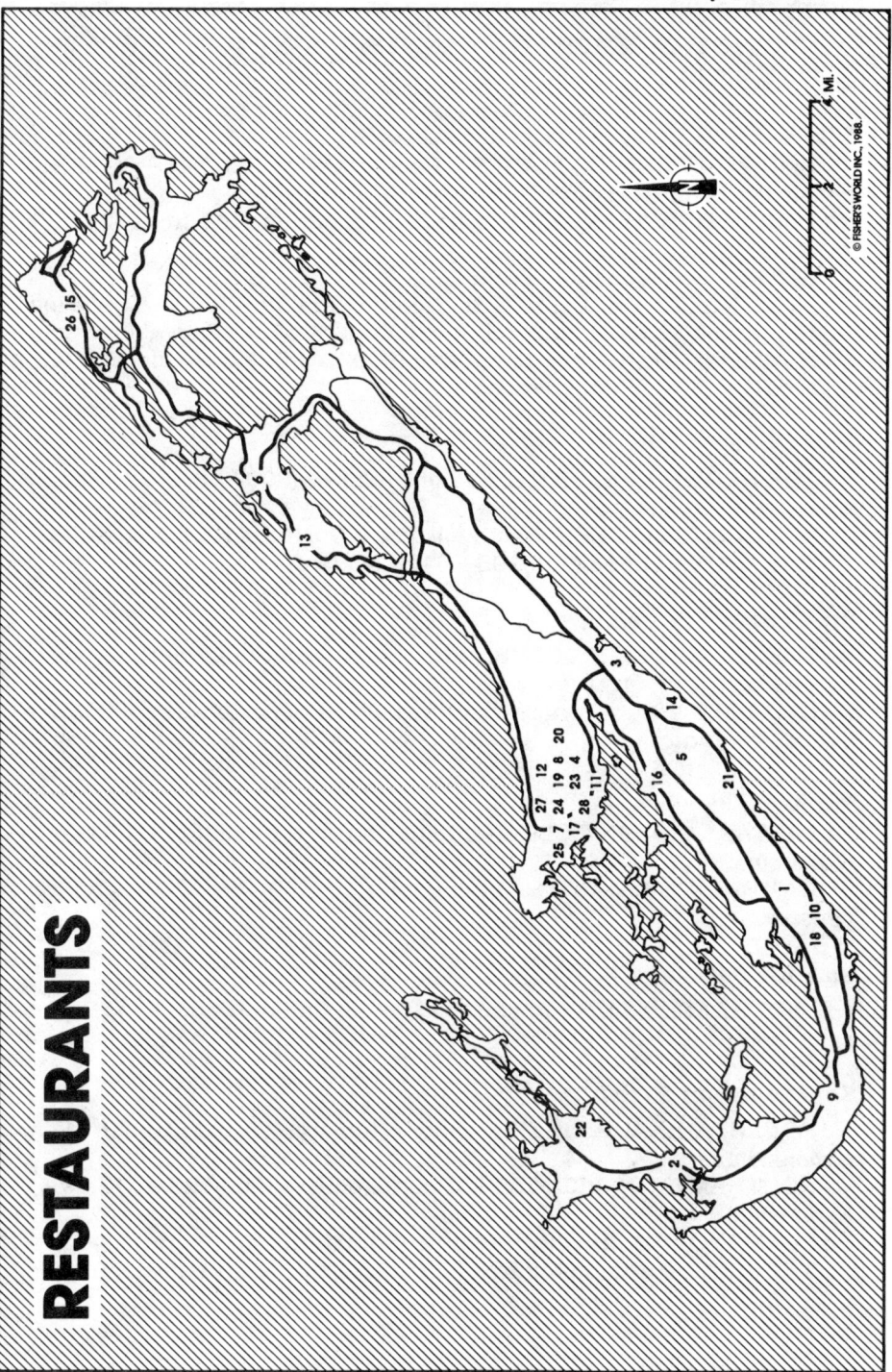

GROTTO BAY BEACH HOTEL AND TENNIS CLUB. Phone (809)293-8333. *Expensive.*

Paget Parish

HORIZONS AND COTTAGES. Phone toll free (800)468-0022. *Expensive to very expensive.*
ELBOW BEACH HOTEL. Paget Beach. Phone toll free (800)223-7434. *Expensive.*
GLENCOE. Phone toll free (800)468-1500. *Expensive.*
STONINGTON BEACH HOTEL. Phone (809)236-5416. *Expensive.*
FOURWAYS INN. Phone toll free (800)223-5581. *Expensive.*
HARMONY CLUB. Phone toll free (800)223-5672. *Expensive.*
PRETTY PENNY. *Moderate.*

Pembroke Parish

THE BERMUDIANA HOTEL. Phone toll free (800)223-5672. *Expensive.*
WATERLOO HOUSE. Phone toll free (800)468-4100. *Moderate.*
ROSEDON. Phone (908)295-1640. *Moderate.*

St. George's Parish

THE ST. GEORGE'S CLUB. Phone toll free (800)268-1332. *Very expensive.*
CLUB MED, St. George's Cove Village. Phone toll free (800)528-3100. *Moderate.*

Sandy's Parish

LANTANA COLONY CLUB. Phone toll free (800)468-3733. *Very Expensive.*
CAMBRIDGE BEACHES. Phone toll free (800)468-7300. *Very Expensive.*

Smith's Parish

PINK BEACH CLUB. Phone toll free (800)293-1666. *Very Expensive.*

Southampton Parish

SONESTA BEACH HOTEL. Phone toll free (800)343-7170. *Very Expensive.*
SOUTHAMPTON PRINCESS. Phone toll free (800)223-1818. *Very Expensive.*
POMPANO BEACH CLUB. Phone (809)234-0222. *Expensive.*
THE REEFS. Phone toll free (800)223-1363. *Expensive.*

Warwick Parish

THE BELMONT HOTEL, Golf and Country Club. Phone toll free (800)223-5672. *Very Expensive.*

Private Clubs

CORAL BEACH & TENNIS CLUB. Paget Parish.
MID OCEAN CLUB. Tucker's Town.

RESTAURANTS

NEWPORT ROOM. Southampton Princess. Phone 238-8167. *Very expensive.*
LATANA COLONY CLUB. Somerset Bridge. Phone 234-0141. *Expensive.*
HORIZONS, Paget. Phone 236-0048. *Expensive.*
PENTHOUSE, Front Street, Hamilton. Phone 295-3410. *Expensive.*
FOURWAYS INN. 1 Middle Rd., Paget. Phone 236-6517. *Very expensive.*
TOM MOORE'S TAVERN, Bailey's Bay, Hamilton Parish. Phone 293-8020. *Very expensive.*
ONCE UPON A TABLE, 49 Serpentine Rd., Hamilton. Phone 295-8585. *Moderate.*
ROMANOFF. Church St., Hamilton. Phone 295-0333. *Very expensive.*
THE WATERLOT INN, Middle Rd. (on the waterfront), Southampton. Phone 238-0510. *Very expensive.*
THE GREENHOUSE, Sonesta Beach Hotel, South Shore Rd. Phone 238-8122. *Expensive.*
THE NEW HARBOURFRONT, Front St., Hamilton. Phone 295-4207/295-4527. *Expensive.*
FISHERMAN'S REEF, Burnaby Hill, Hamilton. Phone 292-1609. *Moderate.*
PLANTATION CLUB, Bailey's Bay, Hamilton Parish. Phone 293-1188. *Moderate.*
THE NORWOOD ROOM, Stonington Beach Hotel, Paget. Phone 236-5416. *Moderate.*
The Margaret Rose, St. George's Club, St. George's Parish. Phone 297-2100. *Expensive.*
GLENCOE, Salt Kettle, Paget. Phone 236-5274. *Expensive.*
THE TIARA ROOM, Princess Hotel, Hamilton. Phone 295-3000. *Very expensive.*
HENRY VIII PUB AND RESTAURANT. South Shore Rd. (near the Sonesta), Southampton. Phone 238-1977. *Expensive.*
BOMBAY BICYCLE CLUB. Hamilton. Phone 292-0048. *Expensive.*
CHOPSTICKS. Reid St. East, Hamilton. Phone 292-0791. *Moderate.*

WATER SPORTS

46 Bermuda–Travel Planner

Map of Bermuda showing water sports locations:

- ST. GEORGE'S HARBOUR
- ST. DAVID'S ROAD
- Ski Bermuda
- Bermuda Water Sports
- Blue Grotto Dolphins
- CASTLE HARBOUR
- SEA GARDENS
- HARRINGTON SOUND
- SEA GARDENS
- Shortz Watersports Centre
- Shortz Windsurfer Sailing School
- NORTH ROAD
- SOUTH ROAD
- FRONT ST.
- BAY ROAD
- PITT'S BAY
- Hartley's Under Sea Adventure
- GREAT SOUND
- Watlington's Windsurfing
- MIDDLE ROAD
- Shortz Windsurfer Sailing School
- Watersports Centre
- South Side Scuba
- Robinson's Charter Boat Marina
- SOMERSET ROAD
- SEA GARDENS
- MIDDLE ROAD
- SEA GARDENS
- Public Wharf
- Skin Diving Adventure Ltd.
- Bermuda Waterski Centre
- Pitman's Boat Tours

© FISHER'S WORLD INC., 1988.

0   ¼   ½   Mi.

THE GOLDEN HIND. South Shore Rd., Warwick Parish. Phone 236-5555. *Very expensive.*
THE SOMERSET COUNTRY SQUIRE. Mangrove Bay, Somerset. Phone 234-0105. *Inexpensive to Moderate.*
LOQUATS. 95 Front St., Hamilton. Phone 292-4507. *Inexpensive to Moderate.*

Lunchtime Restaurants

M.R. ONIONS, Par-la-Ville Rd., Hamilton.
ROBIN HOOD PUB, Richmond Rd., Pembroke.
WHITE HORSE TAVERN. St. George's
CONCH SHELL. Emporium Building, Hamilton.
THE RED CARPET. Armory Building, Reid St., Hamilton.

Tea

WATERLOO HOUSE; CARRIAGE HOUSE; ROSEDON; both PRINCESSES; FOURWAYS INN; TRIMINGHAM'S.

NIGHTLIFE & ENTERTAINMENT

Hotels

THE PEACOCK ROOM. Elbow Beach.
LE CABARET NIGHT CLUB. Inverurie Hotel.
LILLIAN'S. Sonesta.
WINDOWS ON THE SOUND; THE TORCH CLUB. Southampton Princess.
CHEEK TO CHEEK; PROSPER'S CAVE. Grotto Bay Beach Hotel.
THE EMPIRE ROOM. Southampton Princess.
THE GAZEBO LOUNGE. Hamilton Princess.
HENRY VIII PUB; THE GOLDEN HIND; THE HOG PENNY. Loquats.

Other Hot Spots

THE SNIZZLE INN. Middle Rd., near St. George's.
CLAY HOUSE INN. North Shore Rd., Devonshire.

Discos

OASIS. The Emporium Building, Hamilton.
THE CLUB. upstairs from Little Venice Restaurant, Hamilton.
FLAVORS. Middle Rd., Riddell's Bay.

Jazz

THE BAMBU LOUNGE. Oasis/Emporium Building.
THE SPARROW'S NEST. Reid St. East, Hamilton.

48 Bermuda–Travel Planner

BEACHES

HOTEL BEACH CLUBS

ELBOW BEACH SURF CLUB
SOUTH SHORE BEACH CLUB

Charge for non-house guests, reservations required.

SIGHTS AROUND THE ISLAND

St. George's

The Bermuda Journey. 25-minute synopsis of Bermuda's history. Town Hall. Adults $3.50; Children under twelve $2.00.

Deliverance. Replica open to visitors. Ordnance Island. Adults $2.00; Children under twelve .50 cents.

Historical Society. Duke of Kent St. Open 10 A.M. to 4 P.M., Mondays-Saturdays. Adults $2.00, Children under sixteen .50 cents.

St. George's Library, Stuart Hall, Aunt Peggy's Lane. Open 9 A.M. to 5 P.M., Monday, Wednesday, Saturday. Closed one hour for lunch. Admission free.

Tucker House. Water Street. Open daily, except Sundays and holidays. Admission charge.

Carriage Museum. Water Street. Open daily, except Sundays and holidays. Admission free, but donations welcome.

Confederate Museum. Corner of King's Square at Duke of York Street.

Nearby St. George's

Gates Fort.

Fort St. Catherine. Open daily 10 A.M. to 4:30 P.M. Admission fee.

St. David's Lighthouse and Carter House. St. David's Island. Get pass from Naval Air Station to visit Carter House. Phone Lyndell O'Dey, 297-1150.

Tucker's Town.

Sandys Parish

Maritime Museum. North Ireland Island. Open 10 A.M. to 5 P.M. daily except Christmas. Admission fee.

Old Cooperage. Across from museum. The Attack on Washington hour-long multimedia show. Continuous showings begin on the half hour, all day long. Admission fee.

Gladys Morell Nature Reserve. East Shore Rd. near Cavello Bay, Somerset. Open daily.

The Springfield Museum and *Gilbert Nature Preserve,* Somerset Rd., contains the Somerset Library (open Monday, Wednesday and Fridays). Nature preserve open every day, year round.

Southampton Parish

Gibbs Hill Lighthouse. Lighthouse Rd. Open 9 A.M. to 4:30 P.M. daily. Admission fee.

Paget Parish

Paget Marsh. Twenty-six acres owned by National Trust & Audubon Society. For permission to enter, phone the Trust Office at 236-6483.

Botanical Gardens. Guided tours of grounds and greenhouses Tuesday, Wednesday, Friday at 10:30 A.M. Free.

50 Bermuda–Travel Planner

PUBLIC PARKS

- St. George's Island
- Smith's I.
- Great Head Park
- St. David's Island
- Nonsuch I.
- Castle I.
- Nature Reserve
- The Kings Castle
- Coney Island
- Wilkinson Memorial Park
- Spittal Pond Nature Reserve & Spanish Rock
- Palmetto Park
- Botanical Gardens
- Palm Grove Garden
- Admiralty House Park
- Astwood Park
- Spanish Point Park
- Ireland Island
- Somerset Island
- Nelly I.
- Darrell I.
- Burt I.
- Fort Scaur

© FISHER'S WORLD INC., 1988.

Camden House. In the center of the gardens. Open Tuesdays and Wednesdays, noon to 2 P.M. Free.

Hamilton Parish

Aquarium Museum and Children's Zoo. Open 9 A.M. to 4:30 P.M. daily. Admission fee.

Blue Grotto Dolphin Show. Performance five times daily (closed January 11 - February 15). Admission fee.

Crystal Caves. Open 9:30 A.M. to 4:30 P.M. daily. Adults $2.50; Children $1.00.

Leamington Caves. Open 9:30 A.M. to 4:30 P.M. Monday-Saturday (closed part of the winter season). Adults $2.50; Children $1.00.

Devonshire Parish

Palm Grove Gardens. Open daily, except Sunday.

Palmetto House. Three rooms open for viewing on Thursdays only, from 10 A.M. to 5 P.M. Admission is free, but donations are welcome.

Smith's Parish

Verdmont. Collector's Hill, off South Shore Rd. Open 10 A.M. to 5 P.M. weekdays. Admission charge.

Spittal Pond Nature Reserve. South Shore Rd. Open daily. Free admission.

Winterhaven Farm Cottage. East of Spittal Pond. Open Monday and Thursdays afternoons.

North Nature Reserve. Mangrove Lake.

CHURCHES & SYNAGOGUES

Most Christian denominations are represented in Bermuda, but that faith is represented mostly by Anglican (17 churches), African Methodist Episcopal (11 churches), Roman Catholic (6), Methodist (6), Baptist (3), and Presbyterian (2).

Seventh Day Adventists have churches in Hamilton and virtually all parishes while the Salvation Army has branches also throughout the island. Historic churches include the Cathedral of the Most Holy Trinity (Anglican) in Hamilton; St. Theresa's Cathedral (Roman Catholic) in Hamilton; St. Paul's (African Methodist Episcopal), Hamilton; St. Peter's (Anglican), St. George's, and Wesley Methodist, Hamilton.

Other denominations include Baha'i, Christian Science, Jehovah's Witnesses, Lutheran, Mormon, Pentecostal, and many more. There is also a Moslem Mosque in Hamilton.

There is no synagogue or ordained rabbi in Bermuda but the Jewish community meets on the first Friday of the month and on Rosh Hashanah, Yom Kippur, and Passover at the U.S. Naval Station.

TENNIS

1. Belmont Hotel
2. Bermudiana Hotel
3. Grotto Bay Beach Hotel
4. Inverurie Hotel
5. Marriott's Castle Harbour Resort
6. Sonesta Beach Hotel
7. Southampton Princess
8. Hamiltonian Hotel & Island Club
9. Newstead
10. Pompano Beach Club
11. The Reefs
12. Stonington Beach Hotel
13. Ariel Sands Beach Club
14. Cambridge Beaches
15. Horizons & Cottages
16. Lantana Colony Club
17. Pink Beach Club
18. Willowbank
19. Coral Beach & Tennis Club (Private)
20. Mid Ocean Club (Private)
21. Government Tennis Stadium
22. Port Royal Tennis Courts

SHOPPING

Clothing Size Equivalents

Women's Suits and Dresses
American	8	10	12	14
British	10	12	14	16
Continental	38	40	42	44

Women's Hosiery
American	8	8.5	9	9.5
British	8	8.5	9	9.5
Continental	0	1	2	3

Women's Blouses and Sweaters
American	30	32	34	36
British	32	34	36	38
Continental	36	38	40	42

Women's Shoes
American	6	6.5	7	7.5
British	4.5	5	5.5	6
Continental	38	38	39	39

Men's Suits and Overcoats
American	36	38	40	42
British	36	38	40	42
Continental	46	48	50	52

Mens's Shirts
American	14	14.5	15	15.5
British	14	14.5	15	15.5
Continental	36	37	38	39

Men's Socks
American	9.5	10	10.5	11
British	9.5	10	10.5	11
Continental	38-39	39-40	40-41	41-42

Men's Shoes
American	8	8.5	9.5	10.5
British	7	7.5	8.5	9.5
Continental	41	42	43	44

Children's Clothes
American	4	6	8	10
British height(in)	43	48	55	58
Continental height(cm)	125	135	150	155

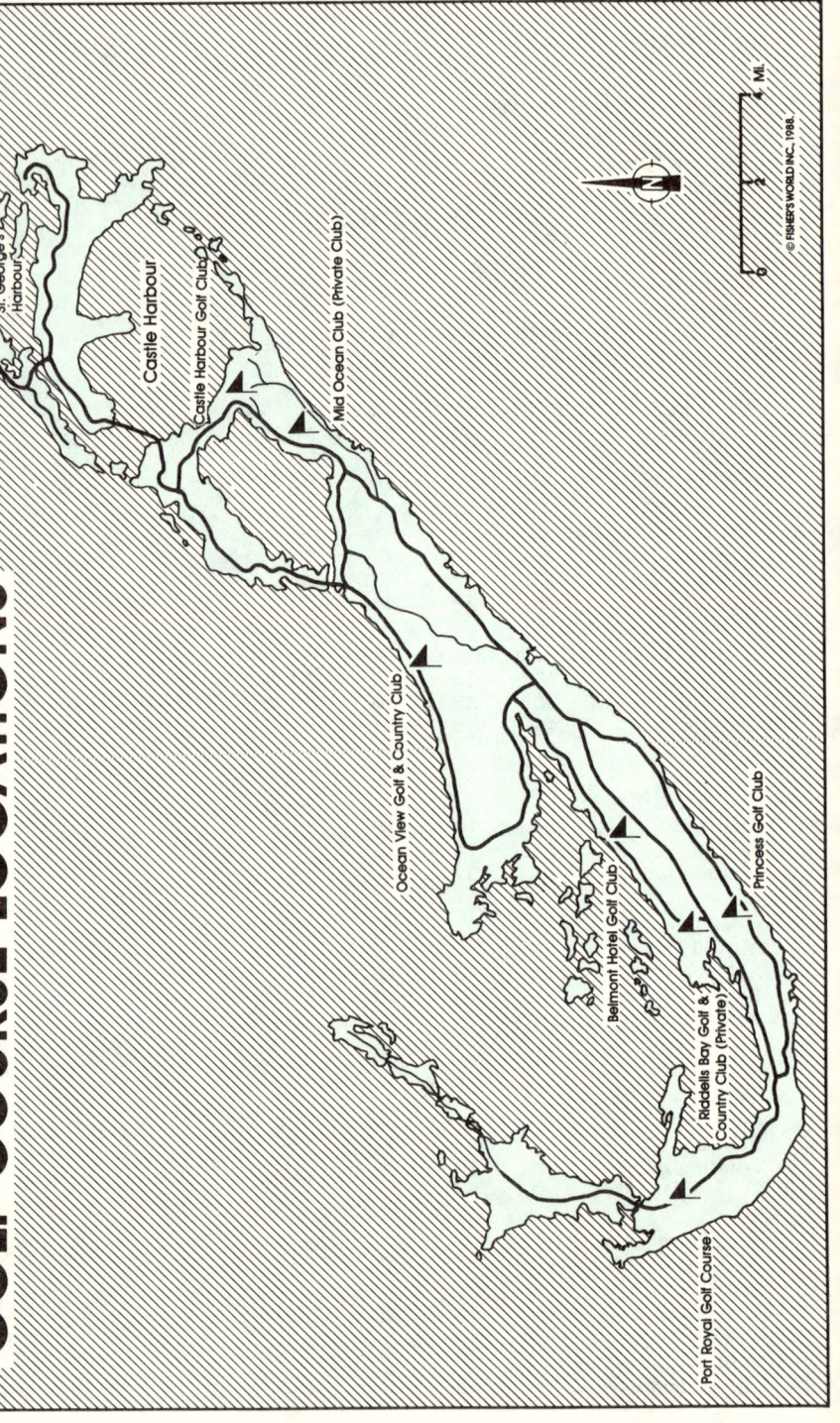

Hamilton

ACCESSORIES. Calypso; Mexicale Rose; Front Street Bananas
BARGIN SHOPPING. St. Michael
BOOKS. The Book Mart; The Book Rack
CASHMERES. Archie Brown & Son; Smith's
CHILDREN. Smith's;Espirit.
CRYSTAL AND CHINA. William Bluck & Co.; Smith's; A.S. Cooper & Sons
DEPARTMENT STORE. Trimingham's
GAMES. Kamla
HAND-CRAFTED ITEMS. Mirage Designs; Vera P. Card; A.S. Cooper & Sons
JEWELRY. Mirage Designs; Kamla; Portobello; Solomon's Jewellers; A. Dickinson; Lote Tree Jewelers; Mexical Rose
LINENS. The Irish Linen Shop
LUGGAGE. Calypso; Harbourmaster
MEN'S CLOTHES. The English Sport's Shop; Archie Brown & Son; Stefance; Sisley; Benetton
PERFUME. Smith's; Calypso; Peniston Brown; Guelain
PRINTS & MAPS. Pegasus Prints and Maps; The Book Mart
SANDALS & SHOES. Kamla; W.J.Boyle & Sons
SPORT CLOTHES. Calypso; Front Street Bananas; Benetton; Sisley
STAMPS & COINS. Portobello; Mexicale Rose; Bermuda Coin & Stamp Co.
SWEATERS. Kamla; Benetton; Stefance
SWIMWEAR. Kamla; Calypso
TWEEDS. Archie Brown & Sons
UNISEX CLOTHES. Archie Brown & Sons; Front Street Bananas; Benetton; Sisley; Stefance
WATCHES & TIMEPIECES. Crisson; Timeless Antiques

ST. GEORGE'S

ART. The Bridge House Art Gallery and Craft Shop
CHRISTMAS ORNAMENTS. The Cow Polly
HAND-CRAFTED ITEMS. Which Craft; The Cow Polly
LEFT-HANDED ACCESSORIES. Which Craft
LINENS. Taylors; Which Craft
SWEATERS. Frangipani; Taylors
TARTAN. Taylors

ELSEWHERE ON THE ISLAND

ANITIQUE REPRODUCTIONS. Thistle Gallery, outskirts of Hamilton.
CLOTHING. The Bamboo Gate, Paget.
HOUSEHOLD GADGETS. The Rising Sun, Southampton.
MISCELLANEOUS. The Old Market, Somerset Village.
SWEATERS. Chameleon Sweater Shop, Paget.

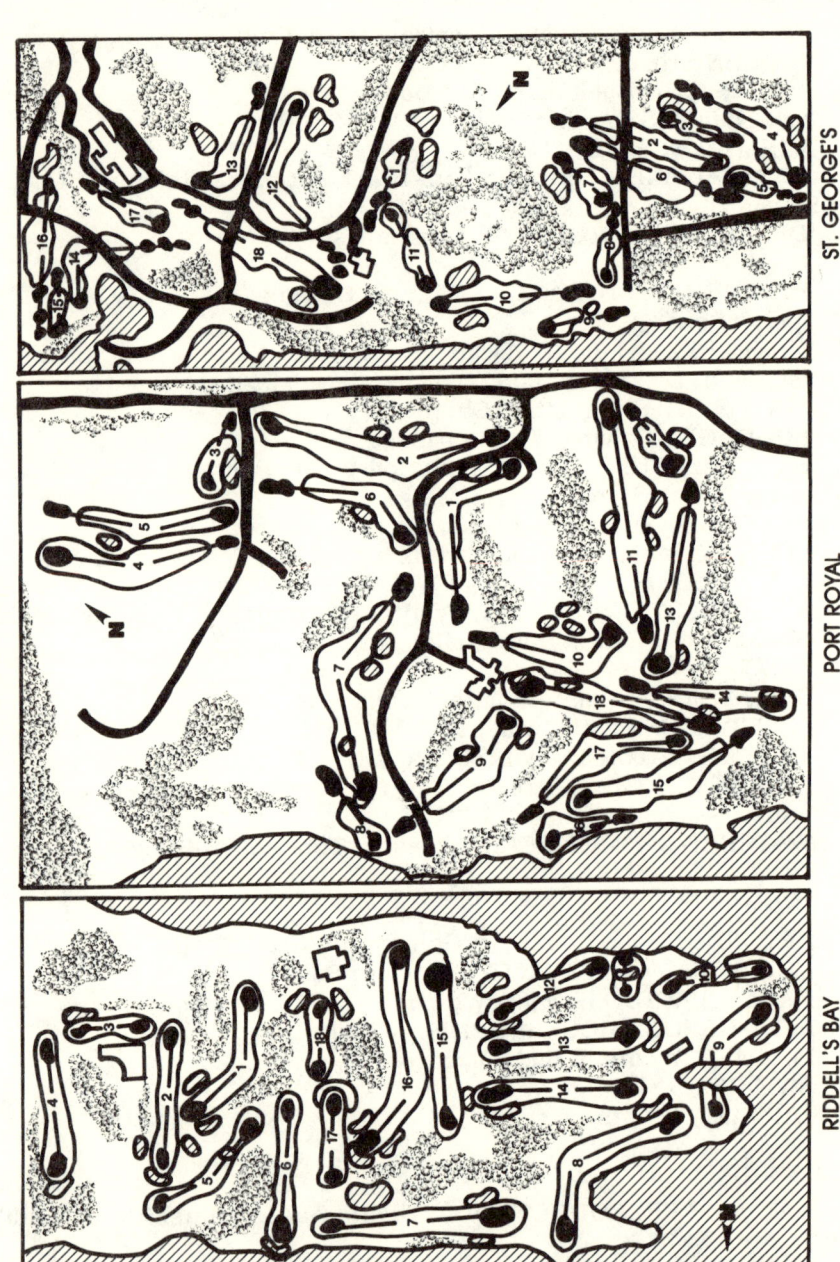

GALLERIES & STUDIOS

The Windjammer Gallery, Hamilton. The Art House, Paget.

Artists who open their studios ask that visitors plan to phone or drop by during traditional business hours (Monday-Friday, 10 A.M.-5P.M.).

Desmond Fountain, sculptor. P.O.Box 317, Flatts 3, Bermuda. Phone 292-3955.

Diana & Eric Amos, oils and watercolors. Warwick. Phone 236-9056.

Captain Stephen Card. Phone 234-2353.

Alfred Birdsey, watercolors and oils. Paget. Phone 236-6658.

Mary Zuill, watercolors. Paget. Phone 236-2439, April-November, Tuesdays-Fridays.

Graeme Outerbridge, photographer. Southampton. Phone 238-2411.

Kathleen Kensley Bell, costume dolls. Paget. Phone 236-3366.

SPORTS

Boat related: Grotto Bay Hotel 293-2640; Salt Kettle Boat Rentals 236-4863; Captain John Shirley Boat Rentals 234-0914; Robinson's Charter Boat Marina 238-9408;) Windsurfing School 236-6218; Shortz Windsurfing Schools 293-2323; Bermuda Water Tours 295-3727; Bermuda Caribbean Yacht Charters 234-0497; Ocean Yacht Charters 295-1180; Mayflower Charters 295-8291; Salt Kettle Boat Rentals-Somerset Bridge Cruises 234-0235; Starlight Sailing Cruises 292-1834.

Diving and Snorkeling

Hartley Helmet Diving Cruise 2924434; Hartley's Under Sea Adventure 234-2861; Grotto Diving 293-2915/292-2592; Nautilus Diving 238-2332/238-8000; Skin Diving Adventures 234-1034/238-0779; South Side Scuba 238-1833/236-0394; Bermuda Cruises 292-7094; Bermuda Water Sports 293-2640; Hayward's Explorer Snorkeling and Glass Bottom Boat Cruises 292-8652; Pittman's Boat Tours 234-0700; Salt Kettle Boat Rentals 236-4863.

Waterskiing

Grotto Bay Hotel 293-2640; A1 Bermuda Waterski Centre 234-3354.

Fishing

Fly Bridge Tackle 295-1845; Four Winds Fishing Tackle 292-7466; Salt Kettle Boat Rentals 236-4863; Captain John Shirley Boat Rentals 234-0914; Bermuda Sport Fishing Ass. Booking Office 295-2370/295-5535.

GOLF COURSES II
OCEAN VIEW
MID-OCEAN
CASTLE HARBOUR
N

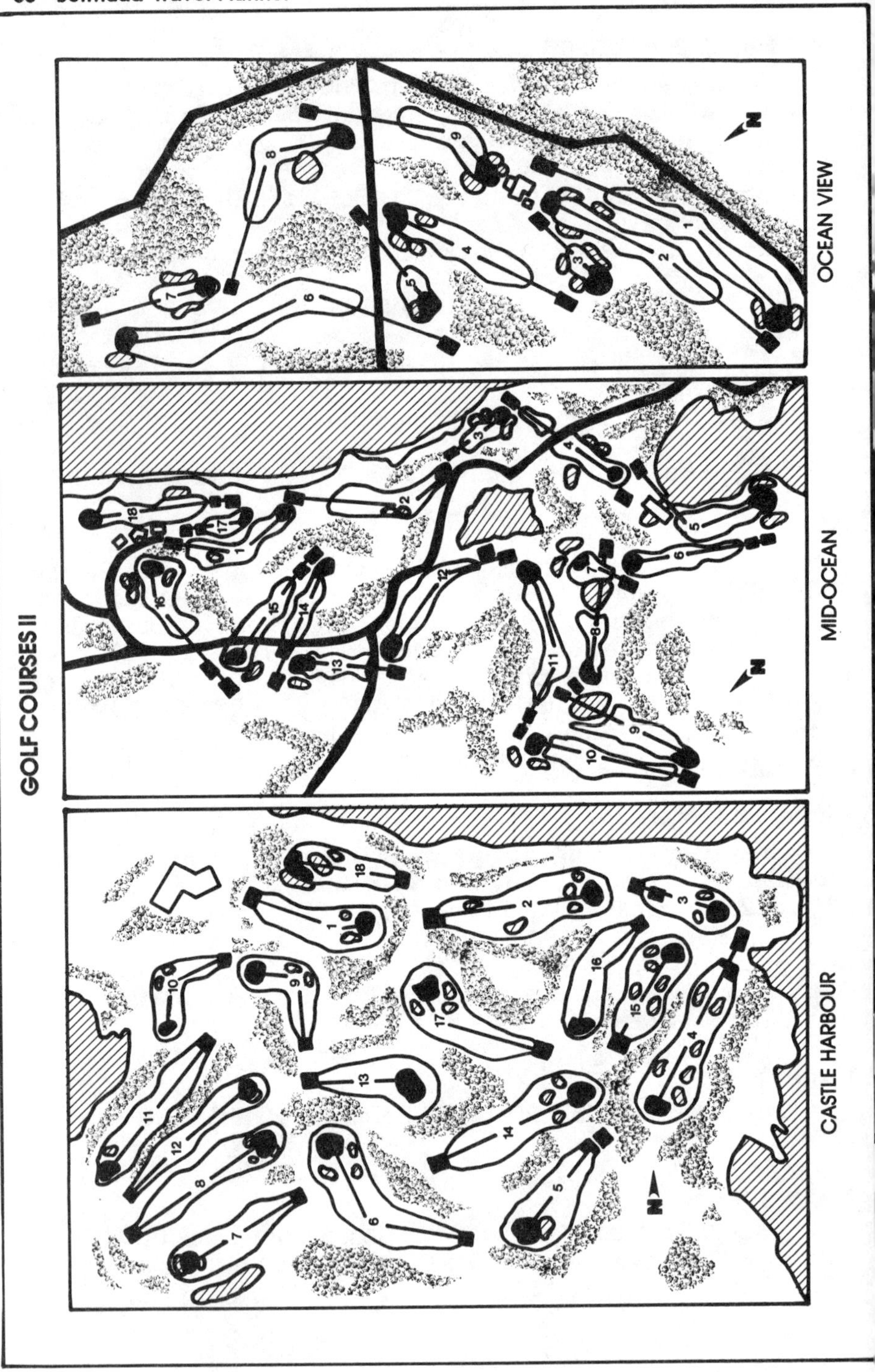

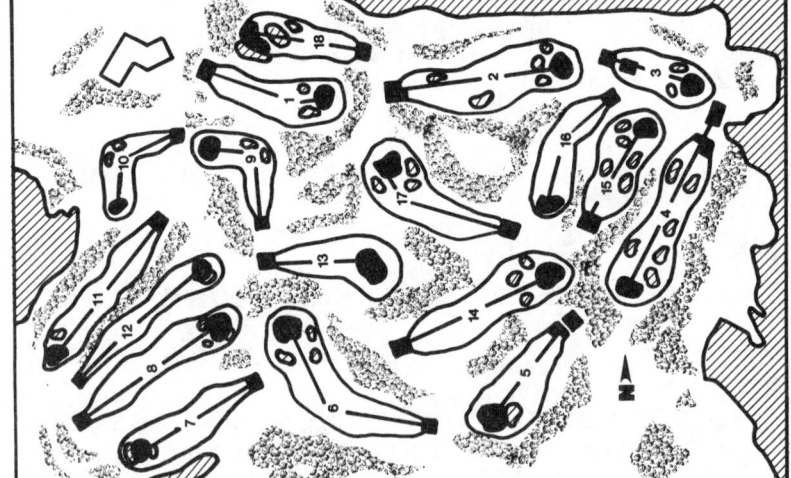

Tennis/Squash

White Heron Country Inn 238-1655; Bermuda Squash Racquets Club 292-6881.

Riding

Lee Bow Riding Centre 229-4181; Spicelands Riding Centre 238-8246/238-8212.

Golf

Public courses: Port Royal Golf Course, Southampton Parish, 234-0974; Belmont Hotel Golf Club, Warwick Parish, 236-1301; Princess Golf Club, Southampton Parish, 238-0446; Ocean View Gold & Country Club, Devonshire Parish, 292-6758; Castle Harbour Golf Club, Hamilton Parish, 293-2040; St. George's Golf Club, St. George's Parish, 297-8067; **Private courses:** Mid Ocean Club, Tucker's Town, 293-0330; Riddells Bay Golf & Country Club, Warwick Parish, 238-1060.

GOING HOME

There is a departure tax of $10.00 levied on visitors leaving Bermuda by air. Children under 2 may leave free of charge; for ages 2-11, the tax is $5.00. The tax for ship passengers is $20, usually included in the ticket cost.

U.S. Customs Pre-clearance

Bermuda is one of the few travel destinations where U.S. Customs is allowed the privilege of "pre-clearance"—and thanks to a recent, major expansion of airport facilities, lines move far faster than in the past. Under these regulations, there are U.S. Customs agents at the Bermuda International Airport to clear all U.S. residents' effects on departure from Bermuda. The same general regulations apply as at U.S. Customs offices on the mainland, including the overall allowance of $400 for duty-free retail value allowed citizens and legal residents of the U.S. once every 30 days after a 48-hour visit.

The next $1,000 worth of goods (above the $400 amount) will be assessed at a flat rate of 10 percent of retail value. After this $1,000 (or a total of $1,400), goods will be assessed at regular rates of duty on estimated wholesale value.

Canadian Customs

If you have been out of Canada over 48 hours, you can return with $100 worth of goods duty free (not including alcohol and tobacco) or $300, after seven days, once every calendar year.

You may also send home gifts up to $15 in value, duty free.

GOLF COURSES III

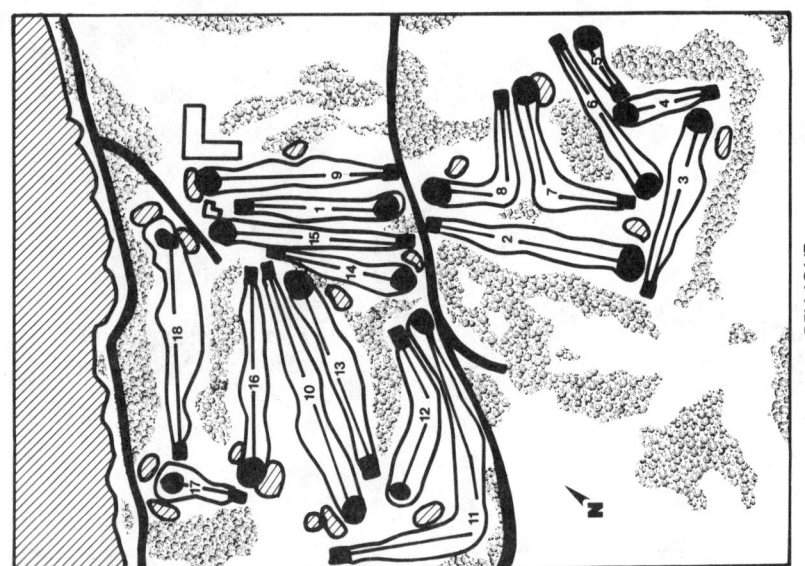

BELMONT

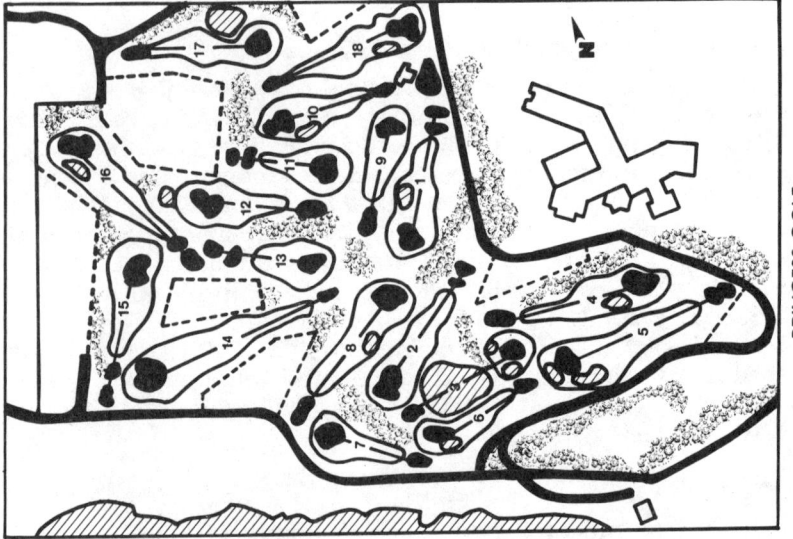

PRINCESS GOLF